Demystifying China

Demystifying China

New Understandings of Chinese History

Edited by
Naomi Standen

ROWMAN & LITTLEFIELD PUBLISHERS, INC.
Lanham • Boulder • New York • Toronto • Plymouth, UK

Published by Rowman & Littlefield Publishers, Inc.
A wholly owned subsidiary of The Rowman & Littlefield Publishing Group, Inc.
4501 Forbes Boulevard, Suite 200, Lanham, Maryland 20706
www.rowman.com

10 Thornbury Road, Plymouth PL6 7PP, United Kingdom

British Library Cataloguing in Publication Information Available

Library of Congress Cataloging-in-Publication Data
Demystifying China : new understandings of Chinese history / edited by Naomi
Standen.
     pages cm
  Includes bibliographical references and index.
  ISBN 978-1-4422-0895-7 (cloth : alkaline paper) — ISBN 978-1-4422-0896-4
(paper : alkaline paper) — ISBN 978-1-4422-0897-1 (electronic) (print)
  1. China—History. 2. China—History—Errors, inventions, etc. 3. China—
Civilization. 4. China—Politics and government. I. Standen, Naomi, 1965–
  DS736.D45 2013
  951—dc23

                                                2012034709

∞™ The paper used in this publication meets the minimum requirements of
American National Standard for Information Sciences—Permanence of Paper for
Printed Library Materials, ANSI/NISO Z39.48-1992.

Printed in the United States of America

With thanks to colleagues and friends at Newcastle University, particularly in the School of Historical Studies and in East Asian studies, who have, despite everything, contributed to the doing of things that mattered but could not be counted.

Not everything that matters can be counted;
not everything that can be counted matters.
—Attributed, in various forms, to Albert Einstein

Contents

Figures

Preface

It's a commonplace that China has become important to us in the last two decades. Actually, it has always been important to the West, but in different ways. In the early twentieth century, Americans saw it as a ripe field for missionary conversion; the British invested millions of pounds in the country. During the era of Mao, China provided the unknown factor threatening to upset the delicate balance between West and East during the Cold War. In more recent years, of course, it has been trade and global power that have been associated with China's rise.

During all this time, however, there has been one common factor: a profound lack of knowledge about China at the heart of Western decision making. To feed this need, there has also always been a significant market in books that seek to explain the Middle Kingdom (as the name for China, Zhongguo, is always translated, even if misleadingly). A century ago, books with titles such as *John Chinaman at Home* revealed more about the author (in this case a clergyman who referred to China as a "topsy-turvy world") than about the country it purported to portray. In our own era, few would dare to publish such openly contemptuous works. Yet there is still a genre of book—quite often aimed at the buyer at the newsstand or the airport—which plays along with this ethos. China is mysterious, possibly dangerous, such books proclaim. Read this and understand how to navigate between the shoals. But of course, such books have a vested interest in fueling the idea that China is indeed mysterious and Other in the first place.

That is where this book is so refreshing. By "demystifying China," it also seeks to place China more firmly within our own understanding of the normal and rational. It portrays a society not in terms of a constructed image of something very alien. Instead it portrays a place that has its own strongly individual culture and society, but was also formed in ways that are familiar from the contours of our own society and history. So, just as Western nation-states created their own "imagined communities" (in Benedict Anderson's penetrating phrase), so China has constantly reinvented itself. The classic narrative of China as a society that has a lengthy continuity of culture, writing system, and governance is not wrong, but it is more complex than the modern cliché of "five thousand years of history" might suggest. This book shows the rough edges behind the smooth language of unity: so we hear about the nonethnic Chinese (an awkward term for a vital collection of groups), the geographical shifts, and the varied relationship with the sea and the Eurasian landmass that make "China" a much less stable but much more exciting idea to think about. We also see the tortuous path to modernity. No "inevitable" Communist victory here, with Mao as some sort of "new emperor" ruling from Beijing, but instead a society constantly thinking about and reinventing its sense of itself. Technology is here too, in the form of medicine, and so is rational bureaucracy in the shape of the thousand years (yes, this time a continuity that has some historical weight to it) of the civil service examination system. And neglected actors in Chinese history, such as the Nationalist Party (for many years merely a villainous foil in a morality tale where the Chinese Communist Party has been the hero) are restored to a more objective historical examination.

China has given rise to a wealth of received wisdom on everything from the Great Wall (even if the rumor that it is visible from space is no longer current) to the nature of Confucius's thoughts (filtered through the philosophically unsatisfactory vehicle of the fortune cookie). This volume provides a much-needed corrective. Scholars of the first rank take a variety of commonplace beliefs about China and carefully, empirically, demonstrate where conventional understandings should be undermined—and where, in some cases, they truly have value.

Rana Mitter
Oxford

Acknowledgments

This book seemed necessary to me, and I would like to thank all those who thought so too—contributors, supporters, the two anonymous readers for the press—and thank and apologize to those whose (sometimes severe) critiques of the project have, I hope, improved where they could not dissuade. I am grateful to the authors for their hard work and patience, and to Susan McEachern at Rowman & Littlefield for her imagination in taking on this project and her still greater patience in seeing it through. As editor, I naturally take responsibility for any remaining (or introduced) faults. This was a project that had to be fitted into stolen moments and nonexistent gaps, and I have to apologize to my family for all the early-morning typing and late deliveries of their wake-up cups of tea.

Naomi Standen
Birmingham

North and Inner Asia	Yellow River region	Yangzi valley and south	Also known as
	XIA? 夏 (Hsia) (late 3rd mill–mid 2nd mill BCE?)		
	SHANG 商 (c. 1600–c. 1050 BCE)		
	ZHOU 周 (Chou) (c. 1050–249 BCE)		Spring & Autumn (722–453 BCE) Warring States (453–221 BCE)
QIN 秦 (Ch'in) (221–206 BCE)			
FORMER (WESTERN) **HAN** 西漢 (202 BCE–9 CE)			
XIN 新 (Hsin) (9–25 CE)			
LATER (EASTERN) **HAN** 東漢 (25–220)			
WEI 魏 (220–265)		SHU 蜀 (221–263) WU 吳 (222–280)	**THREE KINGDOMS**
SIXTEEN KINGDOMS 十六國 (304–439)	WESTERN **JIN** 西晉 (Chin) (265–316)		
		EASTERN **JIN** 東晉 (Chin) (317–420)	
NORTHERN **WEI** 北魏 (386–535) EASTERN **WEI** 東魏 (534–550), WESTERN **WEI** 西魏 (535–556) **NORTHERN QI** 北齊 (Ch'i) (552–577) **NORTHERN ZHOU** 北周 (Chou) (557–581)		**LIU SONG** 劉宋 (Sung) (420–479) **SOUTHERN QI** 南齊 (Ch'i) (479–502) **LIANG** 梁 (502–557) **CHEN** 陳 (Ch'en) (557–589)	**NORTHERN & SOUTHERN DYNASTIES** 南北朝 (420–589)
SUI 隋 (581–618)			
TANG 唐 (T'ang) (618–907)			
LIAO 遼 (907–1125)	LATER LIANG 後梁 (907–923) LATER TANG 後唐 (T'ang) (923–936) LATER JIN 後晉 (Chin) (936–947) LATER HAN 後漢 (947–950) LATER ZHOU 後周 (Chou) (951–960)	TEN KINGDOMS 十國 (907–978)	**FIVE DYNASTIES** 五代 (907–960)
	(NORTHERN) **SONG** 宋 (Sung) (960–1126)		
JIN 金 (Chin) (1115–1234)		SOUTHERN **SONG** 南宋 (Sung) (1127–1279)	
YUAN 元 (Yüan) (1260–1368)			
MING 明 (1368–1644)			
QING 清 (Ch'ing) (1644–1911)			
REPUBLIC OF CHINA 中華民國 (1912–) (on Taiwan since 1949)			
PEOPLE'S REPUBLIC OF CHINA 中華人民共和國 (1949–)			

A Chronology of China's Rulers

Boldface indicates names of official dynastic histories. The central area between the bold lines is the imperial period, from Qin to Qing.

Names in brackets are Wade-Giles spellings; these are widely found in older English-language works.

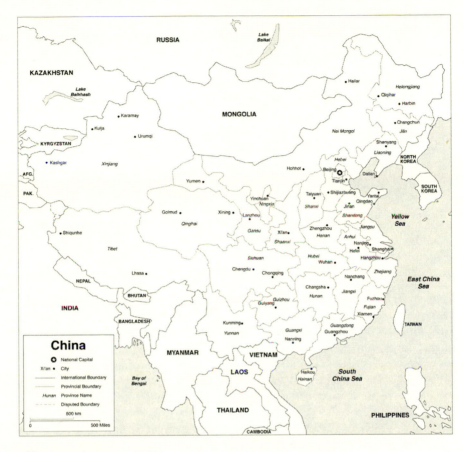

China's Provinces, ca. 2010

Notes on Romanization, Names, and Chinese Characters

The romanization of Chinese here follows the pinyin system. This is characterized by the use as initials of *q*, *x*, and *c*, which bear pronunciations unfamiliar to English speakers (roughly: *ch, sh, ts*). Alternative sound values for familiar letters are also found in the spelling of other languages adopting the Latin script, such as Spanish or, notably, Irish Gaelic.

Pinyin is standard in the People's Republic of China, is now the dominant system used in academic works, and is increasingly found in Taiwan. Many older academic works use a romanization system known as Wade-Giles. This makes extensive use of hyphens and uses apostrophes to mark aspiration, so that *ch'ung* represents a quite different sound from *chung* (roughly: *chong* and *jong*). Wade-Giles spellings show up here in quotations, and in common names and terms like Kuomintang (properly Kuo-min-tang; pinyin: Guomindang).

The spelling of proper names is frequently idiosyncratic. Romanizations of common place names, such as Peking (pinyin: Beijing), are often based on European renderings of local pronunciation, which may not even have been in Mandarin but in another Chinese language. The spelling of personal names may also represent local pronunciation, such as Chiang Kai-shek (pinyin: Jiang Jieshi), or may be the individual's own choice, like Soong Ching-ling (pinyin: Song Qingling). Some of these spellings are found in this volume, accompanied by their pinyin equivalents, in the interests of enabling identification of people across the full range of English-language material, regardless of how their name is written.

In Chinese names the surname comes first, but in Western contexts Chinese names are often reversed so that the surname comes last.

Chinese characters are omitted except where they are essential to understanding the point being made.

Introduction

The Creation of History in China

Naomi Standen

In the last few years, interest in China in the English-speaking world has mushroomed, in response to the emergence of the People's Republic of China (PRC) as a leading world economy and aspirant to superpower status. To deal effectively with this "new China" we need a sound basis for interpretation and response. Yet, while news reporting of contemporary China issues is becoming daily more sophisticated, general knowledge of China's history has lagged behind.

Every place is formed by its history, and references to that history feature in everyday life and sometimes in significant events: President Obama evoked the Constitution and the Civil Rights movement in his "More perfect union" speech of March 2008;[1] the British government, facing financial crisis in 2010, recalled the slogans of postwar austerity, talking of "belt-tightening" and declaring that "we are all in this together." In China, history is notably present on almost a daily basis. Major issues arise out of historical events and their aftermaths, and are profoundly affected—and sometimes created—by historical memories and interpretations. Relations with Japan can always be affected by references to Japan's wartime record, including the Nanjing Massacre of 1937, when Japanese troops slaughtered or raped hundreds of thousands of civilians after the city surrendered, and the use of Chinese and Korean "comfort women" to provide forced sexual services to Japanese troops. These and other examples are compounded by continuing Chinese dissatisfaction with the Japanese government's careful expressions of regret and sometimes apology for such past behavior, which keeps this history a live issue in present-day relations.[2] On a global scale, in climate-change talks in 2009, the Chinese delegation insisted that China be allowed less stringent environmental controls. This demand was justified,

1

not for the first time, by reference to the historical pollution emitted by the more developed countries since the Industrial Revolution, which invoked a narrative that blames China's economic "backwardness" on a history of Western imperialism, war, and internal political turmoil.[3]

Proponents of such arguments read history in ways that support their political agendas, regardless of how this may skew, exaggerate, or distort the record. These and many other historical arguments have been embraced by a significant proportion of China's population, and particularly by young people raised on information that government agencies control and shape, who promulgate these connections between past and present in numerous venues, and especially on the Internet. Furthermore, some claims may be shared or perpetuated by people outside China who simply lack the knowledge to question them.

The regular and serious invocation of the past in China creates issues in its own right and can complicate apparently unrelated matters, which means that sound understandings of present-day China demand reliable knowledge about the underlying historical circumstances, the various interpretations offered for those circumstances, and the uses made of those interpretations. But beyond that, a suitable response to such uses (and abuses) of history requires that we consider how and why such claims are constructed, which entails thinking about how our knowledge is created, accepted, transmitted, and reinforced. And we must think not only about our responses to other people's claims, but also acknowledge the origins of the claims that we make ourselves.

This book thus turns a critical eye on some popular claims about China's history found in the English-speaking world, with two intertwined goals. First, to respond to some commonly held ideas by presenting current scholarly interpretations in compact form. Second, to consider how these commonly held ideas have come into being. Such ideas start from real circumstances, but may distort the historical record, rest upon superseded research or outdated assumptions, or in some cases peddle myth. And although the topics here are specific to China's history, the question of the construction of knowledge applies everywhere.

HISTORICIZING "CHINA"

These short essays present a regionalized or localized China in which diverse groups, ideas, and phenomena jostle for historical recognition. This approach contrasts with a network of common ideas that present China as monolithic. Government sources and general works in English often express such ideas in the singular: "*the* Chinese people," "*the* one-child policy," "*the* system of Chinese medicine." Unsurprisingly over such a large area and so many centuries, not to mention the range of social and cultural groups, all of these things are in fact plural in form. As in other places, individuals in "China," past and present, differed from each other and responded in their own ways to the varied circumstances they encountered. Generalizations too easily collapse this diversity into oversimplified unities, which may be attractive to those trying to comprehend what may appear to be, if not inscrutable, then devilishly complicated. Until we develop more sophisticated general knowledge, China is liable to remain in most Westerners' minds as essentially a singular entity.

Having recognized the plurality of entities included under the headings "China" or "Chinese," we must consider what those two words mean. "China" refers fundamentally to a political unit. Like any other modern country, this "China" at any given moment in history did not always cover the same geographical area but has repeatedly expanded and contracted to sizes ranging from a relatively tiny territory in the middle Yellow River valley to areas even bigger than today's PRC. Each change in the political unit's size and location also changed the set of population groups it governed. Which of these could be categorized as "Chinese" has also changed to suit political needs then or now. The northwestern aristocracies of the third to sixth centuries intermarried heavily with their northern neighbors to create a multilingual elite who founded states regarded in historical works as non-Chinese, in contrast to the states founded by their southern neighbors, which are considered Chinese. However, when some of those multilingual northwestern aristocrats conquered the southern states in the sixth century, modern writers describe the outcome as a long-awaited revival of "China," and its ruling elite—and indeed the whole diverse population—is silently redefined as "Chinese."[4] But "China" was not always under "Chinese" rule, notably in the Mongol (ca. 1234–1368) and Manchu (ca. 1621–1911) periods, and the population always included a range of groups in addition to "the Chinese."

This malleability in the concepts of "China" and "Chinese" does much to enable the claim that "Chinese culture" has a continuous existence over thousands of years, and that this makes it an exceptional case in world history that brooks no comparison. In fact every historical situation is unique, and China's are no more or less exceptional than anywhere else's, and neither are the processes by which their exceptionality is proclaimed. Freed from assumptions of Chinese exceptionalism, we here treat topics such as the position of women or wall-building in what we hope is a usefully comparative fashion. In the same way, the creation of narratives justifying the location and content of the Chinese polity's current political boundaries, or the invention of a singular "Chinese medicine," or the criticism of the Nationalists who lost the civil war of 1945–1949 are compared in the essays here with similar processes of legitimization, nation-building, and "othering" to be found in any modernizing state.

The task is to historicize China not just in scholarship but in general knowledge. Just as readers of this book would not expect Roman Britain to be the same as Tudor England, or the Thirteen Colonies to be like the United States in the Roaring Twenties (let alone like the precolonial period), so we must internalize the idea that the treatment of women and the understanding of political boundaries were different in early twentieth-century Shanghai than in "traditional" Chang'an (now Xi'an), and indeed, that different periods and places in those "traditional" times were different from each other too. The expansive Yellow River empire of 2,000 years ago (the Han dynasty, 202 BCE–220 CE) was not the same as the defeated but prosperous Yangzi River empire of 800 years ago (the Southern Song dynasty, 1127–1276). Attitudes to women were different in urban and rural locations during the same period. Confucian ideas changed in both content and political influence, and were embraced—if at all—to different degrees by different groups at different times. "China" did not always exist as a unified state. We offer here a few specific examples toward the task of historicization, but our wider goal is to provide not only historical toeholds upon which readers may exercise their critical faculties, but also to foster an increased awareness of how everything we commonly think we "know" about "China" is assembled and presented by human beings with their own perspectives and agendas. We should deal with information about China in the same way that we deal with information about anything else on which we wish to draw our own conclusions. What we seek here is a more nuanced view of China, as being unique in its own way—just like everywhere else—but not exceptional in its complexity and strangeness.

CHINA IN HISTORICAL WRITING

Most nonspecialists will disavow any knowledge of an unfamiliar topic, such as the history of China. However, they may ask questions of those who might know more, which typically begin, "Is it true that . . . ?" In other words, such questioners have picked up *something*, although they probably could not say where from, and wish to test that hearsay on someone who might have better information. The assumptions are all around. News reports refer to the Nanjing Massacre or China as a victim of imperialism or offer "human interest" stories about the last foot-bound women still alive or firmly associate antidemocratic and authoritarian government with the Chinese Communist Party. A museum exhibition generates reviews that speak of eighteenth- and nineteenth-century rulers being uninterested in the outside world. A traveler expresses (ironic) surprise that China is not a Confucian society filled with men in long robes and pigtails.[5] These responses invoke generalizations that can only ever be part of the story, that are frequently at odds with the evidence, and yet remain the currency of conversation.

Such views of China's history are transmitted largely via the media, but where do they originate? Some emerge from simple misunderstandings, but few are entirely innocent creations. Here we suggest three main routes: from Chinese sources—official, scholarly, and nonofficial; from Western observers including official sources; and from scholarship, often combining Chinese and Western interpretations. These routes also converge so that, for instance, scholars may relay official Chinese sources and other Western observers may transmit that scholarship. As with anything else, when we are presented with ideas about China, we should always consider where they are coming from and why these are the ones on offer.

Many ideas, as in the essays here on "The Chinese," Chinese medicine, women in Chinese history, and simplified characters, originate at least partly from official Chinese claims designed to meet the needs of nationalism and nation-building. The unchallenged repetition of such ideas has a propagandistic effect that not only seeks to trace back the history of "the Chinese nation" as far as possible, but also to bolster the legitimacy of the current government. There is a further set of claims that aim to legitimate the Chinese Communist Party (CCP) as the only possible rulers of the PRC, seen here in the essays on Xinjiang, Tibet, the Opium Wars, the rise of the CCP, and China's political system.

This connection between history and legitimacy goes back a long way. In imperial times (221 BCE to 1911 CE) rulers claimed legitimacy on the basis that Heaven had selected them for the job of intermediary between Heaven, Earth, and Humanity, which meant they were liable to be judged on how well they delivered desirables such as peace and low taxes. Many modern scholars read China's first historian, Sima Qian (145–ca. 90 BCE), as critical of emperors such as Han Wudi (141–87 BCE), whose military campaigns Sima links to the impoverishment of state and people, thereby raising questions about Han Wudi's selection by Heaven. As dynasties began to succeed one another after the Han period, dynastic founders justified their takeovers by claiming to possess superior virtue, which broadly meant the capacity to deliver on their obligations, and histories that reinforced such narratives became useful elements in legitimation processes. By the fifteenth century some Ming (1368–1644) scholars feared that the legitimacy of the Song dynasty (960–1276) was threatened by the existence of two additional official histories recording foreign-led regimes that coexisted with the Song. For these Ming scholars official histories had such legitimating power that they felt it necessary to rewrite the history of the Song to exclude the foreigners. Legitimacy in the PRC can still be measured by how well government fulfills its obligations, and governments remain keen to control the stories told about them.

The Yellow River states also claimed political and cultural centrality in the East Asia region. Early Chinese texts such as the *Huainanzi* conceive the world in terms of concentric circles or squares with the writer's own ruler at the center, surrounded by increasingly distant adherents and then increasingly barbarous neighbors.[6] Claims to centrality feature in Song-dynasty rhetoric even though it was never preeminent among its neighbors, but rather had to share power with them.[7] In the present day such claims remain necessary because of the sheer geographical size of the PRC: as discussed in the following essays, Beijing's insistence on its right to control Tibet, Xinjiang, and Taiwan rests on arguments that Chinese authority over those regions began centuries, if not millennia, in the past. Asserting historical precedent for territorial claims is not unique to China, but in places like Slovakia, Timor-Leste, and Southern Sudan such efforts have been trumped by demands for self-determination. Unable to silence dissenting voices speaking from outside its borders, PRC governments and their supporters have been forced to respond to interpretations that conflict with the official version, generating disputes that highlight the problems inherent in using contested historical precedents to justify present action.

Chinese critics of their own government are another source of selective claims about China's history. In the reform era of the late nineteenth century, scholars and antidynastic elements developed historical narratives of certain phenomena that supported their political goals. In this book we see how officials' fears of foreign imperialism determined the location of China's borders, and how even the classification of martial arts could imply criticism of the Qing dynasty (1644–1911). Primarily since the 1980s, some seeking policy change have also employed selective historical interpretation. Essays here show how would-be reformers invoke the supposedly meritocratic civil service examinations against present-day social inequality and corruption, and how opponents of the one-child policy exaggerate its failures. Other authors explain how popular sentiment further sustains such approaches by providing, for instance, memoirs about the horrors of the Cultural Revolution, and adopting ideas such as the traditional harmony between humans and nature.

Other claims about China's history are creations of Westerners. Examples in this volume are the "decline of Buddhism," and Tiananmen 1989 as a student movement for democracy. These tend to result from outside observers projecting their own desires onto an idealized China. We see here how foreigners identifying a traditional Chinese harmony with nature were seeking comparisons with which to castigate their own exploitative, industrial societies. More obviously, it was clear even at the time that Western journalists reporting from Tiananmen Square in 1989 were drunk on the idea that the students intended to imitate the Western liberal model, which meant a moral victory for the West in the Cold War that was then still ongoing.

Such wishful thinking has also been applied to antiauthoritarian risings in the former Soviet bloc, the Middle East, and North Africa, among others.

In China this transference also has a lengthy history, as we see in the claim that Chinese society is Confucian. In one of our essays we see how this notion started among the Jesuits and then other Christian missionaries, who represented (and sometimes misrepresented) Confucius and Confucian ideas according to their own interests. This and other ideas have been adopted back into PRC representations for new purposes. When government negotiators argue, as noted above, that the destruction produced by China's development of modern industry is required to overcome the "backwardness" engendered by *Western* imperialism, they suggest an implicit contrast with a *Chinese* tradition of harmony with nature. And Confucius now represents a Chinese culture that is to be spread through Confucius Institutes being established around the world.

Some foreigners have even invented complete myths out of popular fascination with China, inadequate research, and a publishing deal. Although rare, these can make a big impact, as did Gavin Menzies's proposal in his book *1421* that Chinese seafarers discovered the Americas before Columbus, even when every reputable China scholar both inside and outside China rejects this contention outright.

Other claims derive from ideas projected by China's educated elites and transmitted by anglophone scholars. In this volume we have discussions of common Western notions about non-Chinese rule of China, the position of women, and communism in China. These ideas result from Western scholars adopting interpretations presented as fact by Chinese elites, basing scholarly debates on them, and transmitting the outcomes to students and general audiences. One example is "China's response to the West." Some nineteenth-century Chinese reformers felt pride in China's lengthy history, periods of glory, pacifistic character, striving for order, and high level of civilization, but also believed that there were serious obstacles to overcome before China could enter the modern world. Accordingly they sought to marry traditional social and political structures with imported technology and methods. As the study of China within Area Studies became an established academic field in the United States, scholars led by John King Fairbank borrowed directly from their sources to argue that nineteenth-century China had begun to modernize only in response to the impact of contact with the West. Thirty years on this view was critiqued by Paul Cohen for its Eurocentrism and neglect of Chinese internal developments, but in the 1950s and 1960s, when U.S. self-confidence observed China's quest for modernization, these interpretations were fit for the purposes of the time.[8]

Challenges to received wisdom were also discouraged by traditional approaches to studying China in European and North American universities. When Sinology became a field of study in the late nineteenth century, the discipline was philology, that is, cultural understanding through immersion in the language. The model was Classics—the study of an ancient "great civilization" regarded as the precursor of powerful modern nation-states (Britain and the United States, not Greece or Italy)—at a time when this subject was considered suitable preparation for administering empire. The Sinological analogue for ancient Greece and Rome was China's pre- and early imperial periods from the eighth century BCE to the third century CE, with forays as late as the Tang dynasty of the seventh to tenth centuries. As in Classics at the time, the concerns were primarily philosophy and literature, especially poetry. These topics required a demanding training in Classical, or Literary, Chinese, which was often considered more important than the modern or spoken language. The sheer effort and time required to learn Chinese, and especially Literary Chinese, encouraged scholars to emphasize comprehension of the words and what they signified about "Chinese culture" over critique of their content and context, so that the views of the sources were often reproduced without challenge. This approach is noticeable in anglophone accounts of Chinese history even down to the 1980s.[9]

During the Cold War, the Area Studies model became popular, especially in North America. This emphasized the social sciences—often including history—although language study remained at the core of the subject. In history the focus shifted to the modern period, usually starting with significant Western intrusions dated from the Macartney mission of 1793–1794 or the Opium War of 1839–1842. At a time when Mao's China lacked diplomatic relations with the West there was much discussion among anglophone historians of "China's response to the West," and the modern period defined by this relationship was frequently contrasted, in good nationalistic fashion, with "traditional China," portrayed as an unchanging monolith spanning the preceding two millennia.[10]

The majority of China's history—most of the imperial period between about 200 and 1800 CE—remained the object of generalizations projected from readings in the ancient classical texts or observations from the nineteenth century. Since many modern observations seemed to reflect ancient views (for instance, about the submissive role of women), it was easy for both Sinology and Area Studies to agree that China was exceptional for its continuity of culture and political organization, despite the lack of many actual studies of the 1600-year gap between the areas of chief scholarly interest. Accordingly, much was taken for granted, and these assumptions passed into textbooks and thence into "general knowledge" about China.

We should also consider how this "general knowledge" persists and spreads. With new circumstances come new ways to understand China. Change came in the 1980s, and not least among the issues is the very definition of "China" in a situation where Western scholars join others in challenging any kind of unitary conception of people, place, culture, and so on. These challenges are themselves debated, and have elicited reiterations of claims about the unique attractiveness of Chinese culture, China's cultural continuity, and its fundamental political unity.[11] New historical interpretations are always slow to catch on. But scholars may retain old assumptions about Chinese history for reasons that go beyond differences of interpretation. Although anthropologists have now contributed many studies of ordinary people in the present day, the historical record focuses intently on the literati elite and their concerns. This characteristic of the sources, combined with the sheer labor required to gain access to them in the original language, may have nudged the Cold War generation of China historians (both outside and within China) toward an identification with the literati elite and an under-critical approach to the representations they have left us. In China, scholars also feel a powerful reluctance to disagree with their teacher's work but prefer to build upon it. As to the more nationalistic interpretations, particularly as they relate to the governance of the present-day PRC, one cannot entirely discount the possibility of self-censorship by Western scholars afraid of being denied visas to China to do their research.

Outside the academy, there may also be comfort in clinging to familiar impressions of other cultures as a method of making manageable that which is unknown, unavoidable, and even threatening. Such impressions are difficult to address through conventional scholarly means because even if readers turn to academic works, it may not be evident how any particular contribution relates to ideas that may be remarkably deep-seated. Scholars speaking primarily to each other may not explain, for example, how archaeological discoveries in Sichuan or Manchuria speak to the claim that the Chinese are a single people. In their own conversations scholars may stop referring to discredited ideas even though these still circulate in popular works or other academic fields.

The ideas themselves also contribute to their own longevity. One method is shape-shifting: the same claim may be deployed for different purposes by different people at different times. As we see in this volume, everybody regards Sun Yat-sen as the father of the Chinese revolution, but his offspring are diverse, including PRC minorities policy, "guided democracy" in Taiwan, and U.S. admiration for his supposed democratic capitalist impulses. A measured assessment of Sun Yat-sen's role in any one of these will only modify his overall reputation very slowly, if at all.

Many individual interpretations connect to others, creating a self-reinforcing network. Authors in this book explain how ideas about Tibet and Xinjiang contribute to conceptions of China's borders more generally, and other essays show how these link to beliefs about the "Chineseness" of China's population, the Great Wall, and non-Chinese rulers of China. Critiquing one idea invokes its allies and the combination may limit what alternative views may be offered. Contributions here combine to show how questioning the power of "Chinese" culture over "non-Chinese" rulers may founder on the definition of "China" and its borders: if defined politically, then anything within the boundary may be regarded as "Chinese," but if the boundaries are cultural, then "Chinese" ways may be borne outside the line by people defined as "culturally Chinese." Either way, foreign rulers are absorbed into the Chinese world, if not because of their geographical location, then because their officials are "Chinese." These are slippery notions.

HISTORICAL CLAIMS AND ALTERNATIVE INTERPRETATIONS

One might ask by what right the authors writing in this volume presume to criticize other people's claims about their own history. The modern discipline of history began as a handmaiden to nineteenth-century nation-building and imperialism, supplying ancient origins for modern political formations (thus "the Gauls" became the ancestors of "the French," and so on), and narratives that justified colonial expansion. During the twentieth century we came to understand how writing about a place or people creates discourses that shape the way things are seen, and thereby exercises power over them. Often this power of discourse supports and is supported by other types of power: political, economic, and so on, and is particularly evident in relations between imperial centers and their colonial peripheries. This generates resistance from the weaker parties, and some of the interpretations reconsidered here constitute responses from within China against imperialism. Thus Western scholars critiquing those responses for a Western audience risk being accused of perpetuating attempts to exercise control through the power of discourse, which might be regarded as a form of neo-imperialism.

The PRC state also tells its own stories about the past, primarily aimed at people within the PRC but increasingly also in other parts of the world. The international audience includes tourists in China, those reached by the PRC's Confucius Institutes, or watchers of the Olympic ceremonies of 2008. But another thing we learned last century is that mass communications, globalization, and practical discontents with the nation-state have ensured that no government has exclusive possession even of the history claimed as its own. Within any state, including the PRC, there are minorities and First Peoples and other disempowered groups who see inclusive national narratives as encroachments on present and past identities. At the same time there are scholars, including some writing in this volume, who seek alternative interpretations of their own country's history, and may challenge the state's version of events out of conscious resistance or intellectual curiosity.

Furthermore, there are historians from outside the Euro-American world who write in English about countries other than their own. Such scholars may come from places that were themselves subject to colonialism or imperialism, which makes them harder to implicate in any neo-imperialist project, even though many trained or are employed in Western or Western-style universities. The present authors include Chinese specialists on China and China historians from Asia and South America, as well as North Americans and Europeans. They disagree with state-sanctioned historical interpretations, but they are not the only ones raising such challenges, often within China as well as outside it.

Nobody owns history, and historical claims may be associated with political agendas, scholarly trends, personal aggrandizement, or combinations of these factors. Questioning such representations and their uses need not be confined to specialists, and this book aims to present models for critical approaches to some common perceptions about China's history. Many more claims could be challenged than those included here: every reader will be dissatisfied at the omissions. We hope that the selections offered nevertheless speak to some key issues in China's history and in Western understandings of it. The construction of China's (or anyone's) history to suit specific purposes is a game that many have played. Among other things, that means that critical readers should also question the motives of this volume. Readers should note also that because this volume intends to highlight the roles of those who create knowledge, the editor has refrained from imposing a uniform approach to matters such as the use of endnotes and the dating of dynasties, preferring to follow the choice of each individual author taking their own approach to a topic of particular concern to them.

NOTES

1. Philadelphia, 18 March 2008, http://www.youtube.com/watch?v=zrp-v2tHaDo.
2. Konrad M. Lawson supplies a handy list of apologies to China down to 2005, including the original Japanese, on his "Muninn" blog, http://muninn.net/blog/2005/04/japans-apologies-to-china.html; and all of Japan's apologies through 2011 are listed at: http://en.wikipedia.org/wiki/List_of_war_apology_statements_issued_by_Japan; both consulted 28 February 2012.
3. Marlowe Hood, "China, US Clash at Climate Talks," AFP, 10 December 2009, http://www.google.com/hostednews/afp/article/ALeqM5g-mO9Sm2KtNVCQGTZ-1TyOCQlMpwA.
4. Contrast the multiplicity of cultural identities for this period described in Wolfram Eberhard, *A History of China*, 4th ed. (London: Routledge & Kegan Paul, 1977) and David Christian, *A History of Russia, Central Asia and Mongolia* (Oxford: Blackwell, 1998) with the ascription in Denis Twitchett, ed., *Cambridge History of China, Vol. 3: Sui and T'ang China 589–906, Pt. 1* (Cambridge: Cambridge University

Press, 1979), of the Sui and Tang ruling houses, both leading members of the north-western aristocracy, as "Chinese."

5. Pankaj Mishra, "The Barbarian Invasion" (review of "Encounters" exhibition at the Victoria and Albert Museum), *Guardian*, 11 September 2004, http://www.guardian.co.uk/books/2004/sep/11/1?INTCMP=SRCH; Jonathan Watts, "Chinese Communists Dash Hopes for Democratic Reform," *Guardian*, 21 October 2005, http://www.guardian.co.uk/world/2005/oct/21/china.jonathanwatts?INTCMP=SRCH; Gina Cuthbertson and Peter Cuthbertson, "Welcome CTC Cycling Group," *Tandem Club Journal* 240 (February/March 2012): 11.

6. See, for instance, John S. Major, "The Five Phases, Magic Squares and Schematic Cosmography," in *Explorations in Early Chinese Cosmology*, ed. Henry Rosemont (Chico, CA: Scholar Press, 1984), pp. 133–66.

7. Wang Gungwu, "The Rhetoric of a Lesser Empire: Early Sung Relations with Its Neighbors," in *China among Equals: The Middle Kingdom and Its Neighbors, 10th to 14th Centuries*, ed. Morris Rossabi (Berkeley: University of California Press, 1983), pp. 47–65, and Tao Jing-shen, "Barbarians or Northerners: Northern Sung Images of the Khitans," in Rossabi, *China among Equals*, pp. 66–86.

8. Paul Cohen, *Discovering History in China: American Writing on the Recent Chinese Past* (New York: Columbia University Press, 1984).

9. For instance, Denis Twitchett and Michael Loewe, eds., *Cambridge History of China, Volume 1: The Ch'in and Han Empires, 221 BC–AD 220* (Cambridge: Cambridge University Press, 1986).

10. The classic example of this is John King Fairbank and Edwin O. Reischauer, *China: Tradition and Transformation* (Boston: Houghton Mifflin, 1978).

11. For example, Ho Ping-ti, "In Defense of Sinicization: A Rebuttal of Evelyn Rawski's 'Reenvisioning the Qing,'" *Journal of Asian Studies* 57, no. 1 (1998): 123–55; Hugh R. Clark, "Frontier Discourse and China's Maritime Frontier: China's Frontiers and the Encounter with the Sea through Early Imperial History," *Journal of World History* 20, no. 1 (2009): 1–33; Wang Gungwu, preface to *Divided China: Preparing for Reunification, 883–947*, 2nd ed. (Singapore: World Scientific, 2007).

I

IMAGES OF AN ANCIENT AND UNITED NATION

1

The Chinese

Peter C. Perdue

One of modern China's most powerful ideas has asserted that the Chinese people have formed a single collective unit from ancient times through the present. This nationalist claim of primordial unity still retains a strong grip on academic history and popular consciousness. The historian who wants to tell a more nuanced story has to debunk this idea but also explain why it has such broad appeal.

As Chiang Kai-shek, the ruler of Nationalist China, expressed it, "According to its historic development, our Chinese nation (*Zhonghua minzu*) was formed by the blending of numerous clans. These clans were originally branches of the same race, spreading to the East of the Pamir plateau, along the valleys of the Yellow, the Huai, the Yangzi, the Heilongjiang, and the Pearl rivers. . . . During the past five thousand years, with increasing contacts and migrations, they have been continuously blended into a nation. But the motive power of that blending was by assimilation rather than conquest."[1]

Chiang, like Sun Yat-sen, believed that China had been a united nation for "five thousand years," since the dawn of prehistory. The "clans" (*zongzu*) had spread out from the Yellow River valley to settle the historical core of China (China Proper), modern Manchuria, Mongolia, Xinjiang, and Tibet, as well as Taiwan and even the Ryukyu islands (see figure 1.1). The Nationalist Party claimed sovereignty over all the territory occupied by these mingled clans. Although it had overthrown the "barbarian" Manchu Qing dynasty, it laid claim to all the territory controlled by the Qing during its maximal period of expansion in the eighteenth century. But the Qing conquests only restored the deeply rooted unity of peoples that had already existed several thousand years ago:

Figure 1.1. Map of China from Chiang Kai-shek, *China's Destiny* (New York: Roy Publishers, 1947). It indicates Chiang's expansive vision of the peoples belonging to the Chinese cultural realm, including the Ryukyus, Taiwan, Korea, Tanna Tuva, Outer Mongolia, and Tibet.

Within China's territory, the customs of each clan, and the way of life in each locality were different. Yet the customs of each clan were unified to form China's national culture, and the combination of the ways of life in each locality made possible the existence of the Chinese nation. This outstanding fact of China's history is based on her geography, her economic structure, the requirements of national defense, and a common historical destiny (*mingyun*), and is not merely the result of political necessity.[2]

Chiang and his ideologues, fighting against Japanese invasion in the 1940s, insisted on reconquering all the territories lost over one hundred years of foreign incursions. The loss of these territories in the nineteenth century constituted such deep humiliation that the government and its people could not rest until they were all under one ruler:

[I]n the territory of China a hundred years ago, comprising more than ten million square kilometers, there was not a single district that was not essential to the survival of the Chinese nation, and none that was not permeated by our culture. The breaking up of this territory meant the undermining of the nation's security as well as the decline of the nation's culture. Thus the people as a whole must regard this as a national humiliation, and not until all lost territories have been recovered can we relax our efforts to wipe out this humiliation and save ourselves from destruction.[3]

Chiang and the Nationalists, of course, failed to recover the lost territories. After the end of the Pacific War in 1945, a civil war between the Nationalist and Communist parties brought Communist victory in 1949. Chiang fled to Taiwan, where his Nationalist Party ruled continuously until 2000, and returned to power again in 2008. Taiwan is still a separate state from the People's Republic; Mongolia is an independent state, and other territories of the former Qing dynasty are controlled by Russia and the Central Asian republics. The dream of maximal unity of the "Chinese" people has never come to pass.

The orthodox Communist Party interpretation of Chinese history, although it stresses class struggle over culture, expresses similar ideas:

In Chinese history no one ethnic group (*minzu*) has developed in isolation from the others. Each has contributed to the creation of Chinese history (*zu-guo*) and each shares the destiny of the nation as a whole. In the protracted struggle against feudalism, colonialism and imperialism, each group has battled side by side with the others. In every aspect, economic, political and cultural, each group (*minzu*) absorbs nourishment from its fraternal groups for its own enrichment, and each language is under the constant influence of its fraternal tongues. . . . After the founding of the People's Republic, a policy of equality and unity between its ethnic groups was put into effect, autonomous areas for minorities living in compact communities were established, the languages and customs of the minorities were respected, and the state helped each of them to develop its economy and culture. Unprecedented unity has been achieved.[4]

This text summarizes an official multivolume survey of Chinese history that began to appear in 1989. The author, Bai Shouyi, speaks of many different "ethnic groups" (*minzu*) instead of the "clans" described by Chiang Kai-shek, and Bai stresses struggle against "feudal" oppressors; however, he too claims that the "ethnic groups" never fought each other, but joined together in a common struggle for justice. Under the People's Republic, they finally achieved "unprecedented unity." Bai, like Chiang, assumes the continuity of a single Chinese race from ancient times.

It is easy to debunk the simplistic assumptions embedded in this ideology. Genetic evidence does not indicate that all citizens of contemporary China descended from a common ancestor. In fact, recent studies of DNA show that Han Chinese groups divide into two populations, northern and southern, separated by the Yangzi River.[5] Studies of ancient mummies found in the deserts of Xinjiang show closer connections to peoples of Western Asia than to Han Chinese. Biologically, the peoples of China are a mixture of groups from many different places. They are no purer than the peoples of anywhere else in the world.

Modern archaeology also does not support the thesis of a single people inhabiting the territory of modern China. In the early twentieth century, Chinese archaeologists intensively excavated the area called the "Central Plain," around the bend of the Yellow River near the modern city of Xi'an. Scholars concluded that this region was the origin of the Chinese people. This hypothesis, which predominated until the 1980s, held that "the earliest agricultural life and the earliest civilizations first appeared in a nuclear area in the Central Plain."[6] The peoples of this core region, it was said, then spread out to occupy the rest of China.

A similar conception dominated study of the succeeding period of the Shang dynasty (ca. 1570–1045 BCE). The discovery of oracle bones—Chinese characters inscribed on materials from tortoises and oxen—and the excavations at the ancient capital of Anyang from 1928 to 1937 confirmed the existence of the Shang dynasty referred to in ancient texts. It was easy to conclude that this region was "the origin of Chinese civilization" and that succeeding generations of Chinese descended from the people of this region.

Contemporary archaeologists, however, have expanded studies beyond the Yellow River valley, investigating diverse cultures across the Chinese subcontinent. They have examined fishing cultures of the southeast coast, lake cultures in central China, plateau dwellers in the far west, and proto-pastoralists in the northwest. A leading Chinese archaeologist argued in 1981 that "the Yellow River valley did indeed play an important part, frequently occupying a leading position during periods of civilization. Nevertheless, during the same

periods the ancient cultures of the other regions were also developing in accordance with their own respective characteristics and courses."[7] Archaeologists in China and the West now accept more readily ideas of multiple origins
of civilization and interaction between diverse regional cultures.

The Shang period provides even more evidence of diversity. The discovery in 1986 of spectacular, strange bronze figures in a pit in Sichuan, and in
1988 of a rich tomb in Jiangxi, called into question the simple assumption
of diffusion into backward areas of an advanced bronze culture identified
with the Shang capital of Anyang. Such evidence for multiple centers of
cultural innovation undermines the idea of essential unity that supports the
notion of a single people. The bronzes in Sichuan, illustrated in figure 1.2,
showed no signs of contact with Anyang, but they were equally sophisticated. Likewise, bronzes in the northern zone of China, on the border with
the grasslands, used metallurgical techniques originating outside China
Proper, in some part of Central Eurasia. The world of material culture was
wider than that portrayed in the classical texts.[8] Chinese and Western archaeologists still debate the extent to which these multiple cultures formed
a single "interaction sphere," but the assumption of a blended, uniform
culture from ancient times has no empirical support.

Dynastic rulers, however, have repeatedly consolidated control over
much of modern China's territory. In 221 BCE, Shihuangdi founded the

Figure 1.2. Gold Masks from Sanxingdui, Sichuan. These objects exhibit a very distinctive
cultural formation, quite different from the bronzes of north China. http://en.wikipedia.
org/wiki/File:Sanxingduimasks.jpg (licensed for use under Creative Commons).

Qin Empire, and the last empire collapsed in 1911 CE. The twenty-five official dynastic histories present a continuous story of imperial rule over two thousand years. Twentieth-century nationalists rejected the imperial political structures but celebrated their conquests as defining the fundamental unity of China.

The dynastic idea, too, contradicts the evidence. For a large part of the period from 221 BCE to 1911 CE, contending polities divided up the core of modern China (China Proper). If we include the Central Eurasian regions, as the racial idea requires, the periods of unification are even shorter. After the fall of the Han dynasty in 220 CE, no single ruler controlled the core of China until 589 CE under the Sui, followed by the Tang dynasty in 618 CE. By the 750s, the Tang had in fact fallen apart, although it did not officially collapse until 907 CE. The succeeding Song, Liao, and Jin dynasties once again divided the core of China. Only the Mongol Yuan dynasty, by 1279, expanded its reach over all of China Proper and Central Eurasia, but it fell to the Ming in 1368. The Ming dynasty controlled China Proper but not Central Eurasia. The Qing conquered Central Eurasia completely only in the mid-eighteenth century, and it lost control of much of the region after the mid-nineteenth century. In short, the regions claimed as "Chinese" by Chiang Kai-shek were only under a single unified regime for less than two hundred years of China's "five-thousand-year" history.

In any case, political unification is a poor indicator of cultural or racial unity. All of the dynasties ruled over a great diversity of peoples, and they never called them all by a single name. The only feature these peoples had in common was their subjection to an imperial elite. They spoke different languages, made a living in different ways, practiced different religions, and frequently moved around, through, and across borders. The elites of the dynasties whose rulers came from Central Eurasia, like the Tang, Yuan, and Qing, had mixed ethnic origins. The Tang rulers were part Turkish, the Yuan combined Mongols, Persians, Turks, Han Chinese, and even a European (Marco Polo) in its governing class, and the Qing ruled with a triple coalition of Manchus, Mongols, and Han Chinese. The dynasties held together for a long period of time not because they represented a single unified ethnic group. On the contrary, they succeeded because they adapted their policies to meet the demands of multiple distinct ethnic groups. These groups did interact with each other, but they never "blended into a single nation."

We also have considerable difficulty in defining clearly the meaning of the Chinese terms for "clan," "ethnic group," or "race." Anthropologists have repeatedly insisted that the use of the term "race" for biologically based difference between peoples has no scientific basis.[9] The most frequently used Chinese term, *minzu*, has no exact equivalent in English. Until recently, "nationality" has been the standard translation for "*minzu*," but Chinese writers have now begun to translate "*minzu*" as "ethnic group."

They have also used terms like *"zhongzu"* to indicate broader groupings with similar biological characteristics.

But *"minzu"* does not fit very well with the contemporary Western understanding of ethnicity. In China, there are only fifty-six legally defined *minzu*, one indicated on every citizen's identity card, which are generally unalterable after adulthood. There are no hyphenated *minzu*, and one cannot choose freely one's nationality: it depends on your parents. Ethnicity in the West is a much more ambiguous concept, allowing subjective definition of one's identity, and expressed in different ways in different social situations. Ethnic stereotyping is certainly prevalent in Western countries, but these categories are not stamped on identity cards as part of a state ideology.

The notion of Chinese racial unity depends heavily on the concept of fixed nationalities defined by the state, and the ideology of "friendship" between nationalities, which is reinforced in propaganda, films, and historical texts. In principle, no one nationality is superior to any other, but in many practical situations, the majority Han nationality expresses its dominant power, within the Communist Party and elsewhere.

Where did this idea originate? Chinese nationalist intellectuals of the early twentieth century created it, building upon classical foundations. Zou Rong, a young student, wrote in his impassioned text of 1903, entitled "The Revolutionary Army," that "the yellow and white races . . . are fundamentally incapable of giving way to each other." He called for the Han race, "the moving force of Eastern civilization," which had colonized Japan, Korea, Southeast Asia, Tibet, Hawai'i, and the Americas, to lead a racial war against the whites in order to restore its greatness. The repressive rule of the Manchu Qing elite had emasculated this huge Chinese race. Zou Rong and the radical nationalists blamed the Manchus both for repressing the natural right to rule of the Han people and for failing to defend the natural boundaries of China against foreign invasion. Sun Yat-sen, after leading a victorious nationalist revolution in 1911, suppressed the anti-Manchu rhetoric, instead promoting the ideology of the unity of five peoples in one nation (Han, Manchu, Mongol, Muslim, and Tibetan), but the Han still dominated. History textbooks and popular media broadcast these ideas to wider populations. The Nationalists were remarkably effective in embedding their historical and racial concepts in popular consciousness. Even though the Republic of China fell into division among warlords, and recaptured only part of China before losing Manchuria to Japan in 1931, the vision of a deeply rooted united China never disappeared. It pervades historical writing in the PRC, and to a lesser extent in Hong Kong and Taiwan. It embodies the fervent wishes of many Chinese for a single strong state supported by a united population, even though reality fails to fit the dream. No one would take seriously an American historian who insisted that the Iroquois of New York, for example (but not those of Canada), and the Hispanics of New Mexico (but not those of Mexico itself), had always been part of a single American nation. We can respect the strong desire of Chinese for a united nation, while also recognizing that the strong grip of this concept discourages critical thinking.

All myths, however, contain a kernel of truth. By contrast with Europe, where after the fall of the Roman Empire no single entity encompassed all European peoples until the formation of the European Union, China's imperial structures have achieved increasing political and economic integration. Since the eighth century CE, the construction of the Grand Canal, for example, linking southern China with the political capitals in the north, turned the increasingly prosperous south into one of China's two core regions. During the early modern period, from the sixteenth to eighteenth centuries, China generated greater political, economic, and cultural connections and, under the Qing, expanded them to tie Central Eurasian regions more closely to the core. These trends, in fact, paralleled increasing integration in much of the rest of the world, including Southeast Asia, Western Europe, and Russia. Chinese unity was not primordially based, but part of wider global processes. At the same time, forces toward unity constantly struggled against forces of disintegration, and there was no inevitability.

Some thoughtful Chinese historians have promoted more diverse notions of China. Xu Zhuoyun, the distinguished historian of China from Taiwan, recognizes the openness of ancient China and the diverse sources of its culture: "Although China is in East Asia, it is open to Central Asia, and China received influences from the mobile peoples, and learned knowledge of the chariot, combining it with its own highly developed smelting techniques to create its special bronze culture."[10] Hong Kong and Taiwan intellectuals, and some minority leaders in China, have advocated a more pluralist concept of Chinese history and culture, one which recognizes autonomy and diverse regional customs, while accepting the rule of a single state. Advocates of Taiwan or Uighur independence, on the other hand, argue that these regions have experienced such distinct histories that they should not be part of a single governing regime. The PRC government fears than any recognition of regional autonomy will threaten the unity of their party-state.

Would abandoning this notion lead to the breakup of China? What if students learned that contemporary China (including the two states of the PRC and Taiwan) is a contingent product of many political decisions, global processes, accidents, and longer-term cultural and economic trends? Would a closer approximation of historical truth really endanger the unity of China? Wang Gungwu, the distinguished historian of the overseas Chinese, argues that "our understanding of Chineseness must recognize [that] it is living and changeable; it is also the product of a shared historical experience . . . and it should be related to what appears to be, or have been,

Chinese in the eyes of non-Chinese.[11] Intelligent Chinese writers realize that uncritical nationalism closes down inquiring minds. Insistence on racial unity means ignoring the legitimate aspirations of many peoples of China to preserve a distinct culture that earns respect in itself, and is not seen as a "backward" belief system to be merged into a single dominant majority Han culture. China will never become a European Union; it will remain a unitary state. But a greater recognition of its historical diversity would help to open up new ways of thinking about China's identity in the past and present.

SUGGESTIONS FOR FURTHER READING

Scholarly interest in China's minorities, and their relationship to Chinese nationalism, has boomed in recent years. Some of the primary sources for nationalist ideology are available in English, including Zou Rong's passionate anti-Manchu tract (Tsou Jung, *The Revolutionary Army. A Chinese Nationalist Tract of 1903*, trans. John Lust (Mouton, 1968)). The classic statement of the nationalist position is still Chiang Kai-shek, *China's Destiny* (Roy Publishers, 1947), and the Communist version is in Bai Shouyi and Yang Chao, *An Outline History of China* (Foreign Languages Press, 2002). But Western scholars have questioned the standard position in specialized studies. Prasenjit Duara critiques nationalist manipulation of history for ideological ends in *Rescuing History from the Nation* (University of Chicago Press, 1995). The website for the Critical Han Studies project (http://www.hanstudies.org/info.html) contains abstracts of recent papers on this subject.

On the PRC, Morris Rossabi, *Governing China's Multiethnic Frontiers* (University of Washington Press, 2004) contains studies examining challenges to PRC control over minority regions. Susan Shirk, *China: Fragile Superpower* (Oxford University Press, 2007) describes well the ideological insecurity of China's current leadership, as it asserts dubious nationalist claims against Western criticism. Thomas Mullaney, *Coming to Terms with the Nation: Ethnic Classification in Modern China* (University of California Press, 2011) examines how Communist officials in the early 1950s decided the categories for classifying the fifty-six nationalities, and the political compromises involved in ethnic categorization. Uradyn Bulag, *The Mongols at China's Edge* (Rowman & Littlefield, 2002) traces the "friendship of nationalities" idea as developed in Communist and earlier rhetoric about Mongol-Han relations.

Many studies of the Qing dynasty explore ethnic questions. Pamela Crossley, Helen Siu, and Donald Sutton, eds., *Empire at the Margins* (University of California Press, 2006) collects articles on minority peoples and regions within the Qing Empire. Johann Elverskog, *Our Great Qing: The*

Mongols, Buddhism and the State in Late Imperial China (University of Hawai'i Press, 2006) analyzes how Mongols came to view their position within the Qing Empire. C. Patterson Giersch, *Asian Borderlands: The Transformation of Qing China's Yunnan Frontier* (Harvard University Press, 2006) is an excellent regional study.

NOTES

1. Chiang Kai-shek, *China's Destiny* (New York: Roy Publishers, 1947), p. 30, trans. from Jiang Jieshi, *Zhongguo zhi mingyun* (Shanghai: Shanghai Zhongguo shudian, 1945), pp. 1–2.
2. Ibid., p. 35.
3. Ibid., p. 34.
4. Bai Shouyi and Yang Chao, *An Outline History of China* (Beijing: Foreign Languages Press, 2002), p. 16.
5. R. Du, C. Xiao, and L. L. Cavalli-Sforza, "Genetic Distances between Chinese Populations Calculated on Gene Frequencies of 38 Loci," *Science in China. Series C, Life Sciences* 40, no. 6 (1997): 613–21.
6. Kwang-chih Chang, "China on the Eve of the Historical Period," in *The Cambridge History of Ancient China*, ed. Michael Loewe and Edward Shaughnessy (Cambridge: Cambridge University Press, 1999), p. 57.
7. Ibid.
8. Robert Bagley, "Shang Archaeology," in Loewe and Shaughnessy, *Cambridge History of Ancient China*, pp. 124–231.
9. Ashley Montagu, *Man's Most Dangerous Myth: The Fallacy of Race* (Cleveland, OH: World Pub. Co., 1964).
10. Xu Zhuoyun, *Wangu Jianghe: Zhongguo lishi wenhua de zhuanzhe yu kaizhan* (Taibei: Yingwen hansheng chuban gufen youxian gongsi, 2006), p. 50.
11. Wang Gungwu, *The Chineseness of China: Selected Essays* (Hong Kong: Oxford University Press, 1991), p. 2.

2

The Great Wall

Peter Lorge

The Great Wall of China has become a symbol of China itself, and like so many Chinese artifacts and practices its history has been projected back over two thousand years. No tourist visit to modern Beijing is complete without a trip to the rebuilt and refurbished sections of the Great Wall. No visual reference to China can go without an image of the wall snaking its way over mountains. At the same time, the Great Wall itself has been closely connected to an orientation toward defense on the part of all Chinese for all time, and a desire to cut China off from the outside world. For modern Westerners and Chinese alike, the Great Wall is a fundamental and obvious expression of Chinese culture from very early times. What makes this infusion of so much history and meaning into the Great Wall so curious is that over the span of China's history it hardly ever existed. When it existed at all, in some form or another, it was of limited duration and utility, thus representing more of an anomaly than an exemplar of Chinese culture.

As we attempt to separate fact from fiction, and meaning from ideology, modern understandings of the Great Wall can only be seen as a retrospective effort to call into being an eternal Chinese nation. The Great Wall's military value, even when it existed, was always limited, and was in many ways more a sign of policy confusion than of a culturally or strategically based solution to frontier problems. Indeed, as Arthur Waldron pointed out in his *The Great Wall of China*, there is no agreement on what constituted the Great Wall, where it ran at any point in history, or even how long it was. There is not even a term in Classical Chinese for "Great Wall." Yet modern commentators and journalists freely cite widely divergent lengths, paths, and histories for this blurry artifact with the utmost confidence. Every historical map, no matter the period, duly includes a line in northern China indicating where the Great Wall was imagined to be.

The Great Wall has taken on a symbolism akin to that of the medieval castle, and like the castle the image of the Great Wall has been divorced from its original function as one of several reactions to a military problem. Yet there is a real history of the Great Wall, and a history of its modern interpretation. It grew out of an earlier tradition of wall building, culminating in the Qin dynasty (221–207 BCE) and extended through the Han (202 BCE–220 CE). This was followed by another construction program in the Northern Qi (550–574) and Sui dynasties (589–618). The final building program, and the one that provides us with the basis of the modern tourist attraction, took place during the Ming dynasty (1368–1644). However, the myth of the Great Wall belongs not to these historical periods, but to the eighteenth century and afterward, and the arrival of the West.

Oddly enough, the extravagant claims for the Great Wall appear to have begun with the members of the frustrated Macartney mission to China in 1793. Although the mission failed to advance Britain's diplomatic cause, it did give its members the chance to see various sights, including the Great Wall. Macartney and his entourage were duly impressed with the wall itself, and readily accepted Chinese claims regarding its length and antiquity. They took it upon themselves to connect the gun loops in the wall with its supposed antiquity by concluding that the Chinese had had gunpowder for two millennia. Ironically, the wall they saw had been built only a few centuries before, when the Chinese did have gunpowder, and the wall was no longer of any military value.

Over the nineteenth and twentieth centuries the contrast between the grandeur, imagined antiquity, and continuity of the Great Wall on the one hand, and the declining power and military failures of Chinese governments on the other, led to the wall being remade into a symbol of China's core cultural values. Those cultural values were said to be insular defensive mindedness, and stress on self-defense and internal cultivation. The claim to a long history for the Great Wall was intended to prove to foreigners and Chinese alike that these values were fundamental to China. Many among these audiences continue to believe these claims to the antiquity of the wall and the centrality of these values in China, and China's bedrock nonviolence is constantly reiterated in popular culture and government propaganda. Like the misunderstandings of the Great Wall first propagated by Macartney and the members of his mission, there is little truth to these "core" Chinese values, and the real history of the Great Wall seems remote from the symbolic uses to which it has been put.

THE BEGINNING OF THE GREAT WALL

Long walls were built by Chinese governments for more than a thousand years before the construction of the Qin dynasty Great Wall. Remnants of a seven-kilometer wall from the Shang dynasty (1766?–1122? BCE) still stand in Henan in north China. That wall, like all ancient fortification walls that we know of in China, was built of pounded or tamped earth. Layers of soil were placed inside a frame and pounded into a solid mass. This construction method can still be seen in the twenty-first-century Chinese countryside, despite the availability of concrete and bricks. It is a cheap, flexible technique that requires only simple tools and plentiful labor.

The simplicity of pounded-earth construction led to its extensive use not just in domestic buildings and city walls, but also to create border or boundary walls many kilometers long. The first textual reference to a long wall dates from the seventh century BCE, and more than a kilometer of that wall is still visible. Over the succeeding centuries various of the Warring States (403–221 BCE) built long walls, as did some non-Chinese peoples. By the late third century BCE the Qin kingdom completed its conquest of the other Chinese states, and turned to deal with the northern steppe. A massive expedition was followed by an attempt to consolidate those gains through limited fort building.

This process of border consolidation was first described in the *Records of the Grand Historian*, written between 109 and 91 BCE. The passages covering the establishment of a new northern borderline are ambiguous about the nature of this fortified defense line, though its extent is clearer (a rhetorically exaggerated 10,000 *li*, or about 5,000 kilometers). Parts of the northern frontier did have long walls; these predated the Qin conquest and were likely incorporated into the postconquest northern defense line, but modern scholarship both in China and the West has argued against a continuous wall, and since we cannot be sure of that, the Great Wall as we understand the term did not exist. A string of fortified towns was also constructed after the expedition into the steppe, but this did not constitute a long wall either.

The idea that a continuous barrier was constructed crumbles in the light of two facts. First, the description of the new northern border fortifications makes no mention of a large-scale public works project. A continuous wall would have required a vast mobilization of manpower. Given the proclivity of the first Qin emperor for self-inflation through major architectural and infrastructure projects, a failure to mention the scale of work would be surprising. The descriptions simply note that the border was fortified over a great distance. Second, there was simply insufficient time between the final Qin unification of China in 221 BCE and the fall of the dynasty fifteen years later to complete such a vast project. The Qin dynasty ruled China for a very short time; it would have required a near complete mobilization of the empire's labor resources to construct a continuous wall running for hundreds of miles. There is no mention in the sources of any such mobilization.

While there was certainly no Qin Great Wall to defend sedentary China from the northern steppe threat, the threat itself was real, and continued to trouble subsequent dynasties. The Han dynasty, which immediately succeeded the Qin, lost several important campaigns against the steppe nomads and was forced to conclude treaties with them that explicitly mentioned a long wall or walls as the border between the two groups. The long wall in question was nowhere near the putative Great Wall of the Qin, however, though its mention has been used to substantiate, erroneously, the continued existence of the imagined Great Wall.

Long walls on the northern border are also mentioned in the sixth and early seventh centuries and they, like their Han dynasty predecessors, have been morphed into the direct, lineal descendants of the Qin Great Wall. Although these attributions fly directly in the face of geographic and historic reality, the very fact of long walls on the northern border has been enough to maintain a sense that some sort of Great Wall existed, in whatever form or location, at least intermittently, until the early seventh century. Even so, these later long walls were constructed to defend much more limited parts of the border rather than forming a complete system running from the northwest to the coast. What these defensive measures attest is not a real or historic Great Wall, but the persistence of one kind of policy response to the continued threat of raiding.

No border fortification facing China's northern frontier has ever been conceived of as a reliable barrier to a full-scale invasion. Long walls and fortified border outposts were meant to channel and impede smaller-scale raiding. Large invasion forces could always overwhelm local defenses. Fortified towns were always useful, whether as jumping-off points for campaigns into the steppe, or as trading posts. But they were not true defensive bastions. No ruler of sedentary China could pacify the steppe by military means alone, offensive or defensive. Not only were military means limited in effectiveness, but diplomatic and political means were constrained as well. Much of the initiative lay in the hands of steppe leaders far beyond the influence of the Chinese government. When the steppe was politically united or agglomerated into a confederation it could threaten the existence of a Chinese dynasty; conversely, it could also make reliable treaties that pacified the border. When political authority in the steppe was decentralized, individual leaders were difficult to control but did not threaten the security of the Chinese state.

The chronic steppe threat did not support a physically and chronologically continuous Great Wall precisely because such a system was incapable of solving the problem. The relationship of steppe groups to China was dynamic and could not be fixed with a static defensive system. A more dynamic, and successful, system of border defense briefly appeared at the end of the tenth and start of the eleventh century in Hebei province (surrounding what is now Beijing), some distance inside the Song dynasty border. This was a continuous water barrier, linking rivers and dikes and surrounded by irrigated farmland that effectively channeled all but the largest invasion forces into a limited set of routes. Yet once peace was established between the Song and the steppe Liao Empire (907–1125) the water barrier was allowed to disintegrate.

Nothing like a large-scale wall on the northern border was constructed for over seven hundred years, from the seventh to the fifteenth centuries. This was partly because steppe regimes controlled sections of north China, and partly because these regimes came in a continuous series, and were well organized. Mostly, however, walls were not built because they did not work very well. Political and diplomatic means were more effective, and when north China was under steppe rule, the main barrier between Chinese and steppe powers were the major rivers.

THE MING DYNASTY GREAT WALL

The real continuous fortification that underpins our modern idea of the Great Wall was constructed during the Ming dynasty. This reality cuts a millennium and a half off the "history" of the Great Wall, and places it firmly in the late-imperial period rather than at the roots of imperial China. We are therefore left with an artifact a mere five centuries old that arose long after the great accomplishments of Chinese civilization. Perhaps just as surprising to those who imagine the Great Wall to stem from the procrustean bed of Chinese culture is that the Ming Great Wall also included many cannons and firearms in its defensive system. Early firearms were most effective when used from the shelter of a wall, and the Ming took ample advantage of this.

What would eventually evolve into the Ming wall began as a local effort in the late fifteenth century to prevent Mongol raiding in an area of Ming territory without any natural barriers. This was in the loop of the Yellow River. Ming territory did not extend all the way north to the river itself, leaving a foothold of land inside this natural barrier that Mongol horsemen often used to pasture their horses. From there, it was an easy ride into Ming territory if they chose to do some raiding. The raiding itself was mostly local and limited, being done at the whim of individual Mongol leaders. Local Ming officials and military commanders were at a loss as to how to prevent these raids. While they were a minor problem from the central government's perspective, at least initially, they could be catastrophic at the local level.

The imperial government had the option of either mounting an expensive, large-scale military campaign to drive the Mongols entirely out of the region and take control of all the territory up to the river itself, or of withdrawing to more defensible positions further south. Neither was attractive. The gains from a military campaign, even if it succeeded, would be limited and difficult to hold, and they might spark a wider war, but ceding territory to the Mongols was strategically unacceptable and ignominious. While the court dithered, the local officials acted, building long walls to discourage the raiders.

These local wall-building efforts forced raiders to attack neighboring counties. This presented the appearance of a viable solution to the raiding problem, since walls were clearly so effective that they shifted attacks from places that had walls to those that did not. Wall-building took on increasing importance, particularly after a Mongol raid reached the outskirts of the capital, Beijing, in 1550. The walls were then extended to cover greater and greater areas, eventually creating a continuous barrier that also protected the capital region. That wall was gradually upgraded as well, being faced with stone and brick over long stretches to not only improve its defensive value, but also to diminish the maintenance requirements of bare pounded-earth walls.

When the Ming dynasty fell to the invading Manchus, a steppe group, in the middle of the seventeenth century, the Great Wall ceased to have any function whatsoever. It had hardly served any purpose to prevent Manchu incursions into Ming territory. For the succeeding three centuries the Great Wall was allowed to crumble. Its high point had been the century from the middle of the sixteenth to the middle of the seventeenth century, but it was not a glorious or noteworthy history, and it did not gain an important place in Chinese culture until long after it had been abandoned.

THE GREAT WALL IN CONTEMPORARY PERSPECTIVE

In a recent Hollywood movie, *The Mummy: Tomb of the Dragon Emperor* (2008), thousands of enemies of the first emperor of China are buried beneath the Great Wall. The Wall also appears in the animated film *Mulan* (1998), looking very much like the popular tourist attraction rebuilt in the twentieth century from the Ming dynasty ruins. These mishmashes of popular American culture reflect a confusion and mixing-up of different aspects of the various northern frontier walls that began during the Ming dynasty itself. As these distorted representations were transmitted to the West, they were further confused and amplified before finding their way back to China in the twentieth century. Like so many other late-imperial or even twentieth-century Chinese practices and artifacts, the Great Wall was presumed, by Chinese and foreigners alike, to be an eternal Chinese reality. Most Chinese people, if asked, would confidently assert that the Great Wall was built by the first Qin emperor and has existed ever since. Indeed, this is now taught as historical truth in Chinese school textbooks.

Particularly in light of China's twentieth-century history, a period in which the country struggled for internal unity and against foreign invasion, the Great Wall was reevaluated (unfortunately in light of its myths, not its history) as a sign of China's fundamentally nonaggressive culture. China, in this narrative, has a clearly marked border that divides what is Chinese from what is not. Chinese people, it is claimed, have no interest in expanding outside this border and have only wanted to defend themselves against invasion. This story was comforting to people searching for a fixed sense of nation and a higher moral ground than the imperial powers that had attacked it. At the same time, the Great Wall has symbolized Chinese closed-mindedness in the West.

So powerful has this portrayal of the Great Wall been, and so useful as a simplifying conceptual talisman, that it has been used as the outstanding example of China's underlying strategic culture of defense. Created by China's first unifier, the Great Wall is said to have been a declaration that China's territorial interests are fundamentally limited regardless of the power of the Chinese state. Applied to modern China, the representation of the Great Wall as the timeless boundary of China has become a justification for aggressive military action within whatever borders the Chinese government chooses to set. Since China, as defined by the Great Wall, is a nonaggressive and defensive-minded nation, everything it does must therefore be defensive and justified.

CONCLUSION

The idea of the continuous existence of the Great Wall is not only historically unjustified, it is part of a misleading and dangerous mischaracterization of Chinese culture. Chinese frontier policy over the last two millennia seldom involved wall-building and static defense, and Chinese strategic culture therefore had little to do with simply defending a "natural" territorial boundary. Chinese regimes, large and small, have always waged aggressive wars to expand their territory; if they subsequently built fortifications on their border to defend against hostile powers it was because they could not subdue those powers by offensive campaigning. Like all conquerors, Chinese regimes claimed to come in peace, and some of them even built the notion of the Great Wall to prove it.

SUGGESTIONS FOR FURTHER READING

China's Great Wall remains a perennial topic of research. The classic account of the Wall is Arthur Waldron's *The Great Wall of China: From History to Myth* (Cambridge University Press, 1992). Waldron strongly argues for the Ming dynasty origins of our present Great Wall, and that fortification's origin in political and strategic paralysis at the imperial court rather than a directed and ancient strategic program. Of more recent vintage, Julia Lovell's *The Great Wall: China against the World, 1000 BC–AD 2000* (Grove Press, 2006) aims at a more popular audience and provides greater coverage of the place of the Wall in the twentieth century. Lovell's account is nonetheless well researched and reliable. For a stunning visual journey along the wall, Michael Yamashita and William Lindesay's *The Great Wall: From Beginning to End* (Sterling, 2007) is unparalleled. The accompanying text is adequate for casual readers. Lindesay followed this with an intriguing account of the Wall comparing images from the past with the current state of the Wall in *The Great Wall Revisited: From the Jade Gate to Old Dragon's Head* (Harvard University Press, 2008). Finally, Stephen Turnbull's *The Great Wall of China, 221 BC–1644 AD* (Osprey, 2007) provides a simple, clear and concise discussion with ample illustrations. Turnbull also includes much of the day-to-day information not discussed in other works.

3

Foreign Conquerors of China

Naomi Standen

China has often been imagined as an island of civilization amid an ocean of barbarians. Scholars have frequently argued that when uncultured foreigners took over part or all of China, as they did periodically for a thousand years (which is half of the imperial period), they were unable to resist adopting the superior culture of the Chinese and so becoming "sinicized." The moral foundations of Chinese society trumped mere military might, and "China conquered the conquerors." This notion of sinicization once dominated both Chinese and Western interpretations of foreign rule in the traditional territory of China. This was unfortunate because the theory holds no water: it is illogical, narrowly focused, and Sinocentric. Despite this, the claim has been attractive both in China, where it is currently undergoing a revival, and among Euro-American scholars, who have passed it on to wider Western audiences.

WHAT IS SINICIZATION?

The idea of sinicization begins, as do so many, with Confucius. His putative sayings, as gathered in the *Analects*, hardly mention foreigners, but a few brief remarks contrast alien crudity with the civilizing influence of the Confucian "gentleman." Whereas "barbarians" lack civilized attributes such as tying up their hair and having rulers, Confucius proposes that "should the distant . . . not submit, [the Confucian gentleman] will cultivate civil virtues to induce them to come."[1] A century later, the Confucian thinker Mencius elaborated the idea that people will submit voluntarily "to the transforming influence of morality,"[2] which flows outward from Chinese culture: "I have

33

heard of the Chinese converting barbarians to their ways, but not of their being converted to barbarian ways."[3] His point is that Chinese morality is so powerfully attractive that exposure will inevitably lead to its adoption, allowing the transformation of barbarian foreigners into civilized beings. And because Mencius regards China as the fount of civilization, becoming civilized also means a change of identity to become Chinese.

This appears to be exactly what happened in Chinese history, many times over. The barbarians in question were, classically, the pastoral nomadic herders and hunters of the Eurasian steppe: the vast and varied pasture-lands north of the ecological divide represented by the line of the Great Wall. Everything about these pastoral nomads was said to contrast with the sedentary societies south of the line. China's dynasties ruled a largely agrarian population that was focused around walled urban centers and subject to regular taxation organized by a complex bureaucracy staffed by a tiny elite whose defining skill was literacy. China was no slouch militarily, but from time to time circumstances conspired to produce multicultural steppe confederations under charismatic leaders who extended their realms into China Proper. These included first a kaleidoscope of states during the 370 years (220–589) following the end of the great dynasty of Han (202 BCE–220 CE), and then the first two "conquest dynasties" of Liao (907–1125) and Jin (1115–1234), both originating in different parts of Manchuria. Only the largest of these states, notably the Northern Wei (386–534) and the Jin, reached as far as the Huai River that lies between the Yellow River in north China and the Yangzi in the south. But all save the Liao controlled the heartlands of Chinese civilization in the central Yellow River valley. In later centuries, northern invaders took over entirely as dynastic rulers, displacing emperors of the Yellow River region to found the Yuan (1260–1368) under the Mongols and the Qing (1644–1911) under the Manchus, and asserting their authority down to the south coast.

The Mongols and the Manchus inserted themselves over the top of existing structures, from the system of imperial succession, through the taxation and bureaucratic apparatus, to the schools and universities that trained the personnel needed to run everything. These were all retained since they were essential for extracting the tax revenue and adopting the prestige that made China such a bountiful prize. Those who did not take over existing structures found products of the system—trained officials— who were willing to recreate it. In all cases the emperor, his entourage, and a proportion of the new ruling elites also adopted selected elements associated with Chinese culture such as language, clothing, ritual, or religious practices. Governmental systems, literary culture, and ritual in these conquest states were all heavily influenced by Confucian ideas that provided a moral code. In the eyes of many modern scholars, in China and in the West, the adoption of ostensibly Confucian ways could not be separated from attempts to cultivate morality, which equated with becoming Chinese. Thus as nomads were Confucianized, so barbarians learned morality, and foreigners became sinicized.

In short, the conventional interpretation placed upon the aftermath of these conquests was that those coming to China were fundamentally changed by the encounter whereas, by implication, the Chinese never were. The origins of this claim are more modern than contemporary with the events. In the 1940s Chen Yinke wrote a history of the Tang (618–907) that pointed out the many foreign borrowings of the dynasty, starting with a royal family of largely Turkic descent. But by the 1970s, Chinese scholars, willingly or otherwise, generally followed a script that bolstered PRC control of Tibet, Xinjiang, Inner Mongolia, Manchuria, and other "minority" regions. This script claimed the historical rulers of those regions as part of the past of the modern Chinese nation-state, while simultaneously emphasizing the superior cultural level of those claimed as ethnic Chinese, and their role in helping the conquerors to "develop" toward a "Chinese" form of civilization. There has been a greater variety of positions since the 1990s, but the older views have exercised a continuing influence (for instance, in museum displays), and have recently returned in Chinese articles that discuss multidirectional cultural "mixing" while giving the leading role to the "high level" of Chinese culture. Modern anglophone scholarship followed these leads. One strand of research, for instance, reconsiders Chinese "collaborators" from the Song or Ming dynasties who took service with their new Mongol or Manchu rulers and were sometimes criticized for failing to resist the invaders to the death. The "collaborators'" actions were reinterpreted as attempts at sinicization—to instill civilized ways in their new masters or to protect their fellow Chinese subjects from the worst "barbarian" behavior.[4]

Among a new generation of specialists, however, this view has prompted two general responses, particularly in anglophone scholarship but also sometimes in China. First, invaders of China certainly adopted local practices, but they also maintained and developed practices of their own; and second, imports during periods of foreign rule changed the local culture profoundly and permanently. A thousand years is too long to survey here, so I will offer selected examples.

FOREIGN PRACTICES IN CHINA

A recurrent feature of foreign rule in China was dual administration. No two sets of northern rulers did this the same way, but the basic principle was to retain existing administrative structures in the new parts of the empire, and to develop parallel structures to reorganize the old parts. An early example comes from the Liao (established in 907, the same year that

Vikings overran Brittany in northern France and threatened the Byzantine capital of Constantinople). The Liao founder, Abaoji, knew that agricultural taxes could generate enormous sums. During his rise to power, he captured some hundred thousand farmers from north China and resettled them in what is now southeastern Inner Mongolia. The new emperor was from a pastoralist group called the Kitan; he had never ruled a sedentary population, and charged an ambitious young migrant from north China to develop systems for government and revenue collection. What he contrived was modeled on what he knew, which was the organization of the Liao's predecessor, the great Tang dynasty. It worked well enough that the second Liao emperor expanded and refined the system in order to govern newly acquired agricultural districts around modern Beijing and Datong.

The pastoralist population had organizational methods of their own. These were effective for ruling nomads, but now had to be incorporated into a multicultural empire. The solution was to match the sedentary administration, the Southern Region, with a Northern Region for the pastoralists. The Northern Region comprised a ranked official hierarchy, staffing bureaus with distinct responsibilities for the military and state affairs, armies and horses, punishments, literary matters, and rituals. Some offices were borrowed from the Tang system, some titles were continuations of pastoralist offices whose responsibilities we do not always know, though the Kitan surely did.

From this it might seem that not only were the Kitan not being turned into Chinese, but that Liao rulers used Chinese systems to maintain distinctions between the two segments of their empire. But that is simplistic too. The Northern Region was staffed chiefly by members of the two Kitan ruling clans, but certain posts were often given to Chinese officials. Posts in the Southern Region were mostly held by Chinese, except for particular offices that demanded steppe expertise. The principles at work were neither sinicization nor ethnic segregation, but a wish to change as little as possible and to fit the person to the job and the decree to the situation. We can see a similar approach in many other aspects of Liao governance.

The essential pragmatism of the Liao appears in the last of the foreign dynasties too, but that regime, the Qing, also had a much stronger sense of the distinction between conquerors and conquered. The Liao only controlled a tiny portion of north China, which they had received as payment for military services. As Europe was experiencing the Enlightenment, the Manchu founders of the Qing took China by force, installed an army of occupation, and then expanded their realm further still. Whereas the Chinese population of Liao gave the emperors little trouble, the Qing rulers felt the need to engage in a perpetual round of legitimating activities.

Many of those activities were aimed at the Chinese population and especially the literati elite, giving rise to the claim that the success of Manchu rule was down to the sinicization of the Manchu ruling class. But that was before researchers gained access to sources written in the Manchu language, and before they began to look beyond the court and the educated elites. Now we know that the Manchu rulers treasured their own cultural distinctiveness and took steps to maintain separations between Manchu and Chinese. At the same time, the Qing emperors were conscious that they ruled over not just Manchus and Chinese, but also Mongols, Tibetans, Uyghurs and a host of smaller groups.

How to make good on the claims to rule these groups? The Confucian answer would have been to try to turn everyone from the Pacific to Central Asia into a good Confucian (and thus a good Chinese), through education and regulation. The conquerors did at first attempt their own brand of homogenization, most dramatically by enforcing the Manchu pigtail on adult male Chinese on pain of death. But a new answer quickly developed, which was for the emperors to present themselves to each significant constituency in a guise that would tap into that group's cultural expectations about rulership, and foster acceptance of *Qing*—not Manchu—rule.

For the Chinese audience the emperors learned Chinese, continued the Confucian curriculum for the examination system that trained government officials, and sponsored huge literary projects that aimed to collect the best of Chinese writing through the ages. With their Mongol population, the early Qing emperors made the most of old marriage alliances to claim elements of Mongol ancestry, and played up the implicit connection with the greatest of all Mongols, Chinggis (Genghis), by using the title *khan*. By this time the Mongols had adopted Tibetan Buddhism. Tibetan lamas were held to be spiritual companions of the Buddhist universal king, so for the Mongols' benefit the Manchu rulers, starting with the founder Hong Taiji, forged relationships with the lamas and portrayed themselves as *bodhisattvas* dedicated to the salvation of others. Manchus and Uyghurs experienced equally tailored imagery and activity.

So while it is certainly true that the Manchus adopted much from the Confucian palette, this was by no means all they did. Far from becoming merely sinicized, they incorporated not only Chinese but also other elements to develop a form of rulership that was all their own.

IMPORTS THAT CHANGED CHINA

Foreign rule in China often introduced major new elements originating outside China. Proponents of sinicization theory explain these away as examples of China's openness to new ideas, which were then themselves sinicized along with those who brought them. But this is cheating, because it assumes again that China works change but is never itself changed. The most prominent example is the coming of Buddhism to China, but there were also other cases where, as in the Qing, creative interaction produced something quite new, though not always without cost.

Buddhism was an Indian religion that struck roots in China around the same time that Christianity was spreading as the official religion of the Roman Empire. In China Buddhism appealed both to competing rulers and to commoners. The greatest patrons of China's Buddhist age were the Northern Wei. Founded by a group called the Tabgach or Tuoba in 386, their support of the Central Asian translator-monk Kumarajiva underwrote the transmission to China of an improved understanding of Buddhist doctrine. The earliest translators into Chinese had borrowed indigenous Daoist vocabulary to explain the new Indian ideas. This created considerable confusion, for example when the idea of enlightenment (*nirvana*) was translated as *wuwei*, which means not interfering in the natural course of events. From around 400, Kumarajiva and others created a new vocabulary of Chinese words that allowed them to explain, for instance, the differences between the oldest form of Buddhism and the Mahayana version that became most popular in China. By this time, ordinary people, including many women, were flocking to monasteries and nunneries in such numbers that rulers were periodically moved to suppress Buddhism, though never with permanent effect. Buddhism had become a fixture of Chinese society.

Buddhism in China was certainly transformed to suit local conditions, but China would also never be the same again. We can see this best in the transformation of the largely single-story, horizontal architecture of China by the addition of thousands of multilevel pagodas: tall, thin, visible for miles; permanent symbols of change.

Buddhism increasingly bothered Confucians, whose response was neo-Confucianism, which became state orthodoxy in 1240 during the Song dynasty's wars against the Mongols. One characteristic was neo-Confucianism's rigid attitudes toward women, and particularly the insistence on widow chastity: that widows should remain loyal to their dead husbands by not remarrying. Older scholarship attributed the spread of widow chastity during the later dynasties to an entirely Chinese impulse toward neo-Confucianism; if the Mongols were the "least sinicized" of the conquest dynasties, so China remained essentially untouched by their presence. In fact, there seems to have been a gendered convergence of interests between Mongol rulers and the Chinese literati elite.

Neo-Confucian scholars pinned much of their hope for a more moral society onto widow chastity, but this was not a popular option among Chinese widows. Song dynasty law gave these women control of their own dowries, and if that gave them sufficient property, they often remarried into a new family. The Mongols shared the neo-Confucians' distaste for remarriage into a new family, but for different reasons. Many Chinese households were designated to provide soldiers to the Mongol armies in perpetuity, but a military household headed by a widow with no adult son reduced the strength of the armies. Bettine Birge points out that one solution to this problem was the Mongol practice of the levirate. The levirate ensured there would always be an adult male as head of household by compelling a widow to remarry within the clan, usually to one of her dead husband's younger brothers but sometimes to one of his sons by a different wife. Partly to sustain army rolls, the first Yuan emperor, Khubilai, decreed in 1272 that the levirate become compulsory for all widows in his realm, whether Chinese or Mongol. Unfortunately, to Chinese eyes the levirate looked like incest—especially when a man married one of his father's wives—and Khubilai's Chinese ministers protested vigorously.

What to do? Khubilai and his Chinese ministers all wanted to end remarriage outside the clan, but enforcing the levirate on the Chinese risked alienating the literati elite that Khubilai needed to run the country. After a number of compromise responses, the lasting solution was a decree of 1303 that removed women's control of their dowries after marriage. This encouraged Mongols toward the levirate and enforced widow chastity among the Chinese by ensuring that widows had no wealth to offer to a second husband outside their marital family. This Mongol law was perpetuated after the Yuan by the fiercely anti-Mongol Ming dynasty (1368–1644) and for the rest of the imperial period. An effort to maintain the supply of troops to the Mongol armies was turned to advantage by neo-Confucian patriarchs, and Chinese society was changed permanently.

ANOTHER VIEW

So Chinese ways were not uniquely attractive to outsiders, and Chinese encounters with foreigners produced the same kind of multifaceted interactions, inflected by politics, class, gender, and other factors, as you would find anywhere else. Foreign rulers did not adopt Chinese ways wholesale because they were more moral, but piecemeal when they offered solutions to pressing issues like how to extract revenue from the population or legitimate the conquerors' rule. China was also permanently affected by foreign imports, as testified by Buddhist monuments. The new arrivals were certainly domesticated, but Chinese became people who understood accurately what *nirvana* was. Most importantly, among the subject Chinese, elites in particular often engaged in subtle and silent negotiations with their foreign rulers, hoping to further individual, class, patriarchal, and even ethnic interests. To continue to accept the claim that Chinese culture absorbed all others requires a diehard belief in China's inevitable cultural dominance that no longer withstands scrutiny.

SUGGESTIONS FOR FURTHER READING

Confucius and Mencius are most accessible in their Penguin Classics translations. A more technical version, highlighting interpolations, is E. Bruce and A. Taeko Brooks, *The Original Analects: Sayings of Confucius and His Successors* (Columbia University Press, 1998), which provides the translations used here.

The most sophisticated statement of sinicization theory is probably Ho Ping-ti, "In Defense of Sinicization: A Rebuttal of Evelyn Rawski's 'Reenvisioning the Qing,'" *Journal of Asian Studies*, 57, no. 1 (1998): 123–55, which cites equitable taxation and modernization among many other sinicizing developments. The paper has not prompted a mass of supporting scholarship. Rawski's article was published in the 1996 volume.

On the founder of the Liao administration, who was called Han Yanhui, see Naomi Standen, *Unbounded Loyalty: Frontier Crossings in Liao China* (University of Hawai'i Press, 2007). On Qing multiculturalism, see Pamela Crossley, *The Manchus* (Blackwell, 1997). An excellent textbook for post-Han Buddhism is Valerie Hansen, *The Open Empire: A History of China to 1600* (Norton, 2000). On widow chastity and the Yuan try Bettine Birge, *Women, Property and Confucian Reaction in Sung and Yüan China* (Cambridge University Press, 2002). All of these books include up-to-date bibliographies including the best recent studies.

NOTES

1. *Analects*, Book 16, Section 1. See also 3:5; 9:14; 13:16, 19; 14:17.
2. *Mencius*, 2A:3.
3. *Mencius*, 3A:4. See also 7B:4; cf. 1B:11; 3B:5.
4. For instance, John D. Langlois, "Chinese Culturalism and the Yüan Analogy: Seventeenth-Century Perspectives," *Harvard Journal of Asiatic Studies* 40, no. 2 (1980): 355–98.

4

Confucius: The Key to Understanding China

Tim Barrett

This claim supposes that the apparent economic success of East Asian values—first in Japan, Korea, Taiwan, and Singapore, but now most spectacularly in China itself—must stem from the heritage of Confucianism. In China this supposition is encouraged by the waning reliance on the thoughts of Chairman Mao for guidance as Confucius has returned to an even more prominent place than elsewhere in East Asia. But the roots of current success cannot be reduced to such simple causes. The Chinese heritage is far more complex than the description "Confucian" can convey.

CHINA MOLDED BY CONFUCIUS?

Although the name of Chairman Mao has become widely known, Confucius is probably still the most famous Chinese ever outside China. That situation has, moreover, been true for a very long time. Now that the government of China is seeking to promote the knowledge of Chinese language and culture through the foundation of Confucius Institutes, Confucius seems destined to increase his global celebrity. Many places that would probably hesitate to accept a Mao Institute welcome Confucius with open arms. So has it turned out that in the long run understanding Confucius is the key to understanding China?

If only matters were so straightforward, education concerning China would be easy. Unfortunately, the reasons for the modern promotion of Confucius stem from a specific set of circumstances relating to the early spread of an awareness of China in European languages. The current celebrity of Confucius simply repeats a pattern already evident more than half

41

a century ago, when the struggle against Japan briefly brought Nationalist China to the attention of the wider world. Then a Chinese lawyer in Europe, Cheng Tien-hsi, published a volume, *China Moulded by Confucius: The Chinese Way in Western Light* (London: Stevens and Sons Limited, 1946), which on reading turns out to be not solely about Confucius, or even about his influence on China, but rather about what Dr. Cheng thought Westerners should know about his country. The businessman Carl Crow had already published an admiring book on Confucius and the Sinologist Herrlee Glessner Creel was soon to publish another. So Dr. Cheng was perhaps exploiting a degree of contemporary interest. Yet it was an interest with deep roots. At that time most Western knowledge of China derived not from businessmen and scholars but from missionaries, and the missionary interest in Confucius goes back to the start of modern European attempts at evangelizing China.

The men who spearheaded the first missions to China in the sixteenth century were Jesuits, members of a religious order that believed in selecting and training outstanding individuals capable of conveying the Christian message across formidable cultural barriers even when far from home. They were fully prepared to respect the traditions of China. But they believed that the message that they brought was as vital to Chinese civilization as to the rest of humankind. One way they hoped to bring the two together was based on their belief that in early times all humankind had possessed an original awareness of their God. Perhaps in China that awareness had faded more slowly, enriching Chinese thought with values compatible with their own. Confucius could thus be reinterpreted as a figure whose beliefs complemented the Jesuits' religion. Consequently they could appeal to educated Chinese as bearers of a message that added to Chinese culture rather than clashed with it. When reporting back to Europe, the Jesuits emphasized the importance of Confucius as a figure they believed ought to make Chinese acceptance of Christianity easy. This spread great optimism about China's level of spiritual civilization—and about Western missionary prospects.

THE SIGNIFICANCE OF AN UNSUCCESSFUL MAN

About their own chances the Jesuits deluded themselves. But thanks to their writings Confucius gained in Europe, from the seventeenth century onward, a reputation as an ethical thinker of global significance. Some have therefore seen the Jesuits as responsible for manufacturing Confucianism. There is undeniably something in this. Even if Confucius was already a significant figure in China before the missionaries arrived, their interpretation of what was important about him differed notably from the view of his followers in China. What Confucius said about the way people should treat each other was important, but it was the idea of connecting with the past that was central to how he was viewed in late imperial China. Confucius lived at a time when the Chinese world was changing rapidly, and gradually becoming more violent and competitive. The different states composing that world were moving toward coercive unification by the most violent and competitive of them all—Qin, home of the first emperor. Already for Confucius old cultural traditions—especially forms of acceptable behavior—were being lost, and he articulated the necessity for trying to carry on the good legacy of the past.

But he was singularly unsuccessful. The best that can be said of him is that he seems to have been fondly remembered by the students who gathered around him in his later years and preserved some of his sayings. These are far less banal than Western representations would have us believe, though even good teachers cannot avoid attracting students incapable of grasping their ideas. A few writings survive from pre-imperial times by named individuals who looked to Confucius as a key transmitter of earlier traditions; these are all articulate and thoughtful arguments for what might be called humanistic values. But in early China at least some other enthusiasts for times past were reportedly narrow-minded antiquarians, ridiculed by their contemporaries, whereas Confucius was apparently always accepted as worthy of respect from those with a different outlook. But he tends to be taken as representative of "conventional wisdom," especially by those who sought wisdom beyond convention. The greatest embodiment of this they found in a supposed older contemporary of Confucius, Laozi.

After the fall of the first emperor, it was widely believed that his policy toward scholars of the old traditions had been aggressively negative, and that he had murdered many of them. But while he was certainly responsible for many unjust deaths, his surviving inscriptions suggest that he also used the advice of experts in the cultural heritage to vaunt his own rule. The succeeding, more stable, Han dynasty (202 BCE–220 CE) started off showing little interest in such matters. Eventually, however, the empire became more interested in unifying cultural traditions as its struggled against peoples with different ways of life—like the inhabitants of the lands beyond the first emperor's wall to the north. In that situation it seemed more worthwhile to promote a heritage that had now become associated with Confucius. Later admirers of Confucius had long put him on a par with the great kings of old, culture heroes who had instituted all the benefits that belonged to the civilized society of China alone. Now he became more widely promoted as a final "uncrowned king" among this sequence of heroes, responsible for passing on all the literature worth preserving from that tradition: someone so far above ordinary mortals that he could see into the future as well as transmit the good from the past.

The long period of Han rule undoubtedly saw the figure of Confucius become a rallying point for rethinking the core heritage from the past, and especially those texts we recognize today as the "Confucian Classics." But equally, we hear of folk tales from this time in which Confucius is made to look a bit of a fool, unable to answer questions posed by children. And other ways of looking at the problems of empire and culture, and other models of human perfection—the figure of the sage, to use the usual translation—were not displaced. As Han power faded in the second century CE, the figure of Laozi reappeared, not simply as one older and wiser than Confucius, but as a being of cosmic significance capable of providing salvation. Nor was he alone in this role, for news began to reach China of the Buddha and his teachings, and of the hope of *nirvana* as an alternative to an increasingly tumultuous and dangerous world. Soon, too, most of North China had fallen under the domination of peoples who did not speak Chinese and who felt no allegiance to the ancient heritage. Many Chinese meanwhile fled south to the Yangzi River and beyond, where again indigenous, non-Chinese-speaking peoples still abounded.

A few educated Chinese might still be found even in the north, while in the south some refugees had managed to bring their libraries with them, so Confucius was still honored by some who recalled the good old days of their ancestors under the Han. But most inhabitants of what is now China had little time for a sage whose prescriptions for ordering human society seemed less important than immediate issues of life and death—especially the latter. As the graves of ancestors were abandoned by fleeing families, new ways to make sense of the unseen world of the spirits became an urgent necessity. Confucius was not forgotten: he and his immediate predecessor among the sage-kings were remembered as representatives of the tradition that had bequeathed the Confucian Classics to China. More attention was however given to whether Laozi or the Buddha, viewed as figures of supernatural significance, offered the best hope of ultimate salvation in this world and the life to come. Even so, the "Confucian Classics" had been accepted by the state in Han times, and as a knowledge of Chinese civilization spread to Korea and eventually to Japan, non-Chinese who looked back to Han institutions for guidance in state-building learned to respect Confucius too.

When in the seventh century a worthy successor to the Han did appear in the shape of the Tang dynasty (618–907), its rulers honored the tradition to the extent of making sure that official interpretation of the Classics did not stray too far from Han norms. But the Tang rulers claimed descent from Laozi, and the majority of their subjects worshiped the Buddha, so other than supporting scholarship on the Classics little was done. No steps were taken, for example, to prevent Buddhists from affirming that Confucius had been an emanation of a Buddhist figure, though similar claims and counterclaims between the Buddhists and the followers of Laozi were handled much more carefully. We know from Tang-period manuscripts that folktales about Confucius being humiliated by a young child ended with the sage murdering his young tormentor, and apparently some depictions of Confucius even at court were so unflattering that the state did put a stop to them. The purported descendants of Laozi faltered as rulers of the Tang in the mid-eighth century, allowing their capital cities to be sacked by foreign troops, which produced a mood of xenophobia that labeled Buddhism as a foreign religion. Combined with disillusionment at a perceived lack of initiative on the part of the dynasty, this suggested to one or two thinkers that perhaps only the tradition represented by Confucius and earlier sages might provide the spiritual resources to revive the fortunes of the Chinese. Such opinions were clearly somewhat impolitic. Their most articulate proponent was lucky to be granted exile to the borders of the empire rather than execution. But the thought that Confucius had been a failure in his own time no doubt provided some consolation to those who saw themselves in this beleaguered minority.

CONFUCIUS REIMAGINED

This way of looking at the tradition, as something like a religious truth equivalent to Buddhism, was to have important consequences in the eleventh century. By then the Tang dynasty had been gone for over one hundred years and China was a very different place. Profound social upheavals had ushered in a new age in which education had come to the fore as the path to advancement, and the place of Confucius in basic education was now crucial. We know from Tang manuscripts that even under that regime, when Buddhists apparently dominated provision of basic schooling, the sayings of Confucius featured prominently among the non-Buddhist texts studied. By the tenth century his name was usually the fourth character that a Chinese child learned to write. Since to many the regeneration of China entailed a turning back to the roots of Chinese civilization (albeit without rejecting the cultural changes since the fall of the Han), Confucius was at last back in favor.

Yet a few did go further and picked up the hints of their Tang predecessors, approaching the tradition as "true believers." In their view Chinese civilization had lost its way. The truth had been obscured since the demise of the one authentic follower of Confucius, the fourth-century BCE thinker Mencius. Only by reaffirming that truth could China shake off the debilitating influence of non-Chinese peoples. At the heart of this rethinking of tradition was a staggering affirmation of discontinuity, of the irrelevance of Confucius throughout much of Chinese history. Those with a different sense of history did challenge this view, but in the long run the "true believers" stuck to their guns, exploiting their influence and particularly the hold they had over the educational curriculum. The thirteenth century saw the acceptance of their interpretations as state orthodoxy for all who aspired to join the ranks of the mandarins by the examination route.

This new orthodoxy spread in due course to Korea, and even to Japan, where one eighteenth-century figure in that still Buddhist country speaks explicitly of "belief" in Confucianism. But it would be wrong to assume that too much had changed in China, beyond the rhetoric of the mandarins and those who hoped to join them. Practical advice books on family matters show that pragmatic solutions to everyday problems often contradicted the rhetoric put out by the "true believers." Joke books too, show that the believers' intense seriousness often made them the object of ridicule. A growing public acceptance of the value of popular culture was perhaps only prevented by the Manchu conquest of China in 1644, and a subsequent reassertion of the government's duty to police the moral welfare of society. In both China and Japan, moreover, there had arisen far too good a sense of history and philology to take the affirmations of the "true believers" uncritically. The best East Asian scholars of the eighteenth and nineteenth centuries devoted much of their time to a more accurate reconstruction of early China, in which the mind-set exemplified by later "true believer" zealots was shown never to have existed.

Who knows what the upshot of this process would have been, had not East Asia been forced to resist Western imperialism. As it was, once China was on the defensive, Confucius again became a rallying point, first for diehard adherents of the old ways and next for reformers attempting to promote a national alternative to Christianity. The subsequent rise of much more radical solutions to China's problems in the twentieth century saw Confucius made a scapegoat for all the ills of the old society. He was a figure known to all from old-fashioned primary education, but one who had come to be accorded too much symbolic importance by reformers and revolutionaries alike. Such denunciations did however tend to confirm Westerners in the belief that something called Confucianism was the key to understanding the past against which modern China was reacting.

In fact the chimera of a "Chinese key" also goes back to seventeenth-century Europe, when Jesuits first started to report on the Chinese writing system. They knew that learning Chinese characters took time, with no shortcuts possible. But scholars in Europe tended to assume that there was a hidden system to the writing that would make it much easier to understand. In the present day Confucius likewise appears to be a simple key to understanding China's intellectual traditions. But this is because as China learns to live with the contrast of tradition and modernity in more fruitful ways, Confucius is serving as a shorthand symbol for the past.

Yet any movement back to Confucius is likely to be limited. Those who seek to promote a new Confucianism may revive many positive aspects of the Chinese heritage. A thousand years ago it was possible for "true believers" to reject those aspects of the heritage not deriving from early China. Similar rejection of imported elements in the present day may be a temptation, but in an age of globalization it is hardly an option. Besides, guardians of the heritage who do not see the past as exclusively "Confucian" are also gaining ground. Chinese Buddhists, for example, can look back to as many centuries of their heritage within China as Christians can in Europe. Yet Buddhism also has an international, even global, dimension that offers a new middle way between a retreat into narrow nationalism and an uncomplicated acceptance of Western cultural norms. Learning about Confucius and his legacy is certainly a commendable task. But China never was molded by Confucius alone, nor ever will be. Chinese civilization is much richer and more complex than that.

SUGGESTIONS FOR FURTHER READING

Lionel M. Jensen, *Manufacturing Confucianism: Chinese Traditions and Universal Civilization* (Duke University Press, 1997) makes the case for the Jesuit role in creating Confucianism as we know it in the West. Thomas A. Wilson, *Genealogy of the Way: The Construction and Uses of the Confucian Tradition in Late Imperial China* (Stanford University Press, 1995) shows how the prevailing view of Confucian tradition during the past ten centuries has posited a radical discontinuity with the preceding millennium and more. For some of the different phases in the understanding of Confucius, see the essays in Kai-wing Chow, On-cho Ng, and John B. Henderson (eds.), *Imagining Boundaries: Changing Confucian Doctrines, Texts, and Hermeneutics* (State University of New York Press, 1999). For the problems of contemporary Confucianism, see John Makeham, *Lost Soul: "Confucianism" in Contemporary Chinese Academic Discourse* (Harvard-Yenching Institute, 2008).

II

CULTURAL TRADITIONS

5

The "Decline" of Buddhism in China

Tansen Sen

In 845 CE, the Tang emperor Wuzong (r. 840–846) launched a brutal assault on Buddhism and other "foreign" religions in China. According to Ennin (793–864), a Japanese monk visiting Tang China (618–907) at that time, more than 4,600 Buddhist monasteries were destroyed; land and other property belonging to Buddhist monasteries were confiscated; and 260,500 monks and nuns were defrocked, with the remaining monks and nuns all placed under the control of a government bureau. This was not the first time that a ruler in China had tried to suppress Buddhism. There were at least two previous large persecutions, in 446 and 574–577. But this, the so-called Huichang Suppression, named after the reign period of Emperor Wuzong, is considered the most widespread, ruthless, and violent. For many modern scholars this was a "pivotal" event in the history of Chinese Buddhism that marked, in the words of Kenneth Ch'en, "the end of the apogee and the beginning of the decline of the religion."[1]

Sometime in the sixth century BCE in southern Asia, Siddhartha Gautama, popularly known as Sakyamuni (the sage of the Sakya clan) and the Buddha (the awakened one), formulated the doctrine that later became known as Buddhism. Within the preexisting belief system that perceived life as a continuous cycle of birth and rebirth, Sakyamuni proposed that this kind of existence consisted of suffering brought about by desire. This suffering, he explained, could cease only when one has attained *nirvana*, or cessation of existence. Sakyamuni, who lived until the age of eighty, then preached to a large following the ways to awaken to the truth of suffering caused by desire.

By the first century BCE, the teachings of Sakyamuni had spread across the Indian subcontinent through the trade routes. It was also through the

52Tansen Sen

trade routes that Buddhist ideas were first brought to Chinese coastal regions and urban centers. During the third and fourth centuries, Buddhist ideas penetrated different levels of Chinese society, monks from Central and South Asia started translating Buddhist texts into Chinese, and rulers in China began using the doctrine for political goals. Indeed, by the time the Huichang Suppression took place, Buddhism had emerged as one of the three major belief systems of China.

However, in his influential, and still widely used, work called Buddhism in China: A Historical Survey, Ch'en used the title "decline" for the last section of the book which deals with Buddhism in China after the Tang dynasty. This "decline" of Chinese Buddhism, according to Ch'en, resulted from the "moral degeneration" of the monastic community (sangha), the rise of neo-Confucianism, and the decline of Buddhism in India. He argues that no outstanding Buddhist monks emerged after the persecution of 845, no new schools of Buddhist thought were established, and no important Buddhist texts were translated. Ch'en's book remained the only survey of Chinese Buddhism for a long time and contributed to the widespread acceptance of the "decline" argument. In addition, there were few detailed studies on Song (960–1276) and later Chinese Buddhism that challenged Ch'en's views. The situation has changed in recent years with the publication of seminal works on Buddhism during Song and later periods of Chinese history. And while this new research and the total rejection of Ch'en's views have not fully filtered to textbooks and nonspecialists, scholars of Chinese Buddhism agree that the word "decline" is inaccurate to describe Buddhism in post-Tang China.

INDIA AND THE DECLINE OF BUDDHISM IN CHINA

"The glorious flowering of Buddhism in China during the first half of the T'ang (Tang) Dynasty (seventh and eighth centuries)," Kenneth Ch'en writes, "was in no small measure due to the continual stimulus from the fountainhead of Buddhism."[2] With the alleged "disappearance" of Buddhism in India in the eleventh century, he explains, "the flow of Indian missionaries to China and Chinese pilgrims to India came to a standstill. Deprived of this religious and intellectual inspiration, Buddhism in China failed to maintain its position of eminence and excellence."[3] This perception that Buddhism in China was dependent on doctrinal input from India is an issue that needs to be addressed at the outset because it does not do justice to the uniqueness of Buddhism in China or the ingenuity of the Chinese clergy in transforming the foreign religion into a localized belief system.

The view that Buddhism in China relied on India and Indian monks and teachings for its development and subsistence is exaggerated. From the early stages of the transmission of Buddhist ideas to its perceived peak during the Tang dynasty, doctrines and texts introduced from India were not the major reasons for the success of Buddhism in China. Neither were the monks from the Indian subcontinent, who continued to arrive in China until the fourteenth century, crucial for shaping Buddhist doctrines in China. Robert Sharf has pointed out that Buddhism in China developed due to the Buddhist dialogue that "took place largely among the Chinese themselves," rather than with its encounter with Indian Buddhism.[4] Indeed, while India may have been the "holy land" for the followers of Buddhism in China, Chinese Buddhism evolved mostly through internal philosophical debates, discussions, textual production, and artistic representation. Buddhist doctrines from India were never systematically transmitted, comprehensively translated, or completely accepted by the Chinese.

Archaeological and textual evidence suggests that Buddhist ideas seem to have reached Han China in fragmented form, carried by merchants of Central Asian origin. Additionally, early Buddhist images found in Chinese tombs indicate that initially there was a misperception of the Buddha as a longevity-granting deity who was incorporated into the popular religious pantheon. By the time the first monastic rules (*vinaya*) were translated into Chinese, there were already thousands of monks in China. Also noteworthy is that many of the earliest translators of Buddhist texts were not from southern Asia, but Central Asia. In other words, the establishment of Buddhism in China depended very little on the input or stimulus directly from India.

In fourth- and fifth-century China, there was an attempt to faithfully translate and interpret Buddhist texts in accordance with the original intent of their Indian authors. However, for the most part, the Chinese clergy, as Stanley Weinstein points out, "clearly felt themselves free to interpret the sutras of their schools on the basis of their own religious experience, often showing no concern whether a particular interpretation was at all feasible from the standpoint of the original text."[5] Such divergences from Indian texts resulted in the founding of unique Chinese Buddhist schools, such as Zhiyi's (538–597) Tiantai School in the sixth century, and Fazang's (643–712) Huayan School during the Tang dynasty.

A similar phenomenon also can be discerned from the use of sacred Buddhist objects and legends. The relics of the Buddha were widely venerated throughout the Buddhist world. These sacred relics were meant to connect the worshipers to the historical Sakyamuni Buddha. For those who lived far away from the sacred Buddhist sites in India, these relics also served to decrease the spatial distance between the followers of the doctrine and their holy land. The spread of the relic cult is often associated with Buddhist stories related to King Ashoka and his distribution of sacred remains to 84,000 sites in his vast Mauryan Empire. The Indian king is also said to have sent missions to neighboring countries carrying the relics as gifts. The Chinese clergy used these stories to legitimize the presence of the Buddha's remains in their country, even though there is no evidence for Ashoka's emissaries reaching China. Sometimes, the relics are said to have reached China miraculously, appearing magically on the palms of Buddhist monks or under a stupa. Unique ritual practices, mostly associated with Chinese folk traditions, subsequently became part of relic veneration ceremonies in China. For example, at the Famen Monastery, near present-day Xi'an in Shaanxi province, every time the finger-bone relic was worshipped, the Chinese followers burnt or severed parts of their body as offerings to the Buddha. These practices do not seem to have any antecedent in India, but they became ways for the Chinese to spiritually and spatially relate to the Buddha in their own terms and without having to make a journey to India.

Similarly, the Chinese transformed several of their sacred mountains into pilgrimage sites for Buddhist devotees. The most important of these sites was Mount Wutai, located in present-day Shanxi province, which became recognized as the abode of the bodhisattva Manjusri. Through the manipulation of various Buddhist texts, the creation of local legends, and the adornment of the mountain with Buddhist sculptures and cloisters, the Chinese clergy established Mount Wutai as a leading pilgrimage site not only for the Chinese but also for the Buddhists elsewhere in East Asia. By the seventh century, even monks from South Asia traveled to China to pay homage to the bodhisattva who supposedly lived on the Chinese mountain.

Thus, by the time Emperor Wuzong launched his famous Huichang Suppression, Buddhism in China had charted its own course and established its unique schools, practices, and pilgrimage sites. The Chinese Buddhists did not need doctrinal input or guidance from India, nor was there a need to travel to the holy land for pilgrimages since China itself had emerged as a central Buddhist realm. Despite this fact, the "flow" of monks between India and China did not come to a "standstill," as Kenneth Ch'en suggests. During the tenth and eleventh centuries about 80 Indian monks arrived in China, 338 Chinese monks returned after visiting the Indian subcontinent, a total of 1,028 Indian texts were procured, and 564 scrolls of Buddhist texts were translated into Chinese. While Ch'en is correct to point out that this period did not produce famous pilgrims such as Xuanzang and Yijing or Indian missionaries like Amoghavajra, it was not due to a paucity of monks traveling between India and China. Buddhism in China, as the next section will demonstrate, had integrated into Chinese society with little need for eminent bilingual specialists who could translate and interpret new doctrines from India. Instead of a decline, Buddhism had emerged as a Chinese religion.

CHINESE BUDDHISM AFTER THE HUICHANG SUPPRESSION

In 955 there was another anti-Buddhist persecution, this time by Emperor Shizong (r. 954–959) of the Later Zhou dynasty (951–960). The emperor ordered the confiscation of the property belonging to Buddhist monasteries and banned Buddhist practices. Based on this fact alone, it can be discerned that the Huichang Suppression had failed to completely eradicate Buddhism from Chinese soil. In fact, as far as the relationship between the Chinese court and Buddhism is concerned, the subsequent Song period witnessed a renewed interest in the doctrine among Chinese rulers. As Huang Chi-chiang points out, Emperor Taizu, the founder of the Song dynasty, quickly lifted Emperor Shizong's ban on Buddhism, leading to the resumption of public worship of the doctrine. His successor, Emperor Taizong, is said to have "revered the Buddha in private, unabashedly expressing his admiration in writing."[6] Emperors Zhenzong (r. 998–1022) and Renzong (r. 1022–1063) also are known to have venerated or expressed their reverence for Buddhism.

The Song court even revived and funded new translations of Buddhist texts. In 982, under the orders of Emperor Taizong, an organization called the Institute for the Translation of the Sutras was established to procure and translate new Buddhist texts. Later renamed the Institute for the Transmission of the Dharma, it housed some of the leading Indian monks in Song China, trained Chinese monks in Sanskrit, and was also engaged in the printing of the newly translated texts. Despite a severe shortage of qualified bilingual specialists, the Institute, between 982 and 1037, produced translations of 263 Buddhist texts. The Institute also revised and printed new editions of the collection of Buddhist texts known as the Kaibao Canon. Printed copies of the Canon were frequently given as gifts or sold by the Song court to the neighboring kingdoms, many of which had accepted Buddhism as a state religion.

Indeed, during the eleventh and twelfth centuries, there were several kingdoms in East Asia that had adopted Buddhism, facilitating interactions among Buddhist communities in China, Korea, Japan, and Central Asia. These kingdoms included the Liao (907–1125), Jin (1115–1234), and Xi Xia (ca. 982–1227), founded by the seminomadic peoples called Khitans, Jurchens, and Tanguts respectively. Occupying northern parts of present-day China, some of these kingdoms, such as the Xi Xia, developed their own Buddhist translation and printing projects modeled after the Song dynasty.

State support for Buddhism and Buddhist exchanges within East Asia and between China and South Asia continued during the Yuan dynasty. The Yuan ruler Khubilai Khan (r. 1260–1294) was a patron of Buddhism, specifically the Tibetan form of esoteric Buddhism, and made it the state religion in 1268. A Tibetan monk called 'Phags-pa was the Mongol ruler's private teacher, under whom interactions with Buddhist communities in Tibet and Nepal witnessed significant growth. Khubilai seems to have also sent diplomats to India and Sri Lanka to find Buddhist relics. His support for Buddhism can be seen from the court debates between Buddhists and Daoists regarding the superiority of the founder of these two religions. After overseeing and participating in the debate, Khubilai declared the Buddhists as winners and ordered the Daoist leaders punished for forging texts that advocated Laozi, the founder of Daoism, as the teacher of the Buddha.

It should also be noted that Indian monks, albeit in fewer numbers, continued to arrive in China during the Yuan period. The most famous and influential among these was Dhyanabhadra (Chanxian), who reached China in 1322 through the maritime route. Dhyanabhadra was not only active at the courts of three Yuan rulers who succeeded Khubilai Khan, but also played a significant role in Korea and in Yunnan province in southwestern China. Sometime in 1328, Dhyanabhadra visited the Koryo kingdom in Korea, where he quickly gained fame and attracted students, at least two of whom are known to have expressly traveled to Yuan China to study with the Indian monk. Links between Buddhism and rulers in China continued during the subsequent Ming (1368–1644) and Qing (1644–1911) periods. While, for example, the famous Ming ruler Yongle (r. 1404–1424) is known for his contacts with Tibetan monks, Qing rulers identified themselves as incarnations of the bodhisattva Manjusri.

The continued presence and influence of Buddhism in China after the Huichang Suppression is evident from the above examples of imperial patronage of the doctrine from the Song to the Qing periods. More important, however, are the developments that took place within Chinese society, which absorbed Buddhist teachings and transformed them into a Chinese belief system. Recent publications on this topic have successfully challenged the perception of a decline of Buddhism after the Huichang Suppression as outlined by Kenneth Ch'en. In fact, one of the major contributions, a book titled *Buddhism in the Sung*, argues that in regard to the "efflorescence in Buddhism" the Song period might even deserve the epithet of the "golden age."

Focusing mostly on the Chan and Tiantai traditions, one emphasizing the meditative aspect of Buddhism and the other attempting to synthesize the diverse teachings of the Buddha, the essays included in *Buddhism in the Sung* demonstrate the intellectual vibrancy and the widespread impact of Buddhism among Song officials, literati, and lay people. Although founded during earlier periods, both Chan and Tiantai evolved and matured during the Song period due to the ideas and texts produced by contemporary Buddhist monks such as Dahui Zonggao (1089–1163) and Zhili (960–1028). Among the common people, on the other hand, the ideas of a Pure Land, advocating a rebirth in a paradisiacal realm, became more popular than ever before.

This was also the period during which Guanyin, the most important divinity in Chinese Buddhism, attained fully feminine form. In her seminal work on Guanyin, Chün-fang Yü has detailed how the emergence of other cults of goddesses, the development of Chan Buddhism, and even the revival of Confucianism during the Song period may have contributed to the transformation of a male bodhisattva known as Avalokitesvara to the popular female, and uniquely Chinese, Buddhist divinity Guanyin.

Many of these ideas and beliefs that developed during the Song period were represented in various art forms, especially in paintings. These paintings from the Song and Yuan periods, for example, show distinct Chinese ideas that grew out of the above intellectual discourse on Chan and other schools of Chinese Buddhism. Additionally, the paintings and sculptures of Guanyin in her various manifestations also became popular and spread to other parts of East Asia. Indeed, the post-Tang period witnessed an overall integration of Buddhism into Chinese society. What declined after the thirteenth century were the links to Buddhist sites in India that were destroyed due to invasions by Turkic-Muslim forces, and the development of Indian Buddhism into its own Tantric form. However, this did not hinder the growth of Buddhism in China or its further enrooting in Chinese society.

CONCLUSION

During the Song dynasty, the famous Chinese monk Zanning (919–1001), who was influential at the court of Emperor Taizong, argued that Buddhism should be considered as an integral part of Chinese society and culture. After acknowledging that the origins of Buddhist doctrines were in India, he contends that these teachings had already taken new roots in China, from which new trees, branches, and leaves had grown. For him, Buddhist doctrines in China had a new and distinct identity. In fact, he even proposes that a reverse transmission of Buddhism, from China to India, would be necessary for Indians to properly understand Buddhist doctrines.

Zanning was right about the self-reliant and distinct nature of Buddhism in Song China. To understand the development of Buddhism in China, especially after the Huichang Suppression, one has to look at the intellectual discourse within China and the distinctly Chinese practices and beliefs prevalent at the popular level. Just because these discourses and practices did not mirror the Buddhist teachings in India or originate in India does not indicate a "moral degradation" of the doctrine. It is incorrect to discount these Chinese discourses and practices when putting forth an argument for the decline of Buddhism in China. In fact, such an argument is no longer tenable.

SUGGESTIONS FOR FURTHER READING

On international Buddhist links and transmission see Liu Xinru, *Ancient India and Ancient China: Trade and Religious Exchanges, AD 1–600* (Oxford University Press, 1988); Tansen Sen, *Buddhism, Diplomacy, and Trade: The Realignment of Sino-Indian Relations, 600–1400* (University of Hawai'i Press, 2003), and Denise Leidy, "Buddhism and Other 'Foreign' Practices in Yuan China," in *The World of Khubilai Khan*, ed. James Watt (Metropolitan Museum of Art, 2010). On religion and politics, there is Ruth Dunnell on the Xi Xia: *The Great State of White and High* (University of Hawai'i Press, 1996); James Grayson, *Korea: A Religious History* (RoutledgeCurzon, 2002); Peter Gregory and Daniel Getz (eds.), *Buddhism in the Sung* (University of Hawai'i Press, 1999).

On changes in Buddhist artistic production, practice, and doctrine see Wu Hung, "Buddhist Elements in Early Chinese Art (2nd and 3rd Centuries AD)," *Artibus Asiae* 47, nos. 3–4 (1986); Marilyn Rhie, *Early Buddhist Art of China and Central Asia*, Vol. 1 (Brill, 1999); Marsha Weidner (ed.), *Later Days of the Law: Images of Chinese Buddhism, 850–1850* (Spencer Museum of Art, 1994); Chün-fang Yü, *Kuan-yin: The Chinese Transformation of Avalokiteśvara* (Columbia University Press, 2001); and Robert Sharf, *Coming to Terms with Chinese Buddhism: A Reading of the* Treasure Store Treatise (University of Hawai'i Press, 2002).

NOTES

1. Kenneth Ch'en, *Buddhism in China: A Historical Survey* (Princeton, NJ: Princeton University Press, 1964), p. 232.

2. Ibid., p. 399.

3. Ibid., p. 400.

4. Robert H. Sharf, *Coming to Terms with Chinese Buddhism: A Reading of the* Treasure Store Treatise (Honolulu: University of Hawai'i Press, 2002), p. 19.

5. Stanley Weinstein, *Buddhism under the T'ang* (Cambridge: Cambridge University Press, 1987), p. 272.

6. Huang Chi-chiang, "Imperial Rulership and Buddhism in the Early Northern Sung," in *Imperial Rulership and Cultural Change in Traditional China*, ed. Frederick P. Brandauer and Chün-chieh Huang (Seattle: University of Washington Press, 1994), p. 147.

6

Islam in China

Michael C. Brose

When you, kind reader, think of the "Islamic World," is China included? When you think about the kinds of religions practiced in China, does Islam come to mind? You will undoubtedly conjure up images of Daoism, Buddhism, *qigong* and other body-cultivation techniques, and perhaps Confucian family rituals like "ancestor worship." Connecting "Islam" to "China" may also bring to mind sectarian violence involving some members of the Turkic Uyghur community in northwestern China. Although Muslims have lived in China since the seventh century and there are today somewhere between twenty and sixty million Muslims in China, very few histories of China and very few works that describe or analyze the "Islamic World" include any discussion of Islam in China.[1] This is a surprising lack of recognition given that there are almost as many Muslims in China as the entire population of Syria or Saudi Arabia, and more than in Malaysia!

There are probably several reasons for this omission, including the assumptions that Islam is fundamentally incompatible with Chinese civilization, and that Islam is somehow more monolithic than other world religions and demands a uniformity among its adherents that overrides any possible accommodation with local or native culture. Two well-known scholarly treatments of Islam in China make the first argument explicitly, and general discussion of Muslims by the popular press conveys the latter all too vividly. However, the reality of Islamic belief generally, and certainly in China in particular, could not be more different from these assumptions. Muslims can be found in every corner of China, there is a very wide variety of practice of Islam across China, Islam is now an accepted and recognized part of the religious landscape of China, and most Muslims in China would object to being characterized as fundamentally at odds with their home society and state.² Islam's normative position in China today owes much to its long history in China and to how citizenship is defined in the modern Chinese nation.

HISTORY OF ISLAM IN CHINA

China has been home to many foreign religions for millennia, including Buddhism, Judaism, Zoroastrianism, Manichaeism, and Nestorian Christianity. While Islam arrived in China later than most of these other religions, all of them reached an accommodation with or encompassment of Chinese culture. This is perhaps best seen in the fact that they were all denoted as a kind of "teaching" (*jiao*), and their sacred buildings were all referred to by the same Chinese character, *si*, which originally meant an official, or imperial, institution, and were, in terms of architecture, virtually indistinguishable from imperial or administrative complexes.³ The application of that secular imperial architectural style and terminology to religious buildings was intentional, since the power of the Chinese imperium radiated out across the land via its architectural features as much as in the actions of its officials.

Tradition holds that the first Muslim to enter China was an envoy from the Arab state of Dashiguo (on the Arabian Peninsula) to the Tang emperor Gaozong in 651 CE. However, there are no records of mosques having been built at the Tang capital, unlike sacred buildings of other foreign religions. In fact, the earliest mosques in China are all in port cities in the southeast, the earliest being in the important city of Guangzhou (Canton). This is not surprising, since the majority of Muslims who entered China in that era were merchants who came by sea, bringing their religion with them. This first wave of Muslims did not establish Islam as a normative religion in China in any substantial fashion; until the Mongol conquests of the thirteenth century, Islam was only practiced by foreigners in the great trading cities in southeastern China.

The second great source of Islam in China was the Mongol conquests, which began in the early thirteenth century and did not conclude until the mid-1270s. Curiously, it was this wave of Muslim immigrants that really established Islam as a part of the Chinese religious scene. Since the Mongols were a relatively small group they had to rely on others to maintain their power over the settled societies that they conquered. In China they brought in large numbers of personnel from Central Asia, Persia, and points farther west. Many of these people, known collectively as *"semu"* (literally "colored eyes"; in Yuan-period sources this compound meant "various types of foreigners"), were practicing Muslims, and while they were subjects of the Mongols like the Chinese, they actually dominated much of the political and commercial landscape of China at that time. More important, these people settled permanently in China, where they became accepted in their adopted communities, usually as members of the literati class.

The Ming government (1368–1644), which evicted the Mongols from China back to the steppe, continued to employ many of these same personnel in civil and military positions, and was actually much more multiethnic and tolerant than traditional histories have stated. It was also during this era that Chinese Muslim literati brought Islam firmly into the realm of "Chinese religions," and when the shift in identity from "Muslims in China" to "Chinese Muslims" was made.[4] The state sponsored the translation of Muslim terms by an imperial translation bureau, it established the madrasa educational system, and it aided or at least tolerated the production of writing on Islam and eventually the translation of the Quran. As Zvi Ben-Dor Benite eloquently demonstrates, this literary production by Chinese Muslim writers resulted in a body of literature written mainly in Chinese, but also in Persian and Arabic, of over one hundred texts. This genre that he calls Han Kitab (combining the Chinese word for "Chinese" and the Arabic word for "book") was based in a fundamental dialogue, an "encompassment" between Confucianism and Islam that was quite different from "accommodation," which implies an essential element of "sinicization."[5] It shows the true degree to which those writers were both Chinese and Muslim. That process of dialogue, or encompassment, started in the Mongol era and continued throughout the succeeding Ming and Qing (1644–1911) dynasties, down to the present. It spawned a mosque-building and educational program that was nourished by these thinkers and their writings, including Chinese translations of the Quran, and was the key to transforming Islam into a normal and widely accepted part of the larger religious world in China.[6]

The story of Islam in the last decades of the empire and during the Republican era is complex and rather different from earlier times. It is colored for many by the violent Muslim-led rebellions in northwestern and southwestern China. That history is often cited as evidence for the intrinsic incompatibility of Muslims with Chinese culture or the Chinese premodern or contemporary state.[7] But it is equally clear that Islam was also thriving in and posed no threat to many local communities across China in that same period. In fact, it was in the Republican period (1912–1949) that the first regional and national Chinese Muslim associations were started. Of course, all religions were questioned and eventually repressed during the zealous nationalist campaigns ushered in after the founding of the People's Republic in 1949, especially the Cultural Revolution of 1966–1976. It has only been in the post-Mao era with China's "opening up" under Deng Xiaoping and his successors that Islam, like other religions, has again been allowed to flourish in China. In the People's Republic, Muslims and their religion inhabit two spheres, that of the citizen of the state and of the national minority. In order to understand the normative role of Islam in China today, we must examine how these spheres operate and interrelate.[8]

CITIZENS AND MINORITIES IN
THE PEOPLE'S REPUBLIC OF CHINA

The People's Republic of China sees all people living in the nation as citizens, regardless of their religious views. At the same time, all citizens have been categorized into one of fifty-six different "nationality" groups (*minzu*). This notion originated in late nineteenth-century Japan and was adopted by Sun Yat-sen as a founding principle of the new Republic. The founders of the People's Republic elaborated on those principles with borrowings from Stalin's ideas that a "nationality" could be identified by common territory, language, economy, and psychology, and set out to identify every "nationality" group in China. The idea was to separate these nascent groups from religion in order to understand and control all of the peoples who lived in the territory inherited from the Qing state. Of the fifty-six separate nationalities in China, the Han Chinese are the largest group, followed by fifty-five "national minority" groups (*shaoshu minzu*).

There are currently ten separate officially recognized groups of Muslims in China, and nine of these groups are ethnically and linguistically Turkic or Turko-Mongolian (Uyghurs, Kazakhs, Kyrgyz, Tajiks, Uzbeks, Dongxiang, Salar, Bonan, and Tatars), who live predominantly in northern and northwestern China (Xinjiang, Gansu, Qinghai, and Ningxia). The tenth group of Muslims, called "Hui" (often translated as "Chinese Muslim"), are the single largest group of Muslims in China. Of the fifty-five official national minority groups, the Hui are also unique because they have only their religion, and not any specific regional or phenotypic features, to unify them. In fact, Hui are often called "Han Muslims" because they are, apart from their practice of Islam, indistinguishable from their Han Chinese neighbors. This chapter focuses on the Hui Chinese Muslims.

ISLAMIC BELIEF AND CULTURE

Broadly speaking, the vast majority of Hui Muslims in China are Sunni who follow the Hanafi school of Islamic law (known in Chinese as *gedimu* from Arabic *al qadim*, "ancient"). That tradition also informed the Sino-Muslim literati tradition and production of Han Kitab literature discussed above. Less well known but equally important to the Hui "community" was the flourishing of Islamic popular periodical literature written and published by Hui scholars starting in the 1920s in several areas of China. Monthly journals told Hui readers how to pray and worship correctly, related stories of important historic Hui figures, and disseminated reminiscences and stories by local Hui writers. In fact, these Hui writers were following the larger trend of producing a new kind of popular literature for the masses that arose across China as part of the modernizing goals of the May Fourth movement from 1919. One important result of that literary blossoming was that for the first time attention was paid to creating a standardized system of transliterating Islamic terms into standard Chinese. After things settled down following the tumultuous Mao years, a glossary of hundreds of Arabic and Persian Islamic terms used by Ningxia Hui Muslims in their religious and daily life, but which were also thought to be used in common by Hui across China, was published in the 1980s.

MODERNITY AND BELONGING

The post-Mao (post-socialist?) era of economic openness has opened up every religious community and person to new possibilities and problems in China, and the benefits and risks are quite firmly linked to one's *minzu* identity. The Hui have taken advantage of the new spirit of openness and globalization to rescue Islam from perceptions that it is a marginal, dangerous group and to present it as a normative religion in contemporary China. Hui are now routinely appointed as officials in many parts of China. Religious or Islamic names now appear again alongside Chinese names on Hui business cards. Scholarship by and about Hui history and contemporary issues now also is a part of the academy, especially with the regular publication of the academic journal *Huizu yanjiu* (Hui Studies) since 1991. Hui also openly operate schools that teach Arabic language, Islamic history and religion, and Chinese history and culture, with up-to-date websites (such as the English-language website of the Kaiyuan Arabic Institute in central Yunnan province—www.kyaz.com/English/Index.html), faculty from other parts of the Muslim world, and students from many areas of China.

Chinese Muslims have also been a part of the state's newfound role in the international arena. Hui now regularly go on the Hajj pilgrimage to Mecca, and delegations of visitors from other countries regularly visit prominent Hui mosques and communities. Leading Chinese universities have also begun to sponsor academic conferences that are intended to promote China's goodwill to Islamic states; Nanjing University and Harvard University have had several annual conferences that examine new dialogue between Chinese Confucian and Islamic cultures, and Yunnan University now houses a Sino-Iranian Institute that studies and promotes historic and contemporary Sino-Iranian relations. Promoting the notion of Islam as a normal part of

China's history and contemporary society is beneficial both for the state's growing international interests and for the Hui in China.

Another visible manifestation of the strength of Hui communities is in the restoration of historic mosques and the proliferation of new mosques. Many traditional mosques have been repaired and now function both as sacred and tourist sites. Hui communities have also been investing in new mosques that are striking for their adoption of seemingly global Islamic architectural styles: a centralized multistory mosque with a green-tiled dome and white-plaster or tile exteriors adorned with highly stylized Arabic calligraphy. Most interesting, however, is the fact that these new mosques also borrow from Chinese secular modern architectural trends that include multistory concrete buildings with white-tile skins and copious use of clear glass (ubiquitous in new commercial and government urban buildings). Because these new, modern mosques can also be found in almost every city in China, they give the impression of Hui modernity and spiritual and economic vitality. They are firmly part of the "new" China.

UNITY IN DIVERSITY?

This chapter has tried to address two common perceptions: first that China is never considered as a part of the "Islamic World," and second, that Islam is not a part of the normative Chinese religious landscape. Using the largest group of Muslims in China, the Hui, as our case study, it should be apparent that the sheer number of Muslims in China, not to mention the liveliness of their faith, makes China's inclusion in the Islamic World an easy and natural conclusion.

Addressing the second perception, that Islam is somehow historically or culturally not part of China and Chinese society, is more complicated. There are some Muslims living in China, especially some in the Uyghur community, who would side with this view. But their issues and problems with the Chinese state and society have been framed at least as much by state policies toward ethnic minorities and access to resources in specific areas where some minorities live as with any inherent antipathy against Islam. By contrast, the Hui Muslims serve as a good case study to investigate the normality of Islam in China.

Apart from their shared religious affiliation as part of the orthodox Sunni tradition, is there anything that really unifies all of the Hui Muslims into a group with a shared identity? The notion of a shared identity might be seen as a key to regarding any religion as normative in a nation. There is no central religious authority for Islam in China. And unlike other Muslim groups in China, the Hui are not tied to a specific geography, culture, or ethnicity, and local or regional identities matter greatly. Being Muslim is, for the Hui, no different from being Buddhist or Daoist for other Chinese people, since the linguistic, social, and cultural particularities of specific locales transcend or at least compete with any wider religious identity, and also tend to shape specific religious practice.

The fungible nature of their *minzu* identity has also made it easier for Hui to accept their official status. As Dru Gladney has argued, successful accommodation to minority status is a measure of the degree to which these Muslims allow and are comfortable with a reconciliation of Islam to Chinese culture.[9] The encompassment practiced by Sino-Muslim thinkers in late-imperial China that enabled them to be full members of both the Islamic and Confucian literati elite circles continues to inform their identity as good and loyal Hui citizens of the People's Republic who practice one of the world religions long resident in China. It is no surprise to find historic or new mosques in every part of China, and of course the famous Muslim *qingzhen* ("pure and clean") restaurants are ubiquitous and well known even among Han Chinese as good restaurants. It should thus be obvious that Islam is no outlier in the constellation of Chinese religions, and that China should be considered to be a part of the wider Islamic World.

SUGGESTIONS FOR FURTHER READING

Donald Leslie, *Islam in Traditional China* (Canberra College of Advanced Education, 1986) gives a historical survey of Islamic teachings and groups in China into the late-imperial period, while Michael Dillon, *China's Muslim Hui Community* (Curzon, 1999), covers Hui communities in nineteenth- and twentieth-century China, and the role of Sufism in Hui communities and in Chinese Islam generally. Dru Gladney, *Muslim Chinese* (Harvard University Press, 1991), is an anthropological study of the Hui Muslims, centered in northwestern China. Frank Dikötter, *The Discourse of Race in Modern China* (Stanford University Press, 1992), traces the emergence of racial categories in late-imperial China and the modern system of ethnic minorities invoked by the Chinese state since 1949.

NOTES

1. The most recent official census puts the number of Muslims at a conservative twenty-two million. Other estimates range from forty to sixty million. One interesting example of this general omission is John L. Esposito, *Islam in Asia: Religion, Politics and Society* (Oxford: Oxford University Press, 1987), which treats China and Soviet Central Asia in one short chapter. That China is included at all is actually more progressive than most works on Islam outside the Middle East and Saudi Arabia.

2. Some Uyghurs in the northwestern province of Xinjiang argue that they are historically and culturally separate from China, and see themselves as a persecuted ethno-religious minority. This chapter does not discuss the Uyghurs, focusing instead on the largest group of Muslims in China, the Chinese Muslims.

3. Nancy Shatzman Steinhardt, "China's Earliest Mosques," *Journal of the Society of Architectural Historians* 67, no. 3 (2008): 330–61, especially makes this point clear.

4. Donald Daniel Leslie, *Islam in Traditional China: A Short History to 1800* (Canberra: Canberra College of Advanced Education, 1986).

5. Zvi Ben-Dor Benite, *The Dao of Muhammad* (Cambridge, MA: Harvard University Asia Center, 2005).

6. Donald Daniel Leslie, *Islamic Literature in Chinese* (Canberra: Canberra College of Advanced Education, 1981), provides an exhaustive list of these early Chinese Muslim writers and their works, as well as other prominent Chinese Muslim writers in the late-imperial era.

7. See, for example, Michael Dillon, *China's Muslims* (Oxford: Oxford University Press, 1996), and Raphael Israeli, *Islam in China* (Lanham, MD: Lexington Books, 2002). It is in part due to that complex history of the emergence of the contemporary nation-state out of imperial China that some Uyghurs claim they should be separate from China.

8. See for discussion Dru C. Gladney, "Islam in China: Accommodation or Separatism?" *Religion in China Today, The China Quarterly Special Issues*, New Series, no. 3 (Cambridge: Cambridge University Press, 2003), pp. 145–61, and Jonathan N. Lipman, *Familiar Strangers: A History of Muslims in Northwest China* (Seattle: University of Washington Press, 1997).

9. Gladney, "Islam in China."

7

Chinese Medicine

Bridie Andrews

"Traditional Chinese medicine" is a form of healing often described as embodying an unbroken medical tradition reaching back to antiquity. But what is Chinese medicine, actually? Writing in 1869, Scottish medical missionary John Dudgeon wrote that it consisted of "Magic, charms and gymnastics," and dismissed even elite Chinese physicians for dealing in such "superstitions" as *yin* and *yang*. In the modern West, many interpret the long history of medicine in China and its inductive, holistic approach to treatment as a welcome corrective to reductionist biomedicine. For these acolytes, Chinese medicine is something to believe in, like a religion, and is best learned from a "master" who embodies the ancient wisdom of Asian tradition. Somewhere in between these extremes is the Chinese medicine taught in medical schools in China, where it forms a relatively stable, secular, and internally consistent body of theory and practice. How can we explain these different evaluations of Chinese medicine?

MEDICINE AS A CULTURAL SYSTEM

Some decades ago, medical anthropologist and psychiatrist Arthur Kleinman classified the diverse healing practices in Taiwan according to whether they occurred in the formal professional sector, the folk sector of unprofessionalized specialists (often religious, but also including secular healing occupations such as herbalism or bone manipulation), or the popular sector where most healing activity occurs, facilitated by families, cultural expectations, and lay healers. He argued that the totality of activities within these overlapping spheres is what forms a health care system. Within such a system, culture shapes a symbolic reality mediating between the sick person's physical and psychic symptoms and their social and physical environment.

This reminder that health care systems consist of everything from the individual through communities to the organized medical professions alerts us that the term "Chinese medicine" usually refers only to the professional sector. The creation of organized professions—including medicine—was a twentieth-century project in China, and the creation of "traditional Chinese medicine" was a process involving the ideologies and political agendas of successive Chinese governments. As a result of this history, Chinese medicine today is vastly different from anything practiced before the mid-twentieth century.

Before then, there were few regulations governing the practice of medicine in China. Basically, anyone could call themselves a doctor and treat patients for as high a fee as their reputation would allow. Even at the elite end of the spectrum there were many competing currents and medical lineages. Some of the more popular included acolytes of the "Four Famous Physicians of the Jin and Yuan Dynasties"; also southern specialists in epidemic "warmth diseases," *wen bing*, who were differentiated from followers of Zhang Ji's (Zhang Zhongjing) Han dynasty classic, *Shanghan lun*, the *Treatise on Cold Damage*, which offered older ways of treating epidemics. Other medical lineages based themselves on knowledge passed down from father to son or nephew, and occasionally to daughters or trusted outsiders. This secrecy in the transmission of valuable expertise led to great diversity in medical theories and healing practices.

Popular responses to epidemics (whether considered to be "warmth diseases" or the results of "cold damage") might include organizing processions in the streets to expel the "demons" causing the disease. These processions featured loud, frightening noises from drums, cymbals, and firecrackers. Some participants wore animal costumes; others dressed as the imperial officials of the celestial afterworld, bearing placards and banners inscribed with instructions such as "Drive out evil and expel pestilence," "Unite the region in peace," and "Disperse calamity and bring down blessings."

Other healers included midwives, as well as women who specialized in moxibustion and massage, especially to children and other women. The Confucian requirement that respectable women stay within the "inner quarters" reinforced the need for female healers to visit women within their homes, even though the same logic made the occupation disreputable for the generally older women who traveled to their patients. Other kinds of healing specialists combined their healing activities with vocations such as farming or being Buddhist or Daoist monks. For example, people who inoculated children with weakened smallpox scabs (variolation) or with cowpox matter (vaccination) were active for less than two

Figure 7.1. Itinerant Healer Photographed in the 1860s by a Protestant medical missionary, courtesy of the archive of Yale University Divinity School, USA.

months every spring. There were also martial artists who specialized in orthopedic manipulation, shamanic healers, and various medical traders who traveled from town to town to advertise and sell their remedies (see figure 7.1). These less respectable practitioners are scarcely visible in the classical medical literature.

How, and why, was such a cacophony of competing theories reduced to the single, harmonious system of Chinese medicine we know today? The story is one of competing power struggles, both international and internal to China.

FOREIGN IMPERIALISM AND THE SCIENTIFIC IMPERATIVE

By 1860, losing the "Opium Wars" with Britain left China having to pay war indemnities and allow foreign trade in the so-called treaty ports, where foreigners enjoyed extraterritorial exemption from Chinese laws. Increasing use of steam shipping and the opening of the Suez Canal in 1869 greatly increased the volume of foreign trade, and with it, European fears of infectious diseases, especially smallpox, cholera, and plague. All three were regarded to be seasonally endemic in China, and so foreign countries began demanding health certificates for ships leaving Chinese ports, and also for the individual coolie laborers who left southern Chinese ports in growing numbers for the Philippines (an American colony after 1898), Cuba, Mexico, and California. These certificates had to be signed by doctors with accredited, Western-style medical degrees, and awareness of this aspect of foreign control over Chinese trade prompted reform-minded Chinese officials to support training in Western medicine. For example, Viceroy Li Hongzhang established the Tianjin Medical School in 1881, which became the Beiyang Medical College in 1893. In 1894–1895, Japan defeated China in the Sino-Japanese War, causing many Chinese to want to copy Japan's more thorough modernizing reforms. Medicine had been an important element in the Japanese Meiji reforms after 1868, and the Japanese government had passed a law as early as 1873 requiring anyone wanting to practice medicine after that date to have a Western-style MD degree.

Pressure mounted on the Chinese imperial government after the 1900 Boxer Rebellion, which had turned into an antiforeigner uprising and had been suppressed by an allied expeditionary force from eight nations, including Japan. The resulting Boxer Protocol infringed on Chinese sovereignty in several ways and imposed an enormous indemnity of 450 million silver taels. Even conservative Chinese statesmen began to accept the need for drastic reforms, so in 1901 the government embraced the "New Policies," which (among other things) allowed for the confiscation of temple properties to house new schools teaching mathematics, science, and foreign languages in addition to the traditional Chinese curriculum. These reforms were not convincing to many Chinese, who viewed the Qing dynasty as moribund and joined the movement for its replacement by a modern republic.

In medicine, the period saw the first attempt to license ordinary doctors. In 1908, the governor of the two lower Yangzi provinces (now Zhejiang and Jiangsu) ordered all doctors to take a license examination that demanded knowledge of *both* Western and Chinese medicine, but did not require evidence of medical education. One revolutionary was incensed by this half-measure: Chen Yuan (1880–1971) had been influential in setting up a Chinese-run college of Western medicine in Canton in 1908 after leaving a missionary-run college in disgust at the attitude of the missionaries toward their Chinese students. He was aghast at the naïveté of this examination, as without regulated education and evidence that candidates had first mastered basic science, it would not reassure the foreign powers that licensed Chinese doctors were in fact competent. For Chen, this confirmed that the Qing regime was incapable of protecting China from foreign imperialism.

When the Qing regime was overthrown in 1911, and the Republic of China established, the new Ministry of Education included modern medicine in its remit, but not Chinese medicine. This was not a major setback, as it merely continued the status quo: anyone could still practice in whatever way they wished, and there was still no definition of "Chinese" medicine. But in 1915, returned Chinese MDs from the West and from Japan established national medical associations to represent the interests of modern doctors to the new government, and to demonstrate professional competence to the foreign powers in China. They aimed to replace foreigners in strategic medical positions such as Customs Medical Officers, thereby assisting the effort to overturn the "Unequal Treaties" of the mid-nineteenth century and regain national sovereignty for China. Needless to say, even the most educated of the old-style doctors were denied entry to these new professions. The Western-style doctors were in direct competition with Chinese-medical doctors for patients, and they lost no opportunity to berate Chinese medicine as superstitious, unscientific, and unhygienic, just as missionary doctors had done before them. They were joined in this disdain by the young, urban leaders of China's New Culture Movement. For example, in 1915 Chen Duxiu, chief editor of the famous journal *New Youth* (*Xin Qingnian*) wrote that:

> Our men of learning do not understand science; thus they make use of *yin-yang* signs and beliefs in the five elements to confuse the world and delude the people. . . . Our doctors do not understand science; they not only know nothing of human anatomy, they also know nothing of the analysis of medicines; as for bacterial poisoning and infections, they have not even heard of them.[1]

PROFESSIONALIZATION AND THE CREATION
OF A SCIENTIFIC CHINESE MEDICINE

During these same years, the male, literate elite among Chinese-medicine practitioners had also been discussing the new sciences. They established local study societies to share information about modern medicine and to discuss how Chinese medicine should be improved to meet the modern age. Some started journals and even opened medical colleges to teach Chinese medicine. All of these institutions: professional associations, journals, and medical colleges, were modern innovations that mirrored the changes occurring in Chinese society at large. In 1913, representatives of these new Chinese-medicine associations from nineteen provinces sent a delegation to Beijing to petition for the inclusion of Chinese medicine in the Republican government's national education system, and for Chinese-medicine schools to qualify for the new government licenses that would qualify their graduates for government positions. They were turned down flat.

This 1913 delegation shows the beginnings of modern organizations of Chinese medicine, but the political chaos of the so-called Warlord Period of 1915–1928 meant that there was still no real state control of medicine. In 1928, this changed with the success of the Northern Expedition of the Nationalist leader "Generalissimo" Chiang Kai-shek. By persuading many of the regional warlords to join his campaign to unite China, Chiang was able to declare a new Nationalist (*Guomindang*) government, with its capital in Nanjing. Suddenly, the agenda to create a modern Chinese state was again in play, and when the Central Health Committee of the new Ministry of Health resolved to abolish Chinese medicine in 1929, the Chinese-medicine community mobilized to protect their livelihoods. They called a national conference attended by herbal drugs traders and drugstore owners, members of the National Federation of Chambers of Commerce, the Federation of Street Merchant Associations, the Society for Supporting National Goods, as well as doctors of Chinese medicine. They formed a new national association for lobbying the government, and appealed to nationalist sentiment by calling Chinese medicine "national medicine" and accusing Western-style doctors of serving foreign imperialism. A delegation lobbied the government in Nanjing, where they had sympathetic hearings from several government ministers. Ironically, the attempt to eradicate Chinese medicine inadvertently sparked a coordinated movement to protect it, ultimately leading to its incorporation into state medical services under the Communists after 1949.

Political mobilization was just one part of the movement to incorporate Chinese medicine into the modern Chinese state. Just as important was the effort to "scientize" it (*kexuehua*). Inevitably, the scientization of Chinese medicine involved engaging with modern medical science. Many early schools of Chinese medicine included classes in anatomy and physiology in their curricula. In Canton in 1924, for example, the Guangdong School of Chinese Medicine and Pharmacy taught classes in Western physiology alongside a newly designed subject called "Chinese physiology," also Western and Chinese diagnostics, plus anatomy, pathology, chemistry, and "essential Western pharmacy." Noticeably absent from these early medical school curricula is the one technique that Westerners are most likely to associate with Chinese medicine: acupuncture.

By 1936, when the Nationalist government started publishing national regulations to govern the licensing of doctors of Chinese medicine, it also left acupuncture out of the subjects required for qualification. While the practice of acupuncture is as old as Chinese medicine itself, by the late Qing dynasty it had become an artisan-class activity. At the time, acupuncture needles came in several shapes and sizes, from bodkins to straight and curved scalpels (see figure 7.2), indicating that acupuncture was often a kind of minor surgery. As such, it was associated with street tradesmen and itinerants rather than with the literate elite. By the early 1930s, several authors complained that the classics of medicine were either vague or mutually contradictory about the exact positions of the acupuncture points.

Cheng Dan'an (1899–1957) brought Western anatomy to the rescue. In his pathbreaking book *Chinese Acupuncture and Moxibustion Therapeutics* (*Zhongguo zhenjiu zhiliao xue*), first published in 1931, Cheng noted that acupuncture and moxibustion had virtually disappeared from China, and he proposed to revive them. His formula for revival had much in common with earlier Japanese reforms of acupuncture, including using Western anatomy to redefine acupuncture points. His preface explained:

> The pathways of acupuncture points recorded by our forebears are mostly lacking in detail. [. . .] This book employs scientific methods to correct this. Each acupoint must be elucidated anatomically. [. . .] In manipulating acupoints, although our forebears needled into veins, this was really needling the nerves of that area, and certainly not [primarily] rupturing the vein.

Accordingly, Cheng used Western anatomy to ensure that no points were located near major blood vessels (see figure 7.3). His approach marked a major shift in acupuncture theory and practice. Before Cheng Dan'an, acupuncture was frequently used to let small amounts of blood, in order to clear perceived obstructions to the free flow of blood and *qi*. However, after Cheng argued that acupuncture acted through the nerves, drawing blood at an acupuncture point started to be viewed as an indication of the practitioner's clumsiness and lack of experience—a view that persists today.

The demand for Cheng's new, scientific acupuncture was so great that by May 1937, the book had gone into its eighth edition. Prominent

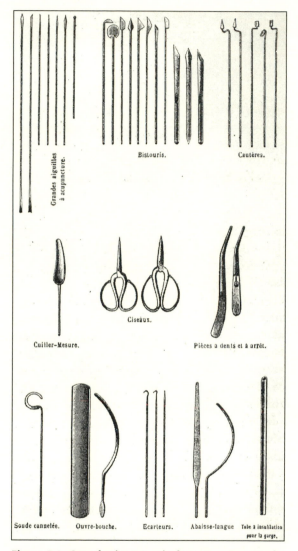

Figure 7.2. Set of Minor Surgical/Acupuncture Tools. Photograph published in Eugène Vincent, *La médecine en Chine au XXe siècle* (Paris, 1915).

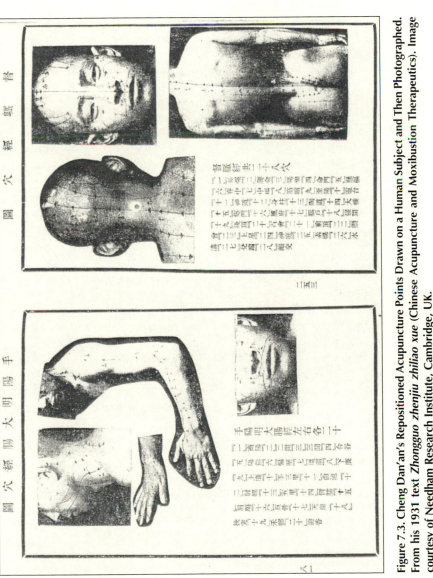

Figure 7.3. Cheng Dan'an's Repositioned Acupuncture Points Drawn on a Human Subject and Then Photographed. From his 1931 text *Zhongguo zhenjiu zhiliao xue* (Chinese Acupuncture and Moxibustion Therapeutics). Image courtesy of Needham Research Institute, Cambridge, UK.

mainland Chinese medical historians describe it as "the most influential work on acupuncture of the last hundred years." In addition to employing Western anatomy to create a "scientific" acupuncture, Cheng rejected the idea of strictly timing acupuncture treatments according to astrological and divinatory formulae. He also condemned as a remnant of superstition the old idea that men should be treated on their left sides and women on their right.

In practical terms, Cheng recommended that moxibustion not be used to cauterize the skin, as it led to ugly and traumatic scars. A prevailing idea that acupuncture and moxa should not be used at the same spot seemed, to Cheng, a product of using thick, coarse acupuncture needles, which caused such damage to the skin that combining them with moxa cautery was likely to leave a considerable wound. If moxa were not allowed to burn the skin, and only filiform needles were used, the two treatments could be combined to great effect. Such revisions heralded major changes in the practice of acupuncture that have survived to the present. Virtually all acupuncture is now carried out with filiform stainless steel needles of varying lengths, with none of the minor surgery or boil-lancing with small scalpels and crude silver or non–stainless steel bodkins that were once part of the acupuncturist's stock-in-trade.

This change in acupuncture theory and practice, which allowed it to seem respectable and scientific enough to be integrated into the modernizing Chinese medicine, is one example of how "traditional Chinese medicine" was constructed out of different cultural resources that were first cleansed of embarrassing elements, and then added to an emerging body of knowledge and practice that was designed to represent a distinctively Chinese medical modernity. A similar process was underway in the Communist base areas in the 1940s. Kim Taylor has documented the remarkable work of a Communist woman doctor, Zhu Lian (1909–1978), who trained in Western medicine, joined the Chinese Communist Party (CCP) in 1935, and served in key medical positions at the CCP wartime headquarters in Yan'an, Shaanxi, between 1935 and 1947. Faced with a shortage of drugs and modern doctors, she noticed that medical teams that included acupuncturists spent substantially less on drugs. After experimentation, she compiled *A New Acupuncture*, a textbook for training medical personnel, published in 1951 just after the establishment of the People's Republic. In this book, the acupoints are called "stimulation points" (*cijidian*), and are arranged in military units: sections, divisions, and lines (as in "front line"). Zhu also "discovered" two new acupoints, named in accordance with the politics of the time: "new construction," *xinjian*, and "new establishment," *xinshe*. As Taylor argues, Zhu's new acupuncture was reconfigured to be the medicine of the Communist revolution.

Zhu Lian also argued that acupuncture would help the Party combat superstition. In rural areas, many people still preferred to consult shamans, drink "holy water" (*shenshui*), or conduct divinations when sick. This behavior needed to be modernized, and Zhu differed from most MDs in making acupuncture part of the Communist solution.

In the early 1950s, the new Ministry of Health promoted the further "scientization" of Chinese medicine, claiming by 1954 to have put over 30,000 Chinese-medicine practitioners through classes at special further education schools where they learned basic hygiene and science along with Party ideology. In July 1954, Chairman Mao demanded that practitioners of Western medicine should now study Chinese medicine so that a Unified Medicine of China could be created. The reluctant first class of eighty-nine new MDs were taught by famous old Chinese doctors, and a committee to create textbooks for them was established in 1956. This class graduated in 1958 after a two-and-a-half-year course. The same year, the first national textbook of Chinese medicine, the *Outline of Chinese Medicine*, was published, which presented Chinese medicine as an internally consistent, coherent system, with citations from the ancient medical classics only where they could be used to undergird this new systematization.

In the meantime, Mao had declared Chinese medicine to be "a national treasure house" and the Ministry of Health had begun to establish Academies of Traditional Chinese Medicine, thus validating education in Chinese medicine in its own right. The ministry also insisted that 30 percent of classes in the new academies should be devoted to Western medical subjects. The result was a system of medical education that required a grounding in modern sciences and acknowledged the epistemic priority of anatomy and pathology, but which then had considerable freedom to develop on the basis of a secular reading of the medical classics.

Several recent anthropological studies of Chinese medicine have demonstrated that at the level of individual practice, there is still a great deal of diversity. Moreover, since economic liberalization began in the 1980s, many of the less "scientific" practices—shamanism, divination, temple medicine— have become available again. But the effort to create a modern, scientific system out of the spectrum of late-imperial healing practices has been so successful that "traditional Chinese medicine" is now among China's most successful cultural exports. Ultimately, the persistence of the perception of Chinese medicine as ancient and unchanging reflects Western patients' dissatisfaction with modern medical practice and their search for a more holistic form of treatment. Which is ironic, as the medical reformers who created Chinese medicine had intended to produce something "scientific" out of the chaotic spectrum of healing practices that existed before. What Chinese doctors rejected because of their enthusiasm for science, Western patients now embrace because of their disillusionment with modern medicine.

SUGGESTIONS FOR FURTHER READING

Bridie Andrews, *The Making of Modern Chinese Medicine* (University of British Columbia, 2013) explores the intertwined histories of modern medicine in China and the modernization of Chinese medicine, while Elisabeth Hsu, *The Transmission of Chinese Medicine* (Cambridge University Press, 1999) offers an ethnography of different kinds of medical training. Volker Scheid, an anthropologist and licensed acupuncturist, combined fieldwork observations in Beijing with modern history in *Chinese Medicine in Contemporary China* (Duke University Press, 2002). Kim Taylor's *Chinese Medicine in Early Communist China, 1945–63: A Medicine of Revolution* (RoutledgeCurzon, 2005) is a detailed examination of how Communist political agendas shaped the development of Chinese medicine.

Nathan Sivin, *Traditional Medicine in Contemporary China* (University of Michigan, 1987), provides a translation of the *Revised Outline of Chinese Medicine* (1978) intended for Chinese doctors of biomedicine, with an introduction on change within Chinese medicine, and Paul U. Unschuld, *Medicine in China: A History of Ideas*, 2nd ed. (University of California, 2010) includes translations from key historic works. Ted J. Kaptchuk's *The Web That Has No Weaver: Understanding Chinese Medicine* (Contemporary Books, 2000) is a clear exposition of modern Chinese medicine. Mei Zhan, *Other-Worldly: Making Chinese Medicine through Transnational Frames* (Duke University Press, 2009), compares Chinese medicine in America and in China.

NOTE

1. David W. Y. Kwok, *Scientism in Chinese Thought, 1900–1950* (New Haven, CT: Yale University Press, 1965), p. 65; Ralph C. Croizier, *Traditional Medicine in Modern China: Science, Nationalism and the Tensions of Cultural Change* (Cambridge: Harvard University Press, 1968), p. 71.

8

Traditional Chinese and the Environment

Ling Zhang

When asked to describe the relationship between traditional Chinese and their natural environment, readers familiar with Chinese philosophy, religion, or the arts might immediately sketch the daily life of Chinese literati of imperial times. These were men who lived in gardens that combined trees, water, and stone to imitate the patterns of nature; who appreciated the beauty of the natural world, communicated with their surroundings, and memorialized them through landscape paintings; who practiced fengshui geomancy and conserved forests on mountains; and who regarded themselves as small creatures in the midst of their father Heaven and mother Earth and as equal beings to other men and things. "The integration of Heaven and humanity" (*tianren heyi*), or harmony between nature and humans, is a convenient answer to the question. The notion that the relationship between humans and nature should be harmonious is widespread, if often left unelaborated, in much Western writing about China. This ideal has been pervasive among Chinese themselves, who comprehend the proposition perhaps very vaguely, but believe in its truth out of pride in their own culture. In recent decades this view has, if anything, strengthened, for the raging environmental problems of present-day China and the lack of effective solutions to combat the crisis tend to arouse nostalgia for the good old days and call for a reversion to traditional environmental values. The belief that there was a harmony between nature and humanity in the past is being formed in company with a surging desire for a harmonious future.

This view of traditional Chinese relations between nature and humanity, however, rests upon a particular assumption. It assumes that the Chinese lived in a more environmentally harmonious way in the past than they do nowadays, a notion liable to lead to the neglect of various inharmonious relations, mainly in the realm of Chinese practices regarding the natural world.

THE IDEALIZATION OF THE RELATIONSHIP
BETWEEN HUMANS AND NATURE

This perception has been generated through several channels. It has certainly been spread by the Chinese classics, scholarly writings, general readings, art works and their interpretations, conservation of historic sites, and the media. Jesuit missionaries and adventurers introduced early-modern Western intellectuals to "Chinese garden" and landscape paintings, which perfectly demonstrated Chinese aesthetics and sensitivity to the presence of nature in daily life. It seems that if they were unable to live near water or travel in the mountains in person, the Chinese would manipulate their surroundings into a smaller-sized "nature" in order to sustain the close link between them and the natural world. The explanation for why they were keen to do so can be found in Chinese philosophy—Confucianism, Daoism, and Chinese Buddhism—which over centuries came to convey a general worldview: that humanity is an organic part of nature rather than superior and external to it. The human body reflects seasonal changes in the natural world, and is a miniature version of the greater cosmos, where the water of rivers and seas corresponds to human blood and mountains correspond to human bones. Joseph Needham, among others, concludes that the basic Chinese attitude is that the natural world is "like the greatest of all living organisms, the governing principles of which had to be understood so that life could be lived in harmony with it," so "the key word is always harmony."[1]

From the 1960s, environmental crisis in the West stimulated a quest for the roots of the developing disaster. Lynn White famously accused Christendom for its possessive and destructive attitude to nature, which for centuries instructed people in behaviors that led them to conquer and deplete their environment. White's view provoked extensive debate and criticism; but more importantly, it encouraged people to seek solutions from the apparently more "harmonious" attitude in East Asia. Knowledge about Eastern cultures and environmental ethics grew rapidly. Zen Buddhism, for instance, flourished in the West in this context. Later on, this fantasy of Eastern environmental ethics was promoted at the theoretical level by philosophers like J. B. Carllicott, who regarded traditional Asian thought on nature as a type of "deep ecology" that opposes anthropocentric worldviews and values the interdependence of humanity and the rest of the ecosphere. This intellectual trend that created an impression of harmony between humans and nature in the East has had wide influence on Western environmental movements.

Inside China, environmental problems are reaching a critical stage as rapidly as its economy develops—with rivers drying up, deserts advancing, air being polluted, and people striving for clean water for the next generation. These facts, however, have not destroyed but rather strengthened the impression of the harmonious relationship between humans and nature in traditional China. Because China's environmental deterioration has been largely caused and exacerbated by modernization and industrialization, it appears to be a recent import from the West, whose ecological curse has extended to the East. Such an observation leads many Westerners as well as Chinese to lament the disappearance of nature's beauties, together with the loss of the profound companionship between the Chinese and the rest of nature. It also brings calls for the restoration of "harmony," hoping that traditional wisdom may help foster environmental ethics and environmental policies in modern China. For instance, we may wonder if it is just coincidence that we see the current prevalence of "national studies" (*guoxue re*), in particular of Confucianism, while the Chinese government advocates the establishment of a "harmonious society," in which pollution, ecological deterioration, and resource depletion are supposed to be substantially controlled. On the other hand, these perspectives echo the same view that traditional gardens, paintings, and philosophies have long nurtured—that in the past the Chinese lived in a world shaped by "the integration of Heaven and humanity."

This view of harmony between nature and humans is flawed in three respects. First, our evidence for the traditional relationship between them is far from comprehensive, and much relies on highly individual instances. Fragmentary motifs extracted from surviving landscapes, paintings, literature, or philosophical writing can hardly delineate the collective circumstances of the majority Chinese population in the whole of the recorded past. Second, historical information is not only scarce but also skewed by its focus on certain social groups, such as aristocrats, officials, and wealthy men, whose lives were associated with gardens, paintings, and books. But how did charcoal burners living at the foot of the mountains perceive and cope with their natural environment? How about swiddening ("slash-and-burn") peasants in south China? Or, how about urban residents who made pastries for a living? These, and other questions regarding the majority, have yet to be answered because of the newness of environmental studies of traditional China.

Third, and more importantly, most of the information accessible to modern readers is ideological and conceptual, little concerned about people's conduct in practice. To a large proportion of the population, their relationship with nature as conceived in idealistic, cosmological, and moral terms was one thing, while their physical involvement in the natural environment was another. The divergence between these two "natures" can also be found among the educated elites. Those possessing timber businesses in Huizhou, for instance, would avoid depleting the entire forest and were concerned about the sustainable development of profits as well as the forests. Nevertheless, the question remains: when these people spontaneously constrained their behavior by not cutting trees, was this in response to their moral and philosophical belief in harmony, or simply because it was pragmatic? The answer is complicated. We should also consider Chinese garden owners who obtained visual pleasure and spiritual meditation when looking from their wooden pavilions over manmade streams and woods. Rarely, however, would they ask where the wood came from and how that place had been affected by the felling of the trees.

After comparing Chinese ideas about nature and the environmental consequences of their conduct, especially deforestation, the geographer Yi-fu Tuan concluded that there were, among Chinese, "discrepancies between environmental attitude and behavior," which sounds quite reasonable. Some, like the philosopher Carllicott, may argue that the ideological harmony between humans and nature and the behavioral disharmony of the traditional Chinese are not comparable. Without denying this opinion, it is important to remember that the perception under question is not rooted in the "discrepancies between environmental attitude and behavior" *per se*, but in modern observers' *understanding* of such discrepancies. The imbalance between our adequate knowledge of environmental philosophy and ethics and our remarkably inadequate knowledge of environmental practices may lead to the false assumption that China's environmental problems are recent, thus resulting in shortsighted conclusions—and shortsighted solutions to current problems. Although quite a number of Chinese environmental problems are caused and worsened by modernization and political mistakes as elaborated in Judith Shapiro's book *Mao's War against Nature*, many of them are rooted much further back in history. Recognizing such assumptions about traditional Chinese practices regarding nature helps to reveal the historical origins of current problems and enables lessons to be learned from the past.

ENVIRONMENTAL DETERIORATION IN THE YELLOW RIVER VALLEY

Historical cases from premodern times provide a glimpse of humanity's collective role in the transformation of China's natural environment, in the related aspects of agricultural colonization, land deterioration, deforestation, flood control, and ecological changes.

Let us start in the Great Bend of the Yellow River in northern Shaanxi province. Neighboring the Mongolian steppe, this area has long been an economically transitional zone between the predominantly agricultural economy of the Han Chinese and the characteristic animal pasturage of nomadic peoples. The ebb and flow between these two has led to changes in the landscape. In 413, when Helian Bobo built the capital for his Xia Kingdom here, this area enjoyed a wealth of grassland and water resources. In Helian's own words, the land was "adjacent to extensive lakes and surrounded by clean streams. I have travelled to many places; none of them are as beautiful as this one." On this promising land, he constructed the "City of Ruling the Myriad" and looked forward to conquering the whole of China.

After the rapid fall of Helian came dramatic change in this area's environmental conditions. The spread of Chinese farmers seeking agricultural land, military colonization sponsored by Chinese governments, frequent warfare and war damage, the continual immigration of nomads who gradually adopted an agricultural life on lands of marginal value for agriculture, and perhaps climatic changes, all contributed to the depletion of this grassland. When a poet visited the region in the 860s–870s, the natural beauty of earlier times had already been fundamentally changed, and Helian's city was found to have merged into the boundless desert known today as the Maowusu.

The desertification of the Great Bend area had far-reaching implications for the environment of the whole of north China. Most immediately there was tremendous soil erosion caused by the denuded land surface. Winds and storms brought sand down into the middle reaches of the nearby Yellow River, causing serious siltation. The deposition of sediment raised the river several meters above ground level, and it overflowed both banks. In the late ninth century the Yellow River flooded or ruptured its banks once every ten years, but this rose to once every 3.6 years in the first half of the tenth century, and then to every 3.3 years in the eleventh century. A giant breach in 1048, for instance, diverted the river's east-west arm farther north, where it swept across the southern half of modern Hebei province. Some one million people were killed or forced into flight. Floods of similar scale occurred once every ten years in the following eight decades.[2]

From the eleventh century on, north China's environmental deterioration fell into a vicious cycle. On the one hand, population expansion and land scarcity drove landless farmers into marginal, often environmentally vulnerable, places like the Maowusu Desert and the Loess Plateau. There, the introduction in late imperial times of new-world crops like maize and sweet potato, while supporting a subsistence economy, might also have stimulated cultivation of the denuded land. Along with these processes came the rapid clearance of forests and consequential soil erosion, due to human desires for arable land, construction materials, and fuel.

On the other hand, unable to prevent environmental damage in the upstream areas in the West, the majority of those living on the crowded central and eastern plains had no choice but to engage in intensive hydraulic works to prevent floods. Given the technological limitations of the time, such works could only be achieved with the input of immense quantities of timber and other plant material. Accordingly, deforestation advanced further upstream into remote mountains and caused even more soil erosion and siltation than anticipated in the central and eastern plains. As early as the eleventh century, the Taihang Mountain range was described as being largely bald, a significant reason being the felling of trees to supply river defenses in the east.

AGRICULTURE, POPULATION, AND ENVIRONMENTAL CHANGES IN SOUTH CHINA

Beyond north China the stories of environmental change are also complex and often tragic. From the eighth century, and in particular from the twelfth, agriculturalists began to migrate south in large numbers to escape wars or seek new land. One case is Jiaxing in the lower Yangzi valley, where the registered population grew from 15 per square kilometer in 980 to 84 per square kilometer between 1080 and 1102, and to 294 in 1290: almost twentyfold in three hundred years. This dramatic population increase was accompanied by heightened agricultural productivity—thanks to the development of new crop species, double-cropping techniques, the construction of extensive sea walls to resist tides, and the application of the polder system and other irrigation methods for rice production. On the downside, deforestation became evident in Jiaxing by the twelfth century. The tremendous demand for firewood, given the lack of alternative fuel like coal, deforested the hills and drove most peasants to live life, in Mark Elvin's words, "on the edge." The peculiarities of the wet-rice economy, such as transplanting rice seedlings in waterlogged paddies and rearing pigs close to human residences, fostered diseases, such as schistosomiasis. This partly explains why Jiaxing people suffered shorter life spans than in some other parts of China, despite their productive economy.[3]

Shifting our gaze upstream to the middle reaches of the Yangzi River, we see the centuries-long expansion and shrinkage of Dongting Lake, the second-largest lake in China today. In the Tang-Song period (seventh to thirteenth centuries), the lake was admired for its vast expanse of open water, and it played an important hydrological role as the catchment and outlet of the Yangzi and other rivers, and prevented the region being flooded. But, following the skyrocketing of the Hunan population from five million at the end of the sixteenth century to nearly thirty million in the early twentieth century, the demand for farmland drove peasants to cultivate the shores of the lake and even to construct polders on the lake itself by erecting dams and dykes. Such efforts, often illegal, not only cut Dongting into small sectors but also destroyed its natural links to the Yangzi and diminished its function of accommodating floods. Clearly, economic interests imposed heavy burdens on the ecosystem of Dongting Lake, which shrank from 6,000 square kilometers in 1825 to 2,740 square kilometers in 1977. As Peter Perdue shows, in Hunan in late imperial times "there was no large lake in the region, but only a series of small lakes, marshes, and river junctions."[4]

Chinese migrants also marched farther south during the Tang-Song or Middle Period, to the Lingnan area in today's Guangdong and Guangxi. Carrying out cultivation on the deposited silt brought downstream by rivers, the migrant and indigenous farmers turned the Pearl River Delta from a collection of islands and marshes into a land of rice paddies. However, the price of such economic development was heavy. Along with forest clearance, the spread of sweet potatoes in hilly terrain, and the local custom of burning off mountain vegetation, came also an increase in soil erosion and flooding in the delta. After 1690, incidents like tiger attacks on humans disappear from the records, leading Robert Marks to suggest that this meant the destruction of the tigers' habitat and the elimination of tigers.[5]

Apart from economic, demographic, and technological forces, often political interventions can recreate the environment too; that is, politics can generate disharmony between nature and humanity. For example, in 1128 the embankments of the Yellow River were breached artificially to generate a flood to thwart the invasion of the Jurchen, similar to what Chiang Kai-shek did to stop the Japanese in 1938; the latter event reportedly killed nearly one million and displaced ten million. During the Yuan-Ming-Qing period (fourteenth to nineteenth centuries), governments built up extensive flood-control levees to constrain the Yellow River within a southern course. The prime reason was to keep the disastrous river away from the political center in Beijing and to protect the Grand Canal, which for centuries transported goods from the south to feed royal families, their bureaucrats, and their armies in the north. The success of these political acts was accompanied by huge environmental, economic, and human costs paid in China's central and eastern plains: frequent floods, rising ground levels due to siltation, sandification damage to arable land, reduced agricultural productivity, population displacement, financial stresses caused by flood-control works, and so on. When these human designs failed and the river ran out of control, catastrophes occurred, and challenges to social stability followed, such as riots by the poverty-stricken in the later years of these dynasties.

CONCLUSION

These are just a few examples of China's environmental history that scholars have begun to investigate. We are still ignorant of the nuances of China's long-term environmental changes on regional and local levels. While more examples await study, it is essential for us, both theoretically and practically, to rectify any presumption that Chinese maintained a more harmonious relationship with the natural world in traditional times than at present. This brief survey suggests that most likely traditional Chinese failed in practice to cope with nature harmoniously, and that the environmental legacies incurred, including deforestation and soil erosion, have formed the base of many modern environmental issues. Heavy industrialization on this land since the mid-twentieth century is not the beginning of all the problems, although it certainly has been exacerbating them at an unprecedented speed. Without a comprehensive knowledge of the historical evolution of China's environment and its human-nature relationships, any solutions for its present environmental crises will be like many of the Yellow River's hydraulic works in the past—a case of erecting levees upon flowing sand, lacking solid foundations and subject to collapse.

SUGGESTIONS FOR FURTHER READING

A good start to reading about traditional Chinese environmental behavior is Mark Elvin, "Three Thousand Years of Unsustainable Growth: China's Environment from Archaic Times to the Present," *East Asian History* 6 (1993). A more comprehensive study of Chinese environmental history is given in Elvin's *Retreat of the Elephants* (Yale University Press, 2004). Readers interested in specific aspects of Chinese environmental studies may consult *Sediments of Time*, edited by Mark Elvin and Tsui-jung Liu (Cambridge University Press, 1998).

Debates on traditional Chinese environmental ethics and philosophy can be found in Yi-fu Tuan, "Discrepancies between Environmental Attitude and Behaviour: Examples from Europe and China," *Canadian Geographer* 15, no. 2 (1971), and J. Baird Carllicott and Roger Ames (eds.), *Nature in Asian Traditions of Thoughts* (State University of New York Press, 1989).

NOTES

1. Joseph Needham, *Science and Civilisation in China, vol. 7, Part II: General Conclusions and Reflections* (Cambridge: Cambridge University Press, 2004), p. 91. Also

Liang Shu-ming, as in Guy Alitto, *The Last Confucian: Liang Shu-ming and the Chinese Dilemma of Modernity* (Berkeley: University of California Press, 1979).

2. Ling Zhang, "Changing with the Yellow River: An Environmental History of Hebei, 1048–1128," *Harvard Journal of Asiatic Studies* 69, no. 1 (2009): 1–36.

3. Mark Elvin, *The Retreat of the Elephants: An Environmental History of China* (New Haven, CT: Yale University Press, 2004), pp. 167–215.

4. Peter Perdue, *Exhausting the Earth: State and Peasant in Hunan, 1500–1850* (Cambridge, MA: Harvard University Press, 1987).

5. Robert Marks, *Tigers, Rice, Silk, and Silt: Environmental and Economy in Late Imperial South China* (Cambridge: Cambridge University Press, 1998).

9

Chinese Martial Arts

Stanley E. Henning

Chinese martial arts continue to be enshrouded by a mist of romance and lack of serious scholarly study. As a result it is widely believed that martial arts were associated with religion and spirituality—Buddhist, Daoist, and, by extension, the beliefs of various heterodox groups throughout Chinese history. In academia, the eminent China scholar Joseph Needham, in his monumental *Science and Civilisation in China*, appears to have influenced scholarly views toward this interpretation. He claims that Chinese boxing probably originated as a department of Daoist physical exercises, and that its subsequent development was likely influenced by Buddhistic monasticism as practiced in Shaolin Monastery. One can see these views echoed in numerous writings on the subject, but they all ignore the evidence to the contrary.

As early as the Western Han period (202 BCE–9 CE), the martial arts were categorized as military skills (*bing jiqiao*). Manuals on martial arts, including boxing and weapons practices, were listed in bibliographies for this period. These military skills spread throughout the population over the centuries and, in the process, were modified into numerous folk styles, although their basic intent, self-defense, remained the same, whether practiced by average citizens or the residents of monasteries. The earliest exposition of Chinese martial arts theory appears in the historical novel *Spring and Autumn of Wu and Yue* (ca. 100 CE). A short passage describes the sword fighting skills of the Maiden of Yue, who was said to have been selected by the King of Yue (497–465 BCE) to train his army against the Kingdom of Wu. In the passage the Maiden of Yue describes the interaction of *yin* and *yang*, and of internal and external attributes, as being among the key principles of all hand-to-hand combat, and these ideas have continued to be central to martial arts practice in general down to the present day.

BUDDHISM, SHAOLIN MONASTERY, AND THE MARTIAL ARTS

As early as the Northern Wei period (386–535 CE) there is evidence that Buddhist monasteries were storing weapons and likely practicing martial arts for the purpose of defending their monastic property. They were even seen as political threats by some ruling monarchs. Shaolin Monastery was not one of them: established in 495 CE, it was not originally associated with martial arts. However, in around 617 it was besieged and largely destroyed in the wars preceding the founding of the Tang dynasty (618–907). Then in 621, Li Shimin the Prince of Qin, who was later to become the greatest of the Tang emperors (Taizong, r. 626–649), asked the head monks at Shaolin for assistance to capture an anti-Tang leader named Wang Shichong. Yet at this point no mention is made of the monks' martial arts.

Shaolin Monastery's recorded involvement in martial arts dates to a much later period, at the end of the Yuan dynasty (1260–1368), when the monastery was laid waste by marauding rebels. It was rebuilt over a number of years, and in 1517, during the Ming dynasty (1368–1644), a commemorative stele was erected. This offered an account of events that failed to mention the monastery's destruction, but claimed that it was saved by a kitchen worker who had miraculously transformed himself into a fierce Esoteric (Tibetan) Buddhist guardian (*vajrapani*) called King Jinnaluo (figure 9.1). As Jinnaluo, he had seized his fire stoker to use as a fighting staff and had run out to frighten away the marauders. Subsequently, during the height of antipirate (*wokou*) operations in the 1550s–1560s, the Shaolin monks developed a reputation as highly skilled staff fighters. So the stele may have served several purposes. First, to divert attention from the monks' failure to protect the monastery in the 1360s. Second, to warn the monks of their responsibility to protect the monastery. And third, to spread stories about fighting monks at the monastery as a way to scare off potential attackers.

Another aspect of martial arts practice at Shaolin during the Ming related to the ethnic origins and political needs of the dynasty. The Mongol Yuan rulers who preceded the Ming, and the Manchu rulers of the Qing dynasty (1644–1911) that followed it, both prohibited Han Chinese martial arts practices, but the Han Chinese founders of the Ming seem to have had less fear of authorizing the monastery to maintain a small militia to protect it. Indeed, in times of disturbance there was good reason to permit such a fighting force, since it could not only protect the monastery but also help to maintain order in the surrounding region. This was particularly helpful to the dynasty because Shaolin occupied prime real estate on Mount Song, the central one of the five sacred mountains to which emperors offered sacrifices. So one could say that the Shaolin monks had a political duty to maintain peace in the area. Some also later participated in bandit suppression operations in Yunnan province. The Shaolin force never exceeded

大聖緊那羅王顯神像

御寨

嵩山

Figure 9.1. Giant Spirit King Jinnaluo Rushes Forth to Protect Shaolin Monastery from Red Turban Rebels at the Close of the Yuan Dynasty (late 1360s). From Cheng Zongyou's *Elucidation of Shaolin Staff Methods* (1621), courtesy of the National Central Library, Taipei, Taiwan.

about 120 fighters, but because of their role of keeping local order, which included the monks' antipirate activities, Shaolin Monastery gained lasting fame as the home of Warrior Monks. These activities did not come from any religious or spiritual impetus, but from the desire to survive.

The spread of this reputation was greatly assisted by the writings of the famous scholar Gu Yanwu (1613–1682). Gu had fought against the Manchu invasion of China in the 1640s and later expressed dissatisfaction with mainstream Han Chinese intellectuals for their lack of concern for social issues. He recorded his observations in the *Record of Daily Knowledge*, which included a section on "Shaolin Monk Soldiers." This concept has stood out in the minds of Chinese ever since, but it was his poem "Shaolin Monastery" that really cemented the image. Gu's poem expressed his disappointment with the rundown state of the monastery and referred back to the prince of Qin who had sought the Shaolin monks' help over a thousand years earlier. Gu's point was to suggest his hope for a new prince of Qin to set things right as the old one had, which was a not too subtle jab at Qing rule. Starting in 1801 and into the twentieth century, this loyalist allusion to Shaolin Monastery was also used by the anti-Qing Heaven and Earth Society, who claimed their founders were wrongly persecuted Shaolin monks.

BODHIDHARMA AND SHAOLIN MONASTERY MARTIAL ARTS

Perhaps the most pernicious belief about the Chinese martial arts is the story claiming that the monk Bodhidharma introduced a form of hand combat to Shaolin Monastery as a series of exercises to counteract the boredom of reading and reciting scriptures. This story is said in one version to have been written by a Tang general, Li Jing, but in fact it is based on apparently forged writings in the *Muscle Change Classic* dating back no farther than the sixteenth century.[1] The story spread during the nineteenth century and appeared in Liu E's *Travels of Lao Can* (Travels of the Old Decrepit One), an immensely popular social satire written between 1904 and 1907. The tale was then incorporated in a popular boxing manual titled *Secrets of Shaolin Boxing Methods*. This was associated with the Heaven and Earth Society and was first published in 1915 under the anti-Qing pseudonym, Master of the Studio of Self-Respect. It enjoyed no fewer than twenty-four editions by 1936. If this was not enough, in 1919 the Fudan University educator Guo Shaoyu included the story in his *Chinese Physical Culture History*, the first book ever published on this subject in China. While there is evidence that Shaolin and a few other Buddhist monasteries did harbor martial arts practices, these should be considered more practical and political than religious and spiritual.

DAOISM, INTERNAL MARTIAL ARTS, AND TAIJIQUAN (T'AI-CHI CH'ÜAN)

For Daoism, by contrast, there are no reliable historical sources tying martial arts practices to monasteries, although individual Daoist priests may have been practitioners. Of the martial arts myths involving Daoism, the earliest is that the Buddhist Shaolin Monastery is meant to have practiced the External School of Chinese boxing while the Daoist hermit Zhang Sanfeng developed an Internal School of Chinese boxing on Mount Wudang. This claim is included in the preface to the *Epitaph for Wang Zhengnan* (1669), by Huang Zongxi, a historian and participant in the Ming resistance to the Manchus, and was repeated in *Internal School Boxing Methods*, by his son, Huang Baijia (b. 1643). However, neither of the Huangs point to any substantive and verifiable differences in basic theory between the so-called Internal and External Schools. Huang Zongxi makes a single mention of theory: "The so-called Internal School uses non-movement to overcome movement; when the transgressor responds he will be dropped to the ground."[2] But this is simply a restatement of universally applicable hand combat theory involving the interaction of *yin* and *yang*, which was espoused way back in the Maiden of Yue story over 1,500 years earlier.

The *Epitaph* (1669) is the earliest text to list a certain Zhang Songxi as a proponent of the so-called Internal School. However, in an earlier *Biography of Boxer Zhang Songxi*, written by a former imperial grand secretary sometime between 1608 and 1615, the Internal School is nowhere mentioned, although the biography does describe Zhang Songxi's martial arts skills as considerably superior to those of Shaolin monks. This suggests that the Internal School was the invention of the *Epitaph*'s author, who may have been inspired by the contrasting skills set out in the biography.

The Ming rulers favored the Daoist Zhang Sanfeng, and Mount Wudang as a sacred location. The Manchus, however, favored Buddhism in the Tibetan-style, esoteric strand (as did the Mongols), and introduced this form to Shaolin. The *Epitaph* distinguishing (Chinese) Daoist practice from (foreign) Buddhist practice likely represented Han Chinese opposition to foreign Manchu rule, and was thus more probably a political jab at China's Manchu conquerors than a serious treatise on martial arts schools. That the Manchus viewed Huang's writings as suspect is suggested by the dynasty's attitude toward the anthology of Huang Zongxi's writings that contained the *Epitaph*. The anthology was originally identified for destruction under Emperor Qianlong's literary inquisition, although ultimately it managed to slip through. Thus it seems likely that Huang wrote the *Epitaph* with political intent.

Despite the dubious authenticity of the distinction between Internal and External Schools, the appearance of the *Epitaph* in 1669 encouraged a few martial artists to jump on the bandwagon by claiming proficiency in both

External and Internal Schools. However, in an extensive volume containing martial arts vignettes published in 1916, only 6 out of 197 items mention individuals as practicing Internal School martial arts. Four of the 6 had supposedly first learned Shaolin martial arts, but none of these short pieces offers specifics to differentiate Internal School from Shaolin martial arts. Furthermore, a limited list of styles compiled just one month prior to the revolution of 1911 fails to include any of the three so-called Internal School styles (Taijiquan, Baguazhang, and Xingyiquan), which only became well known as such after 1911. The vignettes merely note that boxing consisted of two categories, Internal and External Schools, and that the External School was more widespread but, regardless of school, the basic techniques were all similar.

THE APPEARANCE OF TAIJIQUAN

The name Taijiquan first appears around 1852, after Wu Yuxiang (1812–1880), the youngest son of a landowning family in Hebei, learned a boxing routine from Yang Luchan (1799–1872), who had in turn learned it in the village of Chen Family Gulch (Chenjia Gou) in Henan. Wu apparently named this routine Taijiquan after reading a short handwritten manual said to have been obtained by his brother in a salt store. Wu claimed the manual, titled *Taijiquan Treatise*, was written by a man named Wang Zongyue (ca. 1795?), but we really only have the word of Wu's nephew and student Li Yuyu for any of this. We do know that a seventeenth-century patriarch of the Chen family, Chen Wangting (1600–1680) had been designated a military official responsible for maintaining the local militia, had practiced martial arts, and even wrote a short verse titled *A Song Summarizing the Boxing Classic*, which has been claimed to allude to the *Boxing Classic* by the sixteenth-century general Qi Jiguang. In his local military capacity, patriarch Chen Wangting apparently encouraged martial arts practice based on General Qi's thirty-two forms, among others. Twenty-nine of these forms can still be seen in the Taijiquan routine favored by the Chen family (figure 9.2), but this collection of forms was not called Taijiquan in the family. It was not until the outsider Wu Yuxiang adopted the Chen family routine that the family began calling their style by the name Wu had suggested.

Wu Yuxiang's nineteenth-century claim that the salt store manual was written by Wang Zongyue has never been satisfactorily verified, so Wu himself may even have invented the author's name as a subtle poke at the Manchus. Zongyue can mean "one who honors Yue," that is, Yue Fei the famous Southern Song patriot general who in the twelfth century fought against the foreign invasions by the Jurchen Jin. The Manchus were related to the Jurchen and initially called their dynasty the Later Jin. Furthermore, Wu lived in southern Hebei province, where he would have been

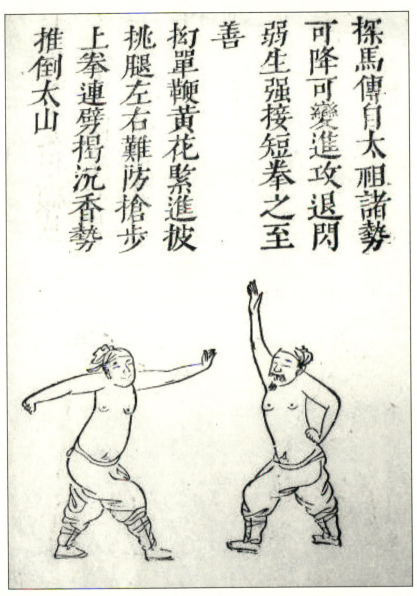

探馬傳自太祖諸勢
可降可變進攻退閃
弱生強接短拳之至
善
拗單鞭黃花緊進披
挑腿左右難防搶步
上拳連劈揭沉香勢
推倒太山

Figure 9.2. Hardly the Product of the Daoist Hermit, Zhang Sanfeng. Two Boxing Forms: Reaching for the Horse (R) and Single Whip (L). From Ming General Qi Jiguang's thirty-two forms in *New Book of Effective Discipline* and also part of the Chen family Taijiquan set known as Exploding Pounder. Twenty-nine of General Qi's thirty-two forms are basically the same as Chen style forms. Illustration from the *San cai tuhui* encyclopedia (1609), courtesy University of Hawai'i Rare Books collection.

well aware of the local School of Practical Learning. Promoted by late seventeenth-century intellectuals, this school emphasized both literary and military knowledge, including martial arts practice. One intellectual, Wang Yuyou, had even written a piece called *Thirteen Saber Methods*, with a section headed "Taiji Sword Essentials." Another intellectual martial artist, Chang Naizhou (1724–1783), lived just across the river from Chen Family Gulch, and had developed his own style of boxing from scratch. He was known in his neighborhood as "The Scholar Boxer," and incorporated the Taiji concept in his own Theory of Central Energy (*zhongqi lun*). Interestingly, both Chang and Wu recognized the Maiden of Yue story as the fount of Chinese martial arts theory, and in their writings quoted the passage, "Strengthen the spirit within, appear calm without." Thus the theory of Taijiquan is essentially the same as for all Chinese martial arts and the real origins of the style appear to lie mainly in its name, not necessarily its content.

The Daoist hermit Zhang Sanfeng, supposed originator of the Internal School, reappeared after 1911 as the originator of Taijiquan. This was claimed in *Taijiquan Studies* (ca. 1915) by the martial artist Sun Lutang, who practiced Taijiquan and two other styles, all three of which thereafter became classed as members of the Internal School. This classification of styles into the so-called Internal School combined with the loose assumption that all other styles must be External and Shaolin-related. This contrast was institutionalized with the establishment of the Central Martial Arts Academy in 1928, which was initially organized into two departments, Wudang (Internal) and Shaolin (External). But leadership of the two departments fought each other over this issue, with the result that both departments were abolished. The division may have been useful as an organizing principle, but it was not essential to the conceptualization of Chinese martial arts.

CONCLUSION

The convenient, but flawed, concept of Chinese martial arts divided into External Shaolin (Buddhist oriented) and Internal Wudang (Daoist oriented) schools continues to hinder a true understanding of martial arts in history and their place in Chinese culture, and has resulted in misperceptions as to their association with religion and spirituality. Martial arts were key skills taught to Chinese soldiers, with generally accepted practice norms from earliest times. These arts were also practiced by locally organized security units, to protect valuable property in wealthy monasteries and other organizations, and for individual self-defense. In other words, they were practiced throughout society, to varying degrees, even into the twentieth century, but for defense, not religious, reasons.

In addition, when places like Shaolin Monastery did things like fighting pirates in the mid-fifteenth century, they were also serving a political role. Politics was even more of an issue under Manchu rule, when numbers of disgruntled Chinese intellectuals practiced martial arts as a kind of subdued form of protest combined with self-respect. On the popular level, the Heaven and Earth Society associated themselves with the exaggerated fame of Shaolin Monastery as a way to attract members. Other secret societies and heterodox religious groups also practiced martial arts for group defense. A number of interpretations associated the martial arts covered here with centuries of Buddhist and Daoist religious practice, but these stories conceal the evolution of these arts in the unsettled conditions of resistance to Manchu rule that ultimately led to revolution.

SUGGESTIONS FOR FURTHER READING

Peter Lorge provides the first ever broad coverage of the sociopolitical place of the martial arts in Chinese history in *Chinese Martial Arts from Antiquity to the Twenty-First Century* (Cambridge University Press, 2012). Brian Kennedy and Elizabeth Guo, *Chinese Martial Arts Training Manuals* (North Atlantic Books, 2005), is an excellent introduction to aspects of Chinese martial arts history through discussion of ancient and modern martial arts manuals. Meir Shahar, *The Shaolin Monastery: History, Religion, and the Chinese Martial Arts* (University of Hawai'i Press, 2008), is strong on Shaolin Monastery's historical involvement in martial arts. Douglas Wile, "Taijiquan and Daoism: From Religion to Martial Art and Martial Art to Religion," *Journal of Asian Martial Arts* 16 (2007), is an interesting article on the issues related to Taijiquan's involvement with Daoism, politics, commercial interest, and national identity. See also Andrew Morris, *Marrow of the Nation: A History of Sport and Physical Culture in Republican China* (University of California Press, 2004), pp. 185–229.

Thomas Green and Joseph Svinth, eds., *Martial Arts of the World: An Encyclopedia of History and Innovation*, 2 vols. (ABC-CLIO, 2010) covers China under a variety of subheadings. Kang Gewu, *The Spring and Autumn of Chinese Martial Arts—5,000 Years* (Plum Publishers, 1995) organizes its content by timeline, with much information from Chinese sources. This generally seems accurate, but some of the translations require cross-checking with original sources.

Tai Hsuan-chih's *The Red Spears, 1916–1949*, translated by Ronald Suleski (University of Michigan Press, 1985), provides a rare firsthand view into the village martial arts groups organized to counter warlords and other lawlessness in the countryside during much of the first half of the twentieth century.

This link, http://seinenkai.com/articles/henning/index.html, provides a complete list of writings by the present author, some of which are available in full.

NOTES

1. As exposed by martial arts historian Tang Hao, in his *Shaolin Wudang Research* (1930).

2. A similar description of this principle can be found in the *Sword Classic* by the Ming general Yu Dayou, which he may have named as an indirect reference to the Maiden of Yue, as her weapon of choice was the sword. This book was actually a staff manual, which General Qi Jiguang included in his *New Book of Military Discipline* (1561).

10

Women in Chinese History

Clara Wing-chung Ho

For one and a half centuries after the Opium War, a prevailing view regarding Chinese women was that they were victims in history. They had no political roles, no educational opportunities, no legal entitlements, no social rights, and because of the practice of concubinage they held shameful positions in their families. They were very much oppressed in all respects.

This view dominated both Chinese and Western scholarship until the late twentieth century, and common perceptions of Chinese women reflect the same attitude. However, during the 1990s, a number of influential scholarly works jointly rejected the notion that women were victims in Chinese history. This chapter will survey the origins of this misunderstanding and explain how scholarship has laid to rest the one-sided image of the passive Chinese woman. Popular views, however, have been slower to change.

THE "WOMEN-AS-VICTIM" APPROACH

During the late Qing and early Republican period after about 1900, China experienced great changes in politics, economics, society, and culture. As part of facing these challenges, reformers often highlighted women's potential contributions as revolutionaries, educators, and social movement leaders. A tide of Chinese publications on women's history and literature witnessed a growing interest in women's issues.

Scholars often take the 1913 work of Xu Tianxiao 徐天嘯 (1886–1941) and the 1928 work of Chen Dongyuan 陳東原 (1902–1978) as the first published general histories of Chinese women. Xu's book adopted a conventional biographical approach to record women's pasts, and was therefore not a full comprehensive history of women, unlike Chen's book, which explored the wider picture of women's lives from the supposed matrilineal age to modern times. But there was also a common theme in both works: women in old China were severely oppressed and enslaved by patriarchal values, and therefore were victims in history.

Xu and Chen argued that scholars should write the history of these dark times as a means to help women to move away from "backwardness" and dependency, and to head toward a liberated era. This basic view was, from the 1930s, shared by a number of publications by Chinese scholars on women's history. Studies on women's literature up to this period also strongly portrayed women as neglected and unrecognized writers, and therefore aimed at reconstructing women's literary history. All these interpretations constituted what Dorothy Ko termed "the May Fourth view of history." This reflected a typical, and politically necessary, attitude among literati-scholars in the decades before and after the 1919 May Fourth movement.[1]

However, Chinese intellectuals were never alone in spreading the prevailing "women-as-victim" view. In fact, Western scholars and writers had a longer tradition of assuming women to be the oppressed sex in Chinese society, also out of political need. Aiming at civilizing and emancipating Chinese women, missionary views often stressed Chinese women's subordination and the usefulness of Christian values in upgrading women's statuses and in improving the quality of women's lives. The victimization of Chinese women spread among Westerners as an Orientalist fascination, and it was believed that only Western values could liberate and modernize Chinese women, a typical "China's response to the West" perspective.

For example, James W. Bashford (1849–1919) remarked upon the "inferior position" and "complete subordination" of women.[2] Samuel Wells Williams (1812–1884) noted that a woman "does not hold her proper place in society simply because she has never been taught its duties or exercised its privileges."[3] Herbert A. Giles (1845–1935) laid down his general belief that "the Chinese hated their female children."[4] Margaret E. Burton (b. 1885) claimed that before China was "opened to foreigners . . . the women of the nation were illiterate and wholly without the benefits of any education."[5] Even as late as the 1930s, Pearl Buck (1892–1973) argued regarding Chinese women, "From the very fact of her sex at birth she has had to submit herself, to endure what she did not like, to do without, in many cases, special notice or even affection."[6] Florence Ayscough (1878–1942) drew the conclusion that "until a few years ago the only world known to Chinese women" was a world behind the door to the inner apartments.[7] Thus countless Western descriptions of China described women as suffering from female infanticide, concubinage, slavery, illiteracy, and so on. In a nutshell, female oppression was a dominating theme in these narratives, although contrary opinions, such as Isaac T. Headland's (1859–1942) doubt about "the credibility of a universal statement" like "Chinese woman is an oppressed creature,"[8] occasionally surfaced.

Moreover, a number of Western accounts also claimed Christianity as the key to making changes for the better. In the year before "the opening of the treaty ports" that "made it possible for Western civilization to enter China,"[9] G. Tradescant Lay already foretold that "should Christianity begin to shed any of her fair beams upon this vast empire, this cruel and revolting practice [footbinding] will be dropped."[10] While Samuel Williams lamented that the Chinese young wife has "little of the sympathy and love her sisters in Christian lands receive,"[11] Lucinda Pearl Boggs (1874–?) stressed that "the greatest thing that we of the West have to give the Chinese woman is the Christian religion in its best interpretation."[12]

THE CONTINUATION OF
THE "WOMEN-AS-VICTIM" APPROACH

The "women-as-victim" approach continued to be a political necessity in works published in the mid-twentieth century. For instance, in 1946 Olga Lang once again pointed to the "low position of women in China" and attempted to explain this phenomenon by "a combination of several economic and ideological factors."[13] As both the Nationalists and the Communists made the emancipation of women a constant element of their agendas, it is not difficult to understand why they reinforced the idea of the victimization of women in old China. Subsequent political campaigns in Communist China as well as the Western feminist movement in the 1960s and 1970s also provided ground for the extension of the "women-as-victim" view. As feminist historians picked up the hot topic of female liberation, they frequently used narratives of historical female oppression to justify the need for liberation, and for advocating that women should stand up and take their place holding up half the sky. Against this background, interesting interpretations continued to exist, such as naming Confucius as "an eater of women,"[14] arguing that the central task of feminist scholarship "should be to increase our understanding of the sources and varieties of the systems which oppress women and of the feminist struggle to overcome that oppression,"[15] and claiming that "few societies in history have prescribed for women a more lowly status or treated them in a more routinely brutal way than traditional Confucian China."[16]

During the first decade or two of the post-Mao era, the "women-as-victim" perspective did not fade away, even though it was no longer used to justify policy. Dorothy Ko has pointed out that even the "highly articulate scholar" Du Fangqin 杜芳琴 has "repeated the May Fourth rhetoric almost verbatim in the conclusion to her recent book."[17] Ko was actually referring to Du's adoption of the concept of the "four thick ropes" (political authority, class authority, husband's authority, and religious authority) as evidence for Chinese women's enslavement. But in fact, Du was only one of many Chinese scholars who held similar views in the 1980s and early 1990s. Opinions treating women as the oppressed sex in general were perpetuated in Tian Jiaying's 田家英 discussion on women's life in early China; Gao Shiyu's 高世瑜 analysis of Tang women; Shi Yun's 石雲 and Zhang Yihe's 章義和 research on Chinese female fidelity; Liu Jucai's 劉巨才, Lü Meiyi's 呂美頤, and Zheng Yongfu's 鄭永福 works on women's movements in modern China; and Meng Yue's 孟悅 efforts to chart women as a blind spot in Chinese history, to name a few examples. In the late 1980s, the Chinese translations of two Japanese works on Chinese women's history were published. Whereas Ono Kazuko 小野和子 displayed "with genuine admiration" the Chinese struggle for women's rights in the modern period,[18] Yamakawa Urara 山川麗 presented a brief account of Chinese women's history from ancient to modern times. The arguments of the latter were quite in line with the general picture of female victimization in Chinese scholarship, as witnessed in the Chinese translators' note.

THE EMERGENCE OF THE "WOMEN-AS-AGENT" APPROACH

A new trend of revising the "women-as-victim" approach began to develop in English-language scholarship in the 1970s and has gradually become the mainstream idea since the late 1990s. A large group of scholars at the academic frontier no longer viewed women as passive victims of patriarchal oppression, but presented them as historical agents.

Early critiques of the "women-as-victim" approach include Margery Wolf's 1972 groundbreaking work, which brought up the notion of the "uterine family" and aptly contrasted the conventional view of women's low statuses in the family.[19] Three important edited volumes published in 1973, 1975, and 1981 jointly reflected a wider awareness of the variety of women's historical experiences.[20] These volumes no longer accepted universal female subordination, but placed more emphasis on women's agency and resistance, thus paving the way for further ventures in this direction later in the 1990s.[21] These reflected not politics but general developments in academic theory: they effectively demonstrated the historical variability in women's experience and integrated an analysis of gender into the discussions of many topics.

During the 1990s, a host of influential works on Chinese women's history witnessed the complete shift from "women-as-victim" to "women-as-agent." In 1993, Patricia Ebrey demonstrated in her well-known *The Inner Quarters* that women in Song China (tenth to thirteenth centuries) occupied positions at vastly different levels of power, just as men did, and that they made choices and contributions that helped recreate and subtly reshape the Chinese family and kinship systems. Ebrey's findings have not only provided readers with new understandings of Song women, but also challenged readers "to reexamine our understandings of history and historical processes." Ebrey argued that Chinese history and culture would "look different after we have taken the effort to think about where the women were."[22] As a review aptly observed: "this book should lay to rest forever the one-dimensional image of the pathetic, downtrodden, and historically immutable 'traditional Chinese woman'—an image that has prevailed too long both within and outside the field of Chinese studies."[23]

Another pathbreaking classic, Dorothy Ko's *Teachers of the Inner Chambers*, came out in 1994. In Ko's own words, the book "seeks to revise the May Fourth view of history, which construed the oppression of women as the most glaring failing of China's feudal patriarchal past."[24] Highlighting the informal power and social freedom enjoyed by the literate women of Jiangnan in southeast China in the seventeenth century, Ko insisted that they were far from oppressed. Furthermore, Ko emphasized that in imperial China "there was much fluidity and possibilities for individuals to constitute themselves in everyday practice," and therefore women sometimes "opened up arenas of freedom for themselves without directly challenging the ideal norms."[25] Ko also proposed a new way to conceptualize China's past by using gender as a category of historical analysis, as Western scholars like Gerda Lerner and Joan Scott advocated.

One of Susan Mann's most representative works, *Precious Records*, came out in 1997. Its tremendous contributions include Mann's outright rejection of the "women-as-victim" notion, and her direct acknowledgment that Eurocentric paradigms may not be applicable to women's history in late imperial China. Mann presented high Qing women as "writing subjects" who enjoyed "remarkable satisfaction and gratification" as writers. By placing high Qing women at the center of her discourse, Mann has successfully put an end to the "women-as-victim" assumption, which she criticized as an Orientalist view of gender relations. In her conclusion, Mann elaborated on her earlier call for "defamiliarizing familiar materials" to "gain new historical meaning" and reasserted that "we cannot ignore the new ways to read the rich sources we already have."[26]

Mann's direction pointing coincides with Kang-i Sun Chang's long-term effort to place Chinese women back into literary history. Chang, in both English and Chinese, has tried to rewrite Chinese literary history from a gendered perspective. She has called for scholarly attention to the fact that China was the only country on Earth to produce thousands of women writers in the decades around 1900. Their voices must be heard and we should not overlook the efforts of the male literati to canonize women's writing.[27]

Chang's argument fits perfectly into the current trend of treating women as subjects and agents.

Among many other such works produced since the 1990s, Lisa Raphals has demonstrated the diversified images of women in early China, while Jo-shui Chen and Ping Yao have opened new channels to understanding Tang women by examining their life histories and especially their connections with their natal families. Kathryn Bernhardt, Bettine Birge, and Xiaonan Deng have reshaped our understanding of Song-Yuan women, drawing our attention to their property inheritance rights. Charlotte Furth, Jen-der Lee, and Angela Ki Che Leung have anchored women's place in Chinese medical history. Francesca Bray has proposed a concept of gynotechnics to explore women's roles in everyday technologies. Dorothy Ko has written a revisionist history of footbinding to argue that not only men should be held responsible for the practice. Janet Theiss and Lu Weijing have rediscovered women's agency within the politics of chastity. Lin Liyue, Yi Ruolan, Wu Renshu, and many others have successfully charted women's active role in the socioeconomic development of Ming-Qing China. Joan Judge and Hu Ying have explored the lives of a variety of late Qing women across different walks of life, and mapped them onto Chinese history at the turn of the twentieth century. Space would not allow me to list here all the representative studies that employ a gender lens to reexamine different aspects of Chinese history, including significant works by Paul Ropp, Beata Grant, Harriet Zurndorfer, Grace Fong, Wai-yee Li, Ellen Widmer, and many more. In short, it is justifiable to conclude that recent scholarship has completely overturned the old, passive and victimized image of Chinese women. Though started in Western academia, this shift is getting more and more recognition in the Chinese intellectual world, as witnessed by modification and abandonment of old views in the recent works of scholars in the field such as Gao Shiyu, Zang Jian 臧健, and Du Fangqin.[28] Scholars now would not accept overgeneralization of women's position in old China as if women belonged to one single group with no diversity whatsoever: in class, region, ethnicity, and age. Further research will doubtlessly follow this irresistible trend to achieve more in-depth integrations of gender analysis into the narration of Chinese history, although how quickly this spreads into popular understandings remains to be seen.

SUGGESTIONS FOR FURTHER READING

The best retrospective account of the "women-as-victim" model is Jinhua Emma Teng's "The Construction of the 'Traditional Chinese Woman' in the Western Academy: A Critical Review," *Signs* 22, no. 1 (1996), which is a constructive review of Western scholarship on Chinese women. A slightly earlier critical evaluation of recent Western studies is Paul Ropp's "Women in Late Imperial China: A Review of Recent English Language Scholarship," *Women's History Review* 3, no. 3 (1994). Two review articles in English are insightful and useful: Ann Waltner, "Recent Scholarship on Chinese Women," *Signs* 21, no. 2 (1996) and Susan Mann, "The History of Chinese Women before the Age of Orientalism," *Journal of Women's History* 8, no. 4 (1997); Li Guotong has reviewed (in Chinese) recent Western studies on Ming-Qing women (2002).

NOTES

1. Dorothy Ko, Teachers *of the Inner Chambers: Women and Culture in Seventeenth-Century China* (Stanford, CA: Stanford University Press, 1994), pp. 7–10. There is no space here to list all that was published, but they are easily found in bibliographies of studies on Chinese women.

2. James W. Bashford, *China: An Interpretation* (New York: Abingdon Press, 1916), pp. 127–28.

3. S. Wells Williams, *The Middle Kingdom* (New York: Wiley, 1851), p. 784.

4. Herbert A. Giles, *The Civilization of China* (London: Williams & Norgate, 1911), p. 97.

5. Margaret E. Burton, *The Education of Women in China* (New York: Fleming H. Revell Company, 1911), p. 33.

6. Pearl S. Buck, "Chinese Women: Their Predicament in the China of Today," *Pacific Affairs* 4 (1931): 905.

7. Florence Ayscough, *Chinese Women, Yesterday and Today* (London: Jonathan Cape, 1938), p. 3.

8. Isaac Taylor Headland, *China's New Day: A Study of Events That Have Led to Its Coming* (West Medford, MA: Central Committee on the United Study of Missions, 1912), p. 50.

9. Burton, *Education of Women*, p. 33.

10. G. Tradescant Lay, *The Chinese as They Are* (London: William Ball & Co., 1921), p. 32.

11. Williams, *The Middle Kingdom*, pp. 794–95.

12. Lucinda Pearl Boggs, *Chinese Womanhood* (Cincinnati, OH: Jennings and Graham, 1913), p. 125.

13. Olga Lang, *Chinese Family and Society* (New Haven, CT: Yale University Press, 1946), pp. 42–53.

14. Julia Kristeva, *About Chinese Women*, trans. Anita Barrows (London: Marion Boyars, 1977), pp. 66–99.

15. Judith Stacey, "A Feminist View of Research on Chinese Women," *Signs: Journal of Women in Culture and Society* 2, no. 2 (1976): 486.

16. Kay Ann Johnson, *Women, the Family, and Peasant Revolution in China* (Chicago: University of Chicago Press, 1983), p. 1.

17. Ko, *Teachers of the Inner Chambers*, p. 3.

18. See Joshua A. Fogel and Susan Mann's Introduction in Ono Kazuko's *Chinese Women in a Century of Revolution, 1850–1950*, ed. Joshua A. Fogel (Stanford, CA: Stanford University Press, 1989), p. xxv.

19. Margery Wolf, *Women and the Family in Rural Taiwan* (Stanford, CA: Stanford University Press, 1972).

20. Marilyn Young, ed., *Women in China: Studies in Social Change and Feminism* (Ann Arbor: University of Michigan Press, 1973); Margery Wolf and Roxane Witke, eds., *Women in Chinese Society* (Stanford, CA: Stanford University Press, 1975); Richard Guisso and Stanley Johannesen, eds., *Women in China: Current Directions in Historical Scholarship* (Youngstown, NY: Philo Press, 1981).

21. See, for example, Rubie S. Watson and Patricia B. Ebrey, eds., *Marriage and Inequality in Chinese Society* (Berkeley: University of California Press, 1991); Christina K. Gilmartin et al., eds., *Engendering China : Women, Culture, and the State* (Cambridge, MA: Harvard University Press, 1994); Ellen Widmer and Kang-i Sun Chang, eds., *Writing Women in Late Imperial China* (Stanford, CA: Stanford University Press, 1997).

22. Patricia Ebrey, *The Inner Quarters: Marriage and the Lives of Chinese Women in the Sung Period* (Berkeley: University of California Press, 1993), p. 270.

23. Beverly Bossler, in *Journal of Asian Studies* 53, no. 2 (1994): 529–30.

24. Ko, *Teachers of the Inner Chambers*, p. 7.

25. Ibid., pp. 9–10.

26. Susan Mann, *Precious Records: Women in China's Long Eighteenth Century* (Stanford, CA: Stanford University Press, 1997), pp. 219–26. See also her "What Can Feminist Theory Do for the Study of Chinese History? A Brief Review of Scholarship in the U.S.," *Research on Women in Modern Chinese History* 1 (1993): 241.

27. Kang-i Sun Chang, "Gender and Canonicity: Ming-Qing Women Poets in the Eyes of the Male Literati," *Hsiang Lectures on Chinese Poetry* 1 (2001): 1–18. Also Kang-i Sun Chang and Haun Saussy, eds., *Women Writers of Traditional China: An Anthology of Poetry and Criticism* (Stanford, CA: Stanford University Press, 1999).

28. It is worth noting that although the major call for moving toward the "women-as-agent" approach flourished in Western scholarship, individual Chinese publications voiced similar opinions as early as the late 1980s. For example, Li Yu-ning 李又寧, an American-based Chinese scholar, made it clear in a 1989 article that the time was ripe for scholars working in women's history to turn away from protesting male-oriented views and to step into a stage of objective academic research. Similar views are seen in various articles by Gao, Zang, and Du since the late 1990s. Du's more recent publications revise her earlier views, which stressed female oppression.

III

IMPERIAL CHINA

11

China's Age of Seafaring

Ruth Mostern

THE 1421 MYTH AND ITS POPULAR APPEAL

In 2002, Gavin Menzies, a retired British submarine commander, published a book entitled *1421: The Year China Discovered the World*. The best-selling *1421* is inspired by the voyages of the Ming admiral Zheng He (1371–1435), whose vast fleets made seven voyages across the Indian Ocean between 1405 and 1433.

When Gavin Menzies decided that certain features of early European world maps were difficult to explain, he jumped to the conclusion that they must have been based upon Chinese originals. Against all historical and scholarly consensus, he set out to make that case. Menzies misread historical maps and tied them by conjecture to anecdotes about currents and shorelines. He posited a world-girdling voyage that reached every continent except Europe, and both the north and south poles. Ignoring all scholarship about Chinese seafaring, early modern cartography, material culture, and natural history, Menzies launched an invented view of Chinese history.

According to the historical record, Zheng He's sixth voyage returned to China in 1421. Menzies imagines that only a few ships returned home, and three armadas, each comprised of twenty-five to thirty ships with 7,000-person crews, set sail for lands unknown. According to Menzies, they were joined by the Venetian merchant traveler Niccolò di Conti (1385–1469), who met the Chinese fleet in India, submitted Chinese maps and charts to Portuguese cartographers upon his return to Europe in 1424, and inspired subsequent European seafaring. During the two-and-a-half-year journey, the fleets would have sailed at speeds twice those of the known voyages, not counting time out for shore-side adventures: establishing mining, trading, and farming colonies in Australia, New Zealand, and North America; introducing livestock, crops, giant sloths, and sea otters to new lands; building stone towers marked by indecipherable inscriptions, and surveying the lands and seas. Menzies believes that upon returning to China in 1423, the explorers produced a world map, but by the end of the decade, officials had burnt the records, sunk the ships, and embargoed trade.

The book strains credibility and logic. It also misconstrues the aims and context of Ming seafaring policy. There was no motive for Ming sea captains to sail giant armadas on perilous missions into the unknown. Moreover, the book is concocted from discredited evidence, misrepresented sources, and undocumented conclusions. Menzies mocks experts and rejects evidence that contradicts his preconceptions. In fact, the Chinese record fully accounts for the fleet's presence in the Indian Ocean during the "missing years" of 1421–1423 and all of the ships' return to China. For more information, *1421 Exposed* (http://www.1421exposed.com) debunks the most glaring errors in the Menzies book. In summary, no archaeological, archival, scientific, or textual evidence supports any of Menzies's key claims. Anomalies on early modern European maps are decorative elements or evidence of Arab Atlantic seafaring. Di Conti's travel memoir makes no mention of a world journey or Chinese maps, nor does any other European or Chinese source. As the scholar Geoff Wade concludes on the *1421 Exposed* site, Menzies demonstrates "utter and complete contempt for truth." As historian Robert Finlay puts it, "the author's 'trail of evidence' is actually a feedback loop that makes no distinction between premise and proof, conjecture and confirmation, bizarre guess and proven fact."[1] Responsible scholars have called upon librarians and publishers to classify *1421* as a work of fiction.

CLAIMS BEHIND THE MYTH

It is no surprise that *1421* has attracted a large readership and significant attention. It is written in an engaging and anecdotal style that incorporates the author's own travel adventures, and Menzies portrays himself as a practical military man unafraid to confront scholastic orthodoxy. Moreover, the book appeals to an understandable curiosity about antecedents for contemporary China's rise to world power. It also resonates with trends supporting a more global perspective on the history of seafaring. According to Menzies's account, the early Ming state, positioned "at the summit of the civilized world" (36), sought a maritime empire and had navigation technology capable of "pinpoint accuracy" (19).

Chinese authors celebrate this image of Ming seafaring, albeit with somewhat closer adherence to historical truth. They tend to ignore the military aspect of the voyages and depict Zheng He as a great explorer, a diplomat, a commercial trader, and a man of peace. The 2008 Beijing Olympics opening ceremony featured blue-robed performers bearing oars and enacting Zheng He's epic voyages, and a team of Chinese archaeologists has just disembarked in Kenya in search of the material record of the expeditions.[2] These activities focus upon Zheng He as an individual rather than upon Ming maritime foreign policy in general. In doing so, they portray the voyages as an anomaly, and they construe the end of the seafaring age as a personal conflict between Zheng He and civil service officials threatened by his status, fostering an image of modern mercantilism sacrificed to conservative moral politics.

Still, all of the Zheng He claims, even *1421*, are responses to older, equally pernicious interpretations that were overdue for revision. When the nineteenth-century Chinese court resisted foreign demands to participate in global trade on disadvantageous terms, their efforts gave rise to a stereotype that China was arrogantly xenophobic, culturally earthbound, and closed to the wider world. Scholars who absorbed these notions have overlooked China's seafaring history until recent years. The current attention to it is a welcome corrective.

MARITIME CHINA BEFORE THE MING

In fact, China has been engaged with the South China Sea and the Indian Ocean for over two thousand years. Evidence of seafaring between China, India and Southeast Asia dates to the first century BCE, and trade grew throughout the first millennium of our era. Supported by technological advances, the southern expansion of the Chinese state, and the role of Buddhist and Muslim networks, maritime contacts intensified during the Tang dynasty (618–907). During the Ten Kingdoms era (907–978), southern China was divided among multiple commercially oriented states that competed for dominance and supported overseas trade. By the tenth century, a maritime merchant community based in China's southeastern coastal provinces had outposts in Manila in the modern Philippines, Nagasaki in Japan, and other ports.

Trade expanded further during the wealthy and urban Song era (960–1276). During the first millennium, most traders were Persian, Arab, or Indian; but during the Song, Chinese merchants began to travel to India and the Persian Gulf in person. The merchant community was largely independent of the imperial state, which did not perceive significant political or financial benefit from foreign trade, and did not protect capital investments or shipping routes. Song scholar-officials did not prevent trade, but they did not develop a legal or military framework for supporting it either.

In 1225, Zhao Rugua (1170–1228), customs inspector at the Fujian port of Quanzhou, used information gathered from Quanzhou merchants and from foreign traders in order to catalog China's maritime trade partners based on the content and volume of commodities that they tendered. A ship of Chinese origin wrecked at Quanzhou in 1271 was full of goods from Africa, the Persian Gulf, India, and Southeast Asia.

With the conquest of Yunnan, formerly an independent state on the Chinese-Burmese border, the Mongol Yuan dynasty (1276–1368) oriented China even more toward Southeast Asia. The Yuan court also sponsored a state-run maritime network, seeking trade revenue, political and military influence, and particular commodities, notably pepper. Conflict between the Yuan dynasty and the Chagataid khanate in Central Asia elevated seafaring into the best route for maintaining trade and alliance with the Persian Ilkhans. Yuan navies displayed military might, intervened in local politics, established commercial relations, and sponsored numerous Indian Ocean missions. Yuan-era travel writers, the Venetian Marco Polo (1254–1324) and the Moroccan Ibn Battutah (1304–1368), described Chinese ships in foreign ports, and Ibn Battutah declared that "on the sea of China, traveling is done in Chinese ships only."

EARLY MING MARITIME POLICY

During its first sixty years, Ming (1368–1644) foreign policy was shaped by Yuan precedent. Immediately after the regime was founded, maritime missions led by civil officials proclaimed the new dynasty to kingdoms overseas, conducted imperial ceremonies on behalf of deceased rulers and newly enfeoffed allies, sought gift and ritual exchanges, distributed Confucian texts, and conducted tribute and trade missions. As in the Yuan, private and tributary trade were intermingled. Differences soon emerged, though. Ming rulers faced endemic coastal piracy, conflicts with Vietnam and Champa (now southern Vietnam), difficulty suppressing Yunnan independence, and conflicts with Tai peoples along the Ming southern border. Seeking a more orderly coastal perimeter, the Ming court attempted to limit and control foreign contacts and foreign trade. Fearing unrest and insecurity along the coast, the Ming banned private maritime commerce and removed profit-making trade from the official tribute missions conducted through garrisoned ports. The policies were calamitous for merchant communities in the southern coastal provinces of Fujian and Guangdong. Chinese mercantile ports declined, and merchants ceased to be a political constituency. There were no longer private advocates for maritime engagement.

The early Ming rulers were more engaged with the maritime world than those of any earlier point in history, but the relationships that they fostered were entirely oriented toward China's civilizing influence and imperial legitimation, not profit. From the Ming court's perspective, foreign countries derived their meaningful existence from personal relationships between their rulers and the emperor of China. The Ming founder declared a Sinocentric world order and sought symbolic acknowledgment of China's cosmological centrality.

Early Ming rulers willingly used military might to pursue that objective. The Ming dynasty used force in the south, from both land and sea. Ming armies invaded and occupied tribal polities in Yunnan and Guangxi and expanded Chinese power on the southern periphery. Ming forays reached as far as the Brahmaputra River and the Indian province of Assam. Ming armies occupied Vietnam for thirty years, beginning with a coup attempt in 1406. Vietnam was a highly militarized Ming province from 1407 to 1428, intended as the forward base for China's maritime interests. There were three maritime trade supervisorates there, the same number that existed in the entire rest of the empire, and Vietnam owed taxes in the form of maritime commodities. In addition to the occupation of Vietnam, the early Ming court maintained permanent and garrisoned treasuries at Malacca on the Malay Peninsula and at Sumatra in the Indonesian archipelago.

ZHENG HE AND THE TREASURE FLEETS

An important aspect of Ming maritime policy was the sponsorship of large naval voyages, among which Zheng He's are the best known. The boy later known as Zheng He was born into a distinguished Central Asian Muslim family in Yunnan. After his father was killed resisting the Ming conquest, he was taken prisoner and castrated for service as a eunuch. He joined the household of the future Yongle emperor (1360–1424). As imperial household managers, trusted eunuchs directed large construction projects and chaperoned honored guests and treasures to the palaces. Overseas, civil officials conducted diplomacy and performed rituals; but eunuch admirals, often, like Zheng He, from a Muslim background, collected tribute and escorted envoys, commanding overseas missions that extended from Java in the Indonesian archipelago to Persia.

Zheng He's fleets made six voyages between 1405 and 1422, and a seventh near the end of the Chinese seafaring era in 1431. They traversed established trade routes through the South China Sea and the Indian Ocean, itineraries organized around the annual cycle of the monsoon winds. They traveled long distances, but never into uncharted lands. The first three voyages set sail from Fujian and traveled from Ming Vietnam south to the kingdom of Champa, across the South China Sea to Java and Sumatra, onward to Sri Lanka and the Malabar coast of southwestern India, and back to China on the following year's monsoon winds. On the later voyages, the whole fleet, or at least some ships from it, reached the Persian Gulf, the Arabian Peninsula and the Muslim holy city of Mecca, and the trade ports of East Africa. The voyages asserted awe-inspiring power, carrying almost 30,000 personnel on about 250 ships: the largest armadas and the largest ships to set sail prior to the twentieth century. Edward Dreyer's book *Zheng He* details the remarkable technology that these giant ships employed. They were staffed primarily by military men, and each voyage battled coastal and naval enemies. As Zheng He's biography in the official *Ming History* declares, the Yongle emperor "wanted to display his soldiers in strange lands in order to make manifest the wealth and power of the Middle Kingdom." They issued imperial proclamations acknowledging local rulers as legitimate monarchs of their own homelands, offered silk, Ming currency, and other gifts to them, and returned to China with ambassadors and exotic luxuries, famously even including a live giraffe from Africa.

There were twenty-five eunuch-led voyages between 1403 and the 1430s, including Zheng He's seven. The voyages helped to personalize the relationships among rulers, support gift exchange between them, and establish symbolic submission to the Ming court. In the context of unrest in and between Indian Ocean states, Zheng He and the other commanders also became embroiled in local politics. They suppressed coups and usurpations against Chinese allies, which mocked the rituals of recognition that the emperor promulgated. Seeking a *pax Ming* in the Sinocentric maritime world, the fleets conducted military actions in Sumatra and Java, and leveled military threats against Burma, Sri Lanka, Samudera on the island of Sumatra, Ayudhya in Thailand, and other locales. Presumably under duress, some Southeast Asian rulers traveled on the armadas to China as envoys: owing to security issues and ritual requirements in their own kingdoms, they would not have left home lightly.

The mission of the fleets was not to occupy territory, profit from maritime commerce, or explore new lands: it was to legitimate the Ming in the maritime world by gathering acknowledgments of its supremacy and convincing maritime rulers to accept the performance of Chinese rituals and the conferral of Chinese titles in their domains. China's allies could benefit from Chinese ceremonies and military assistance as well. Fifteenth-century Indian rulers were aware of China's willingness to arbitrate and intervene in local disputes. On at least one occasion, a ruler requested such service, and Ming envoys complied. Nevertheless, early Ming maritime policy was not sustainable. Zheng He's voyages and those of his contemporaries represented a new kind of foreign policy framework that was based upon regular and overwhelming naval presence: an expensive proposition requiring vast personnel, new government institutions, and an ongoing commitment to military force and gift exchange. The tradition of tribute exchange had evolved to support regular but minimal foreign policy, not active international politics, and was not intended for resource-intensive ventures. The missions offered no tangible economic or security benefit to the court. If they had been intended to foster profit-making trade, they might have generated enough economic activity to pay for themselves. Otherwise, as historian Wang Gungwu explains, "more money, power and ceremony applied in the same old way was simply bound to fail."

MARITIME CHINA AFTER ZHENG HE

Beginning in the 1420s, the Ming court gradually reversed earlier modes of engagement with the south. Motivated by growing conflict with Mongol armies on the steppes, the court turned its military spending and its policy orientation toward the north. The capital moved to Beijing, close to the Mongol border and away from its previous location at the Yangzi river metropolis of Nanjing. In 1449 a Mongol army captured the Ming emperor and came close to occupying the new capital. At the same time, rising coastal piracy, which was a transnational Chinese, Portuguese, and Japanese enterprise, made the shipping lanes more treacherous. The tribute system, focused upon relationships among sovereigns, was poorly suited to monitoring piracy, let alone combating it. With the rise of piracy and the subjugation of Yunnan, Southeast Asian trade shifted toward overland routes. With the imperial coffers empty and Ming territorial integrity threatened, the armadas were abandoned. Tribute missions lost their political significance, and atrophied once pressure from the Chinese court disappeared. By the turn of the sixteenth century, the court had lost interest in maritime relations, tribute missions, envoy exchanges, and the entire *pax Ming* vision. When armed and aggressive Europeans dislodged the earlier traders and transformed the maritime world beginning in the late 1400s, the Ming court was no longer paying attention.

Nevertheless, China's maritime age left real legacies. It fostered new political alignments, new economic networks, and new trade entrepôts. The Chinese maritime era spread technologies including copper currency, shipbuilding, firearms, and ceramics, and cultural legacies like Vietnamese Confucianism. Ming requirements for silver specie and an outlet for its growing southern population meant that the later court tolerated more trade and migration than official policies would have dictated. In spite of prohibitions, private trade flourished, Chinese merchant ships sailed the seas, and overseas Chinese merchants worked with rulers and traders throughout the maritime world. In spite of changing government policies, China's late imperial era remained one of close integration between China, Southeast Asia, and the rest of the world. Connections fostered by the early Ming voyages continued to bring Indian, Arab, and Persian traders to China, creating markets and networks that stimulated subsequent Portuguese, Spanish, and Dutch commercial and political activities.

SUGGESTIONS FOR FURTHER READING

On the Menzies fabrications see Robert Finlay, "How Not to (Re)Write World History: Gavin Menzies and the Chinese Discovery of America," *Journal of World History* 15, no. 2 (2004), and Geoff Wade, Kirsten Seaver, et al., *The "1421" Myth Exposed: Chinese Admiral Zheng He Did Not Discover the World in 1421*, http://www.1421exposed.com/index.html.

Good work on Zheng He and the Ming voyages includes Edward Dreyer, *Zheng He: China and the Oceans in the Early Ming Dynasty: 1405–1433* (Longman, 2007); Tansen Sen, "The Formation of Chinese Maritime Networks to Southern Asia, 1200–1450," *Journal of the Economic and Social History of the Orient* 49, no. 4 (2006); Geoff Wade, "The Zheng He Voyages: A Reassessment," *National University of Singapore Asia Research Center Working Papers Series* No. 31 (October 2004), and "Engaging the South: Ming China and Southeast Asia in the Fifteenth Century," *Journal of the Economic and Social History of the Orient* 51 (2008). Louise Levathes had earlier popularized and speculated, but with reference to the evidence, in *When China Ruled the Seas: The Treasure Fleet of the Dragon Throne, 1405–33* (Simon and Schuster, 1994).

Chinese emigration is considered by Wang Gungwu, *China and the Chinese Overseas* (Singapore: Times Academic Press, 1992) and Philip Kuhn, *Chinese among Others: Emigration in Modern Times* (Rowman and Littlefield, 2008).

NOTES

1. Robert Finlay, "How Not to (Re)Write World History: Gavin Menzies and the Chinese Discovery of America," *Journal of World History* (2004), http://www.history-cooperative.org/cgi-bin/justtop.cgi?act=justtop&url= www.historycooperative.org/journals/jwh/15.2/finlay.html (accessed 5 October 2010).

2. Xan Rice, "Chinese Archeologists' African Quest for Sunken Ship of Ming Admiral," *Guardian*, 25 July 2010, http://www.guardian.co.uk/world/2010/jul/25/kenya-china (accessed 5 October 2010).

12

Civil Service Examinations

Elif Akçetin

From the sixteenth century on, Western commentators who wrote about Chinese governance spoke highly of the civil service examinations. They praised them as a source of harmony and order, and a system where anyone, regardless of social background, could aspire to an official position in government. In their view, years of studying Confucian values and ethics to prepare for the examinations inculcated in the Chinese literati a compliance culture, creating obedient and dutiful officials who followed the rules in the service of the state. It was such long-held idealized views that led some policy makers in Britain in the nineteenth century to request the implementation of competitive examinations for public service adapted from the Chinese model. One ardent supporter of this idea, Thomas Taylor Meadows, argued in 1847 that "the long duration of the Chinese empire is solely and altogether owing to the good government which consists in the advancement of men of talent and merit only."[1] Therefore, a similar meritocratic system could also ensure good governance in Britain and its overseas colonies. British interest in the Chinese model of examinations emerged from the need to solve certain pressing problems. By establishing a recruitment system for public service based on merit, many hoped to curb corruption and patronage—which had reached its apogee in the late eighteenth century—among the East India Company officials who amassed fortunes in the colonies and formed their own clique in government. The objective was to establish an efficient government in the British colonies run by loyal and dutiful officials in the service of the state.

While Britain adopted a form of civil service examinations in 1855, in China the centuries-old examination system—the backbone of Confucian education—was criticized for being an obstacle to China's modernization and was abolished in 1905. A century later, however, new circumstances and needs changed attitudes toward traditional Confucian values. In the 1980s, the opening of the Chinese economy to international trade brought rapid economic growth while creating severe problems of social inequality and corruption. Corruption in central and local governments, in particular, has evoked serious dissident voices and even violence. Hu Jintao, China's president since 2003, has attempted to take the edge off popular anger by embracing a new rhetoric of "social harmony," a concept retrieved from Chinese tradition. In conjunction with this ideological change, some intellectuals have proposed a return to "Confucian ideas of meritocracy" to achieve political and social justice, and have argued for the reestablishment of competitive examinations for leadership positions in government. All these suggest that Western and Chinese policy makers alike have perceived the civil service examinations as a token of certain ideals—merit, talent, honesty, loyalty, and order. But was this really the case? Scholars in imperial China were often critical of the examinations, and their perspective and experiences will allow us to draw a more nuanced picture.

THE PURPOSE OF THE CIVIL SERVICE EXAMINATIONS

Written examinations to recruit officials for government were first held in the Sui dynasty (581–617).[2] They were briefly halted in the early Yuan (1270–1368) and Ming (1368–1644) dynasties but remained among the most important Chinese imperial institutions until 1905. From the start, merit was not the main concern. Rulers in the seventh and early eighth centuries used the examinations to end the aristocratic monopoly over government positions, and their dominance in politics. The idea was to create a new class of loyal officials whose position would depend on the ruler. So from the beginning, power politics were an important factor in the establishment of the examinations.

Moreover, the examinations also satisfied practical and ideological concerns. In practical terms, the ruler could not personally govern and administer a country the size of China. He depended on the services of trustworthy and capable officials, and the examinations provided in theory an efficient way to identify such individuals. On an ideological level, the Confucian tradition legitimized the preservation of the examinations for centuries. The *Analects* stressed the necessity for a ruler to employ talented and virtuous individuals in order to rule in peace. Confucius's influential follower, Mencius, judged a ruler by the quality of his officials: In D. C. Lau's translation, "if you honour the good and wise and employ the able so that outstanding men are in high position, then Gentlemen throughout the Empire will be only too pleased to serve at your court." This meant that, to be thought ethically outstanding, the ruler had to employ capable and incorruptible officials. The ruler was also accountable for official corruption, such as bribery, imposing extra fees on the local populace, and seeking personal profit, which could seriously undermine his legitimacy. The examination curriculum thus became an important means for the state to inculcate Confucian ideals of virtue (benevolence, humaneness, frugality) in aspirants to office, and simultaneously to project the image of virtuous rule.

Examinations also established a tie between central government and local society. Successful students were respected by the populace, which positioned them for leadership in society. They were a source of local pride, and their names and degrees were recorded in district gazetteers. Conversely, the dynasty reinforced its legitimacy and local control through the degree holders, especially when they were from prominent families. The dynasty's power was validated to the extent that degrees and government positions were coveted. Emperors valued this aspect of the system and even organized special examinations to incorporate local notables within the state. The elites of the richest provinces—those south of the Yangzi—were particularly important for any dynasty aiming to maintain control over the country. In 1679, the Kangxi emperor (r. 1661–1722) organized special examinations to select scholars for the Ming history project. What was on the surface a routine scholarly endeavor, in reality disguised the wish to gain the allegiance of the lower Yangzi literati to the Manchu Qing dynasty during the critical War of the Three Feudatories. In contrast to the Kangxi emperor's lenient approach, his son the Yongzheng emperor (r. 1723–1735) used the examinations as a bargaining tool. Faced with increasing dissidence from Zhejiang province against Manchu rule, the Yongzheng emperor declared that no Zhejiang student be allowed to take the metropolitan examinations in 1727.[3] This was a real threat to the Zhejiang literati and showed how an emperor could use the examinations to convey a message. However, this remained largely symbolic. By Yongzheng's time the lower Yangzi elites dominated the examinations, supplying the most students and examiners, not only because the examinations were integral to preserving their status and enhancing their social and political recognition, but also because the Manchu rulers needed this powerful elite's participation in government.

EXAMINATION DISSENT

Many literati actively sought an official career via the examinations but they were also often critical of the system, generally complaining that the examinations failed in their goal of promoting real learning, and instead encouraged the quest for fame and profit. Even though these criticisms might have reflected conventional student complaints, they acquired a new meaning after the fall of the Ming dynasty to the Manchu conquerors in 1644. Chinese scholars who sought explanations for the Ming's fall argued that the blame lay with the corrupt and incompetent officials who had permeated the late Ming bureaucracy, and ultimately in the examination system that produced them. The logic was that such widespread corruption had created resentment among the populace, promoted banditry, and left the country prey to invasion. As Wang Fuzhi (1619–1692) summarized it succinctly: if a country lacked employable people, it was doomed to be lost.

One of the most active critics of the examinations was the scholar Gu Yanwu (1613–1682). Gu argued that the Ming examinations had fostered mediocre scholars with a superficial understanding of the Confucian Classics, and corrupt and opportunistic individuals who sought only position and prestige. More seriously, the examinations had failed to encourage independent and critical thinking, qualities believed necessary to deal with everyday problems in government. Students simply memorized passages from the Classics without contemplating their broader meaning, or discussed historical events without understanding their implications for current affairs. To Gu and his contemporaries, intellectual creativity and analytical skills had been hampered by the "eight-legged essay," which became the required format for essay writing in the Ming examinations. The eight-legged essay was an inflexible form of composition that followed strict stylistic rules (it had to be in eight parts and contain a fixed number of characters). Unsurprisingly, the rigid structure made for predictable questions and answers, and candidates often memorized model essays that had circulated widely since the late Ming publishing boom. There were even instances, as Gu Yanwu related, when rich families commissioned famous scholars to write essays on the most frequently occurring themes, which the candidates parroted in the examinations.

The views of the Ming-Qing transition scholars remained influential with the postconquest generation. Dai Mingshi (1653–1713) did not personally experience the fall of the Ming but grew up listening to family memories of the conquest and loyalist struggles against the Manchus. It is no surprise that he echoed late Ming–early Qing mainstream beliefs blaming corrupt officials and the decay of the examinations for the fall of the Ming. For instance, Dai deplored that people did not value learning any more, only titles. The focus on style in the eight-legged essay had turned the study of the Classics and Histories into a meaningless endeavor. Worse still was the proliferation of examination guidebooks, which Dai complained spread erroneous commentaries that students reproduced instead of developing their own analyses.

Dai Mingshi's criticisms had a personal dimension as well. He failed the examinations several times, and was fifty-two before he earned the highest degree, the *jinshi* ("presented scholar"). Thus it was empathy that led him to voice the disappointment felt by failed scholars. There were outstanding scholars who could have been officials, Dai wrote, but after the rejections and injustices they suffered in the examination halls, they could only wander on a desolate mountain humming poetry, laden with grief. Dai expressed the feeling of uselessness endured by failed examination candidates.

Such frustration was understandable. Examination preparation involved years of intense study. Candidates began to memorize characters at the age of five and were expected to have by heart the 400,000 characters of the Four Books (the *Analects, Mencius, Doctrine of the Mean,* and *Great Learning*), plus Zhu Xi's (1130–1200) commentaries on them, and Five Classics (*Book of Documents, Book of Songs, Book of Changes, Spring and Autumn Annals,* and *Book of Rites*) by age eleven. Candidates first took the preliminary examinations at the county seat. If they qualified, the second-level examinations were at the prefecture. The third level took place at the provincial capital, and the fourth in Beijing, the latter being given at the palace by the emperor himself. Candidates usually tried several times before progressing to the next level, and most did not advance beyond county level. It was the feeling of injustice at failing after decades of hard work and stress that bred examination dissent.

In the 1720s, dissenting voices, and especially that of Wang Jingqi (1672–1726), acquired a sharper tone and targeted specific imperial policies. Wang was born into a scholar family from Zhejiang province. His father occupied high official positions before he was dismissed in 1706, accused of corruption while conducting the metropolitan examinations in Beijing. Wang Jingqi passed the provincial examinations in 1714, but failed to obtain the *jinshi* degree despite several attempts. His failure was not uncommon at the time, as the Qing government during the Kangxi reign reduced the *jinshi* quotas radically, and actively promoted scholars from well-established Chinese families who had sided with Manchu rule during the conquest.[4] In 1724, Wang decided to travel to the headquarters of the famous military official Nian Gengyao to ask for employment. On the way he took notes, which he entitled *Casual Jottings of My Journey to the West.*

Unlike Dai Mingshi's controlled criticism, Wang was unreserved in expressing his disappointment and anger. He lamented his poverty and failure in the examinations and was particularly sensitive about his future reputation, declaring that his failures at the examinations would be ever remembered in the annals of history. His tone in the diary hinted that, like other older candidates whose advancement had stalled, he might have suffered mockery for his failure. His personal experiences led Wang to believe that merit was not the guiding principle of the examinations. How many court officials, he asked, genuinely understood the Five Classics, and how many of those who had worked diligently, endured hardships, and successfully answered the questions had been able to earn the *jinshi* degree? Wang portrayed a stagnant picture of the Qing bureaucracy where upward mobility was practically nonexistent. An underlying theme was the detailed description of corrupt Manchu and Chinese officials who pursued extravagant lives and bribed their way up the hierarchy. He described the Manchu high officials, who drained people's wealth, as not only greedy, but also illiterate, using their underlings to handle official documentation. Wang intended to demonstrate the decaying morale of the bureaucracy and the failure of the examinations to select capable and incorrupt individuals. Even more daring was his denunciation of the continual wrong judgments made by the Kangxi and Yongzheng emperors in their evaluation of individuals for official positions.

Wang's criticism of Qing examination policies and the emperors' ineptness in choosing the right people were reiterated by another Zhejiang native, Zha Siting, in 1727. Confronted with such accusations, the Yongzheng emperor was anxious to prove that he was a fair ruler. He declared to the entire bureaucracy in an edict that he watched his officials' performance carefully and stayed awake all night to select those most suitable for the vacancies. Yet four years later another disenchanted scholar, Zeng Jing, condemned the moral depredation created by the system. "In the examinations," he wrote, "fame and profit are preached openly, corrupt and vile practices [abound] shamelessly. With a sweep of the pen thought is nullified and humanity is destroyed."[5]

LIMITS OF THE EXAMINATIONS

For many, there was nothing sacrosanct about the examinations. The imperial government tried to ensure impartiality and prescribed strict punishments, but cheating and bribery were a pervasive problem. Candidates employed various tactics, including the use of cheat shirts on which they copied excerpts from the Classics in tiny characters (see figure 12.1).[6] Corruption occasionally incited riots by failed candidates. Sometimes, the examinations could become a stage for factionalist politics. In the late Ming, the eunuch faction and their adversaries used secret codes in the examination questions that signaled their affiliation to certain examinees. The pursuit of individual and group interests hardly corresponded to the ideals of duty and compliance to which the examinations were later believed to contribute.

The role of the examinations as a merit-based institution was limited because, as so often in modern times, success depended on wealth. Preparation for the examinations required financial resources that disqualified many from the beginning, and candidates from prosperous provinces were

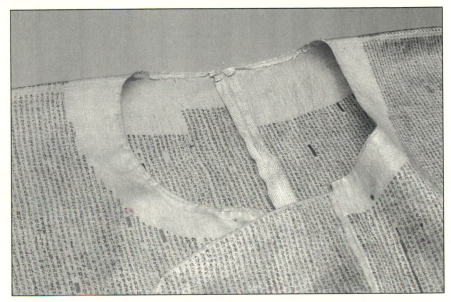

Figure 12.1. A "Cheat Shirt" Used by Examination Candidates. This one is from the Qing dynasty and contains a selection of model eight-legged essays. Courtesy of the East Asian Library and the Gest Collection, Princeton University. Photograph by Heather Larkin, 2004.

in an advantageous position. For instance, the wealthy Zhejiang province produced 2,808 *jinshi* graduates between 1644 and 1904, whereas the number of graduates from the poor northwestern province of Gansu during the same period was only 255.[7] Along with economic prosperity, the south had strong lineages in which several related families banded together to provide for their members' education. Ming and Qing emperors tried to compensate by establishing higher quotas for northerners.

Two external factors also contributed. The first was population growth. In the eighteenth century the population doubled from approximately 150 million to 300 million. Competition in the examinations became more intense as the probability of success at the higher levels decreased considerably while the number of county-level degree holders increased. The second factor was the annual fluctuation of examination quotas. In his story collection *Censored by Confucius*, the scholar and poet Yuan Mei (1716–1798) related a dream he had just before the county examinations in 1732. In this dream, his family's old doorman pleaded with him not to sit the examinations on the grounds that he will surely fail: "They are only passing a very few talented scholars this year. Wait until they plan to pass a lot of scholars before you sit the examinations."[8] As the doorman predicted, Yuan Mei failed that year. Whether he really had this dream or not, the story reflected how individuals coped with failure and the increasing unpredictability of the examinations in the eighteenth century.

Over the centuries the examination system was the central imperial institution but the government also sanctioned unorthodox avenues to officialdom. Military success (for example, quelling rebellions) could earn promotion. Family also mattered. Being the son or grandson of a famous official opened the way for promotion without having to pass the examinations. Individuals could sometimes purchase a post or degree, and by associating with the right people, they could rise quickly. However, members of the literati regarded the purchase system as a debasement of the examinations. One of Wang Jingqi's diary entries, for instance, tells of Wang Yuanshi, who bribed his way to a post away from central control, where he funded an extravagant lifestyle on the profits from selling degrees. Wang Jingqi, like many others, believed that the sale of degrees bred corruption.

Like any institution, the civil service examinations had their limitations. They did not promote merit and equal opportunity for every participant. Both the imperial government and the literati pursued their own interests, which did not always coincide. And the government did not hesitate to bypass the examinations if that suited its interests. These are serious considerations, but there was also an important strength of the examinations, which was their significance as a symbol of state building. Whoever aspired to rule China, rebels and foreign conquerors alike, understood that a centrally controlled examination system was necessary for political legitimization. Hong Xiuquan, leader of the Taiping Rebellion, failed the examinations several times. But when he took Nanjing with his rebel armies in 1853, his first act was to institute civil service examinations. His disappointment in the examination halls did not eradicate the symbolic value of this rooted institution.

SUGGESTIONS FOR FURTHER READING

There is an abundant literature on the civil service examinations. Ichisada Miyazaki's *China's Examination Hell*, translated by Conrad Schirokauer, provides a good introduction to the system's working in its most developed form in the Qing. John Chaffee's *The Thorny Gates of Learning in Sung China* (Cambridge University Press, 1985) examines the social aspects of the examinations in an earlier period. On the late imperial period, see Benjamin Elman's *A Cultural History of Civil Examinations in Late Imperial China* (University of California Press, 2000).

A Ming-Qing transition scholar, Huang Zongxi (1610–1695) wrote in detail on the selection of degree holders for official positions. His views can be found in Theodore de Bary's translation, *Waiting for the Dawn: A*

Plan for the Prince (Columbia University Press, 1993), pp. 111–121. On Gu Yanwu's criticisms, see Lung-chang Young, "Ku Yen-wu's Views on the Ming Examination System," *Ming Studies* 23 (1987).

Examination dissent was not always expressed with the intense emotions seen in Wang Jingqi's diary. Wu Jingzi (1701–1754) voiced his criticism by writing a satirical novel, *The Scholars*. Paul Ropp's *Dissent in Early Modern China* (University of Michigan Press, 1981) examines in detail the literature of dissent in the Qing, including *The Scholars*. Jonathan Spence's *Treason by the Book* (Penguin, 2001) sheds light on the world of disenchanted county-level degree holders.

NOTES

1. Quoted in Ssu-yü Têng, "Chinese Influence on the Western Examination System: I. Introduction," *Harvard Journal of Asiatic Studies* 7, no. 4 (1943): 289.

2. The idea of recruiting officials by examination materialized first in the Han dynasty (206 BCE–220 CE), but the scope was limited and examinations were oral only.

3. Jonathan Spence, *Treason by the Book* (London: Penguin, 2001), p. 52.

4. Lynn A. Struve, "Some Frustrated Scholars of the K'ang-Hsi Period," in Jonathan D. Spence and John E. Wills, eds. *From Ming to Ch'ing: Conquest, Region, and Continuity in Seventeenth-Century China* (New Haven, CT: Yale University Press, 1979), p. 342 and 362, fn. 41.

5. Quoted in Paul Ropp, *Dissent in Early Modern China: Ju-lin wai-shih and Ch'ing Social Criticism* (Ann Arbor: University of Michigan Press, 1981), p. 100.

6. See Andrew H. Plaks, "Research on the Gest Library "Cribbing Garment": A Very Belated Update," *The East Asian Library Journal* 11, no. 2 (2004): 1–39.

7. Ping-Ti Ho, *The Ladder of Success in Imperial China: Aspects of Social Mobility, 1368–1911* (New York: Columbia University Press, 1962), p. 228.

8. *Censored by Confucius: Ghost Stories by Yuan Mei*, ed. and trans. Kam Louie and Louise Edwards (Armonk, NY: M.E. Sharpe, 1996), p. 154.

13

Modern China's Borders

Andres Rodriguez

Students who first encounter China in a textbook rapidly become familiar with broad attempts to characterize this nation across a number of aspects. There are, for example, standard references to its language (and many dialects), ethnic diversity, and the influence of Confucianism, while its varied geography and sheer size are illustrated by maps that help students to clearly identify the contours and borders that form the shape of present-day China within East Asia. Most of these textbooks, however, tend to omit an important part of the wider picture, leading to misunderstandings about China's present-day territorial configuration. The China we recognize today on a map was far from being an unchanging entity from the past until now. Rather the present-day shape of China is a product of global processes assailing the world at large, which saw the relatively recent formation of various nation-states that included, among others, China.

However, few people would question the usefulness of maps in a classroom when introducing students to a new country. After all, starting in our own childhood we are exposed to maps that teach us what our countries look like and their fixed geographical position in the world. Most present-day students in the People's Republic of China (the PRC, 1949–present), for example, would never question the shape and dimensions of the country they identify on a world map as their own; indeed, PRC education teaches that this territory has always been part of China. And yet, these boundaries are really very recent.

In fact, maps and the lines on them that differentiate countries are somewhat misleading when we attempt to understand *how* modern China—that is, the PRC—acquired the borders that everyone today takes for granted. The apparently objective nature of maps makes it easy for us to overlook the historical processes and fluctuations underlying the formation of China as a nation-state; that is, a political unit conceived as an ethnically bounded community with a shared history and a well-defined territory. This process of formation only began with the consolidation of China's frontiers in the eighteenth century, through a series of military campaigns conducted by the Qing dynasty (1644–1911).

Accordingly, it is important to recall that outlying territories such as Tibet, Xinjiang, and Mongolia, which are now conceived as part of China, are relatively recent additions that were acquired as a result of these campaigns. Although longstanding relations existed between the imperial center and these regions, viewing their incorporation as an inevitable historical outcome, or even as sheer imperial expansionism, is not all that convincing as an argument. Rather, we should seek to understand the complexities, negotiations, and global setting underlying the formation of China as a nation-state during the Qing period, and its subsequent troubled border consolidation as a Republic during the early twentieth century.

"WHEN DID CHINA BECOME CHINA?"

At first sight, this question of William Kirby's seems deceptively simple.[1] Yet it should make us aware of the recent nature of modern state formation within which "China" emerged as a nation along with others in the world during the nineteenth and early twentieth centuries. If indeed, as Kirby argues, the establishment of the Republic in 1912 literally created "a new country," now labeled "China" (*Zhongguo*) by both the foreign powers and the (Han) Chinese elite who overthrew the Manchus, it is also important to understand how such a new sovereign territorial unit acquired its vast shape and form.

Perhaps what is striking for most students who compare maps of the late Qing dynasty and the present-day PRC is how little variation we find in their territorial composition. With the exception of Mongolia, where China's ruling Guomindang regime relinquished all territorial claims in the years after the Second World War (in Chinese terms, the Second Sino-Japanese War or War of Resistance), most of the domains under Qing rule remain today integral parts of the People's Republic. Despite the embattled divisiveness that characterized most of China's political history during the early twentieth century, the one issue that found a consensus among all the vying regimes and parties was that of the sovereign claims over outlying territories such as Tibet, with just some variations in the degree of autonomy to be granted. This marked continuity in outlining China as we know it is a powerful reminder of the legacies bequeathed by Qing imperial rule. Yet it was only in the eighteenth century that the Qing dynasty began a series of campaigns that encompassed large swaths of territories in Inner Asia such as Mongolia, Tibet, and Xinjiang, as well as consolidating direct control in the southwestern province of Yunnan. Prior to this, such territories were under the control of nomadic steppe societies who engaged in both trade and battle with imperial China, leading to a series of uneasy political alliances and truces. Over time, these territories and their ethnically diverse inhabitants were gradually incorporated into the maps and minds of the Qing elite as being part of a larger and unified territorial unit. The seedlings had been sown for what were to become China's modern national borders, transcending the imperial borders of what some authors have termed the Qing colonial enterprise.

However a solely China-centered perspective provides a rather incomplete picture of this issue. The history of the expansion of the Qing and the establishment of modern national borders at the fringes of its empire was far from being unique. It was part of a global process of national state formation out of former empires in both Europe and Asia, which had far-reaching consequences that still literally shape the countries on our globe up to the present. Alongside the Qing, the Muscovy (Russian) and Ottoman empires were also gradually expanding and establishing demarcated linear boundaries between themselves. Asian empires bordering Yunnan, such as Burma and Thailand, were also expanding during the eighteenth century and also contributed to the shaping of new territorial units in the region.

One cannot underestimate the significance of this process that began to pave the way for a complete reorganization of the ways states related to each other. Empires by their very nature claimed to represent a universal order that theoretically allowed for a boundless expansion of territory and its peoples. Fixed boundaries on the other hand literally marked the beginning of a new way for states to organize and confine their space, territory, and most importantly their population, a modern practice that continues today. Despite the universal claims found in Confucianism regarding the boundless reach of Chinese civilization, the Qing, like the Russian Empire, soon recognized the need to delineate their frontiers where they met in the east, and enshrined that realization in what later became known as the Treaty of Nerchinsk (1689).

Yet the period ranging from the nineteenth to the early twentieth century brought new challenges that further reconfigured the establishment of sovereign territories. The presence of Western imperialism and the rise of modern nationalism arguably shook the Qing Empire from within and without, and as a result boundaries were pushed and pulled in the same fashion.

Imperialism had a catalytic effect on attempts to secure and consolidate sovereign rule over the Qing's borderland territories. British interests in Central Asia and the subsequent British invasion of Lhasa by the Younghusband expedition (1903–1904) prompted a series of Qing reforms seeking to insti-

tute direct rule instead of relying on local elites in those territories bordering
Tibet that were known as Kham. Rebellions within the Qing Empire in the
northwest, led by Yakub Beg and stoked by Russia, ultimately led to the formal establishment of the territory of Xinjiang as a province in 1884 securing
direct administrative control in place of Muslim elites for whom Qing rule
had previously brought little interference in local affairs. Similar alarm bells
were rung in light of China's defeat in the Sino-French War (1884), which
allowed France to take over Vietnam and as a result weakened the Qing dynasty's influence on its southwestern border. The growing presence of Japan
in Manchuria and the loss of Taiwan sanctioned under the Treaty of Shi-
monoseki (1895), after the Qing's humiliating defeat by Japan in that same
year, led to a rising concern among scholars to find new ways to strengthen
China, and as a result, its borders as well. Recent scholarship has shown, for
example, that the Qing's New Policy reforms (1901–1911) placed great emphasis on developing geography in schools in order to strengthen the bonds
of students not only toward the dynasty but to its territory. Through the
extensive use of maps that displayed the vast and diverse territorial holdings
claimed by the Qing, students were made aware of China's position—and
dimensions—in the world. Such an enterprise endured well into the Republican period in light of Japan's occupation of Manchuria in 1931. Major Chinese newspapers such as the *Shenbao* sold huge numbers of national atlases
of China seeking to counter Japanese claims to the Chinese Republic's territory, and to trace in the minds of young readers across the nation a picture of
China and its inalienable borders.

Nevertheless, nationalism also played an important role in reconfiguring
notions of territorial belonging and the establishment of borders. A growing trend of racial ideology imported from the West empowered a segment
of discontented Han Chinese who in 1911 finally overthrew what in their
eyes was the most dangerous enemy of the Chinese nation: the foreign
and nomadic Manchu, who had come from beyond the Great Wall and
established the Qing dynasty in 1644. However, one of the main problems
faced by these strident Han nationalists was the enormous potential territorial loss that lay behind the vanquishing of all non-Han ethnic groups.
If "China" was to be confined only to those territories belonging to the
Han Chinese, then outlying regions such as Xinjiang, Tibet, and Mongolia
would have to be removed not only from maps but from Chinese control.
"China" as a nation had become a contested concept, not only in terms
of who was to be considered "Chinese" but also in defining the extent of
its territories. It comes as no surprise that soon after 1911 early Republican governments began to preach a more ample definition of Chinese
nationhood (enshrined as the Unity of the Five Races, *Wuzu gonghe*) in its
attempts to preserve the former Qing dynasty borderlands that had rapidly
claimed autonomy as central authority crumbled.

Despite the above picture, China, in contrast to other parts of the world, arguably displayed a remarkable level of resilience in its often troubled and bumpy transition from empire to nation-state. It is easy to forget that sizable portions of the world were undergoing a similar process in which national borders were being redrawn. Ideals of nationalism and self-determination in Europe, coupled with the effects of the First World War, led to the demise of the Habsburg and Ottoman empires, the complete redrawing of political boundaries, and the creation of new countries. The former Russian Empire, on the other hand, managed to retain most of its territorial integrity once the October Revolution and its ensuing civil war (1917–1923) were over, and it remained united until the final demise of the Soviet Union in 1991. Earlier on, the United States was establishing its hold over the continent and later the Pacific, led by the idea of a Manifest Destiny opening the pathway for agrarian settlers and railways to consolidate the final contours of the nation, often at the expense of the indigenous populations who inhabited these regions. The same can be said for the young Latin American republics that were shaking off the remnants of Spanish colonial rule during the nineteenth century. They engaged in a series of localized wars over natural resources and agricultural expansion, leading to a number of treaties that reshaped national boundaries over the continent.

The Chinese Republic that emerged after 1912 undoubtedly inherited a troubled legacy in which for the most part the central state remained powerless to exercise any true sovereignty over its outlying territories. Maps depicting the vast extent of a unified China with clearly demarcated borders during this period reflected a nationalist aspiration rather than anything else, in face of the challenges posed by local warlords and foreign imperial projects.

Japan's incursion into Manchuria and other provinces in China before the outbreak of war in 1937 sought to establish common ethnic and religious ties under a larger discourse of Pan-Asianism in order to assert Japanese sovereignty in the region. On the other hand, during most of the 1920s and 1930s the Chinese government also faced, on its southwestern border, a series of territorial disputes with both France and Britain. The diverse ethnic nature of many of these territories posed a significant political problem, as many of the inhabitants were adamant in claiming autonomy from both sides. In effect, as empires and later nation-states expanded, those peoples caught in between also attempted to carve out their own niche of influence either by transferring loyalties to one of the states or by simply rejecting both of them. It is no coincidence that during this same period a large number of geographical and ethnographic surveys were launched by Japanese, British, French, and Chinese authorities in order to provide information for formulating policies that would ultimately allow for firm control of these outlying and contested territories. Over time, the ambiguous gaps and interstices forming between nation-states and empires would finally come to an end. Nevertheless, for most of this period until the end of the Second World War little could be done by the authorities to foster the loyalties of these societies, who had a scant understanding of what a nation or territorial borders actually meant.

There is no doubt that the Second World War and the Allied conferences that discussed its settlement were a key factor in establishing a new world order dominated soon afterward by the United States and the Soviet Union. This new world order not only meant the end of all the imperial aspirations of Nazi Germany and Imperial Japan, but also the colonial interests of Britain and France. As a result, the outcome of the Second Sino-Japanese War (1937–1945) and China's rising position among the Allied powers was to have a profound effect on the configuration of China's territories that has endured to this day almost in its entirety. In effect, most of the contested territorial claims made by China at the time were finally upheld by international treaties at the end of the war. Upon signing the Cairo Declaration in 1943, China's leader Chiang Kai-shek not only secured the end of extraterritoriality but also ensured that Manchuria and Taiwan, in Japanese hands during the war, were to be part of China. The latter, despite only becoming a province of the Qing Empire in 1887, resurfaced as an important symbol of Chinese territorial integration both during the Guomindang's takeover of the island in 1949 and later on during the bitter struggle that ensued between the governments of Mao Zedong and Chiang Kai-shek through much of the Cold War.

As the Chinese Communist Party (CCP) came to power in 1949, the CCP's own discourse of ethnic self-rule for China's borderland territories in effect followed the grander geopolitical blueprint laid out by its Qing and Republican predecessors. Although proudly proclaiming the creation of a "New China" on the world stage, the CCP's newly secured borders were for the most part neatly aligned with those established during the Qing dynasty.

The China we know and recognize today on a map is far from being the result of some inevitable or unilinear evolutionary process, even though this is what most historical narratives of nation-states around the world during the nineteenth and early twentieth century seem to suggest. Rather, China's borders were a product of unique historical wranglings and negotiations that also shaped the world at large. As empires expanded and subsequently nations were imagined into being, tracing the geographical contours of these new countries onto maps and into people's minds became essential for the establishment of a firmly rooted nation-state. China was no exception to this process, and as it slowly became aware of its position in a world of nation-states its scholars and officials resorted to a wide array of historical, geographical, and ethnographic resources that allowed them to redefine what peoples and territories they claimed as being "Chinese," and as a result to trace what are now assumed to be its permanent borders in the twenty-first century.

SUGGESTIONS FOR FURTHER READING

Only general texts are cited here. Works on specific border regions of China (Tibet and Xinjiang) are referred to by other authors in their respective chapters.

The eighteenth-century campaigns of the Qing Empire into Central Eurasia that laid the foundations for most of China's present borders have been masterfully studied by Peter C. Purdue, *China Marches West* (Harvard University Press, 2005). Laura Hostetler's *The Late Qing Colonial Enterprise: Ethnography and Cartography in Early Modern China* (University of Chicago Press, 2001) shows the importance of mapping techniques in the Qing's state-building project and its relationship with a new global order in the making. The Qing's encounter and accommodation with other expanding Asian empires and peoples in the southwest border regions during the same period has been insightfully studied by Patterson Giersch, *Asian Borderlands* (Harvard University Press, 2006). The incorporation of Taiwan as part of the Qing Empire can be found in Emma Teng, *Taiwan's Imagined Geography: Chinese Colonial Travel Writing and Pictures, 1683–1895* (Harvard University Press, 2004). Discussion on the Qing's engagement with ideas of modern Chinese nationalism can be found in Gang Zhao, "Reinventing China: Imperial Qing Ideology and the Rise of Modern Chinese Ideology in the Early Twentieth Century," *Modern China* 32, no. 3 (2006): 3–30.

William C. Kirby's brief but thought-provoking essay "When Did China Become China? Thoughts on the Twentieth Century," in *The Teleology of the Modern Nation-State*, ed. Joshua A. Fogel (University of Pennsylvania Press, 2005) on the origins of "China" as a new (Republican) territorial unit is the best starting point for the twentieth century. The dispute over Manchuria in the northeast during the Republican period and the various techniques deployed by both China and Japan in order to assert sovereignty and delineate borders has been studied by Prasenjit Duara, *Sovereignty and Authenticity: Manchukuo and the East Asia Modern* (Rowman and Littlefield, 2004). For the attempts of the Guomindang state to incorporate borderland territories under Chinese sovereignty see James Leibold, *Reconfiguring Chinese Nationalism: How the Qing Frontier and Its Indigenes Became Chinese* (Palgrave Macmillan, 2007). A series of useful essays on borders from both a historical and contemporary perspective can be found in Diana Lary ed., *The Chinese State at the Borders* (UBC Press, 2007).

NOTE

1. William C. Kirby, "When Did China Become China? Thoughts on the Twentieth Century," in *The Teleology of the Modern Nation-State*, ed. Joshua A. Fogel (Philadelphia: University of Pennsylvania Press, 2005), pp. 105–14.

14

Xinjiang at the Center

Judd Kinzley

The rapid expansion of empires into Central Asia during the nineteenth century helped to create the image of modern China's Xinjiang Uighur Autonomous Region as an inhospitable backwater. This impression of the region, which is located on the farthest western border of the People's Republic of China, was propagated during the last hundred years by travelers and explorers from both East Asia and the West. More recently, the Chinese Communist Party (CCP) has been attempting an aggressive integrationist policy in the province in order to strengthen their claim to this resource-rich, once highly contested territory, and this has frozen Xinjiang in the minds of many people as a barren, dusty borderland tacked on to the end of the Chinese nation.

The diversity of the population that makes up modern Xinjiang, or "New Dominion" in Chinese, offers a hint that perhaps this commonly held image needs to be questioned. In addition to a long history of links to the east with China, the ethnically Turkic indigenous population of Xinjiang (the largest group of which is known as the Uyghurs) shares substantial cultural and ethnic ties with the peoples that make up modern-day Kazakhstan, Kyrgyzstan, Afghanistan, Mongolia, Tajikistan, Pakistan, and India, which sit across the rugged international borders that surround Xinjiang on three sides. For much of its history, the region that would become Xinjiang was a place where different ethnic and cultural groups met and faced off—a destination for migrants and a prize for conquerors and empires.

XINJIANG AND THE RISE OF NOMADIC EMPIRES

Xinjiang (figure 14.1) is larger than Alaska, three times the size of France, and is located a dusty 2,000 miles from China's capital city of Beijing. The region is hemmed in by the towering Kunlun Mountains and the Tibetan Plateau to the east and the 20,000-foot Pamir Mountain Range to the west. The southern half of the province is defined by the massive Taklimakan Desert, while the north sits astride the Zungarian Basin—an arid grassland that connects Xinjiang to the broad Eurasian steppe.

A cohesive, unified "Xinjiang" with borders reflecting its current shape was only created following the conquest of the region by forces from the China-based Qing dynasty in 1755, but the landscape and the peoples that came to populate it have a much longer history. Scholars today believe that the region that would later become Xinjiang is the farthest eastern outpost of an Indo-European civilization that first spread out of the Caucasus region, between the Black and Caspian Seas, around 4,000 years ago. Descendents of Indo-Europeans (who can be tracked by their languages) came to populate Europe, India, and Iran, as well as much of Central Asia, and by 2000 to 3000 BCE, a branch of this group had reached as far east as the fertile oases of the Taklimakan in present-day southern Xinjiang. This early group is known to experts today as the Saka (or in Chinese the Sai), but by the middle half of the first millennium BCE this group had given way (either through conquest or intermixing) to another related Indo-European group known in Chinese sources as the Yuezhi. Perhaps the most well-known evidence of the early Indo-European presence in Xinjiang is the famed "European" mummies. These are desiccated corpses, kept intact by the arid Taklimakan desert, that exhibit several physical features commonly associated with Europeans, including high cheek bones and red or blondish hair.

The physical remains of these Indo-Europeans, as well as a growing amount of archaeological evidence, points to a network of trade relations that linked the region that would become Xinjiang—nearly 3,000 years later—to long-distance commodity networks stretching from the Mediterranean in the west to the Yellow Sea in the east. Silk, lacquer, and cowrie shells uncovered in Xinjiang, as well as jade and various distinctive bronze and iron products produced there but found in present-day "China Proper"[1] point to interactions with China-based cultures to the east. Particular types of pottery, burial objects, weapons, as well as evidence of shared copper-production techniques, cotton textiles, and the adoption of stringed instruments are evidence of the broader connections that link the region to Central Asia and also to cultures based in present-day India and Iran.

That these communities based in present-day Xinjiang make an appearance in classical works of history emerging from ancient Greece as well as China testifies to their integration into a world system. These textual

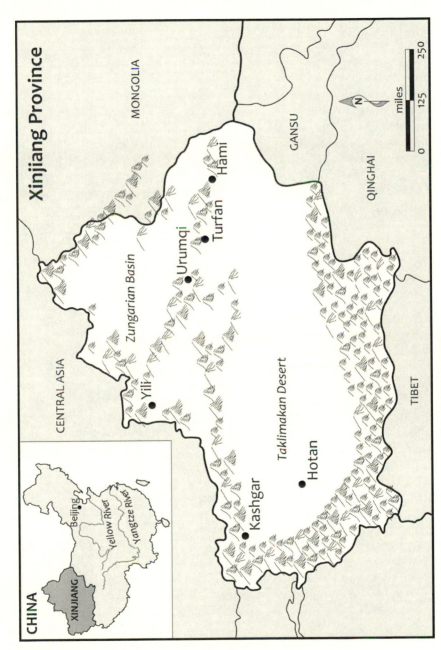

Figure 14.1. Xinjiang Province (cartography: Debbie Newell).

sources are spotty and frequently open to interpretation, but scholars are beginning to find a consensus that for ancient "Western" historians of the classical tradition, Xinjiang was no isolated land on the edge. The Greek historian Herodotus discussed groups linked through trade and other ties to the Indo-European "Scythians" in his work *The Histories*—groups that almost certainly included the peoples populating the region that would become Xinjiang. Likewise, the Roman-era scholars Pliny the Elder and Ptolemy appear to be referring to the peoples of Xinjiang in their discussion of the "Seres" people. In China, various classics, from the *Classic of Mountains and Seas* (*Shanhaijing*), the *Guanzi*, and the renowned *Records of the Historian* (the *Shiji*), also discuss the peoples who populated present-day Xinjiang and afford them a prominent role along the edges of the Middle Kingdom. These peoples as they appear in the ancient Chinese classics were not simply poor residents of a harsh frontier; rather, they were recognized as producers of the jade being voraciously consumed by the imperial court and wealthy elites. Equally importantly, as far as the two latter classics are concerned, these peoples are also the forerunners of nomadic warriors who came to terrorize a succession of imperial Chinese dynasties.

Despite their central role in a trade network that spanned the Eurasian landmass, the nomadic Yuezhi fell victim to a more powerful group that was on the rise in the Mongolian steppe to the northeast of present-day Xinjiang. Scholars speculate that the conquest of the Taklimakan oases by the powerful, united Xiongnu tribes in the second century BCE was probably an attempt to gain access to the wealth produced in this region in the form of taxes and tribute but also, for a nomadic people in need of grain to support their growing population and armies, a bid to gain control over these fertile agricultural areas. The Xiongnu conquest of the region that would become Xinjiang made it part of a vast nomadic empire that stretched from Mongolia to Central Asia. For the young Han dynasty growing in the Yellow River valley to the south, the Xiongnu campaigns of conquest served as a terrifying new development that threatened the Han empire's very existence.[2] From a Xinjiang-centered perspective, however, the conquest of the Yuezhi by these neighboring nomads from the north was only the first step in a pattern that replicated itself over and over again for nearly 2,000 years, as a long list of nomadic groups saw the acquisition of fertile southern Xinjiang as a key to their ability to feed and clothe their armies, and to produce the wealth needed to develop and project their power well beyond the Central Asian and Mongolian steppes.

In the centuries following the Xiongnu conquest of the Yuezhi, a succession of nomadic confederations would rise in the north and either sweep into the oases of the Taklimakan seeking wealth and grain, or else extract these in the form of tributary payments under the threat of violence. Beginning in fourth-century Mongolia with the Ruanruan, which followed the latter strategy, seven nomadic empires rose to power based either on the Mongolian steppes to the northeast or else in Central Asia to the northwest. A succession of exotic-sounding groups like the Hephthalites, Kok Turks, Uyghurs (not to be confused with the ethnic group), and Karakhanid rose to power and subsequently faded into obscurity. Others like the Mongols led by Chinggis Khan, and later the Mongol tribe known as the Zungars, were able to gain a more lasting name for themselves by using the wealth produced in Xinjiang's southern oases to control broad swaths of territory.

AGRICULTURAL EMPIRES STRIKE BACK

In 138 BCE, China's Han dynasty imperial court dispatched an envoy named Zhang Qian from the Han capital of Chang'an, today in modern Shaanxi province, to the northwest through Xinjiang to try to rally the remnants of the Yuezhi and other potential allies for a campaign to take on the Xiongnu. While Zhang's mission was largely a failure, the intelligence he gathered resulted in a series of successful military campaigns in the region. These campaigns were spearheaded by the famous Han emperor Wudi (141–87 BCE), who finally wrested Xinjiang from its nomadic overlords in the first century BCE, a maneuver that many experts suggest helped lead to the downfall of the Xiongnu a few years later. Han Wudi's military successes are often held up as having helped create the famed "Silk Roads," which linked China culturally and economically with Central Asia and Europe.

The Han dynasty's reaction to the Xiongnu set up a model for interactions with nomadic groups to the north that would be reused repeatedly well into the nineteenth century. Responding to the Xiongnu threat, Han dynasty thinkers were the first to begin holding up nomads as the barbarian antithesis of China's agricultural society, which was also claimed to be morally righteous.[3] But they certainly were not the last, and this central dynamic, which pitted northern nomads against the agriculturalists in China's central plains to the south, became infused into the strategic policies of China-based dynasties for the next 2,000 years. Within this dynamic, Han Wudi's successful campaign in Xinjiang appeared to lay out a blueprint for a potent new strategy for dynastic courts: conquer Xinjiang in order to deny the region's wealth and productive capacity to their nomadic adversaries. And indeed, later China-based dynasties like the Sui, Tang, Yuan, early Ming, and Qing, through either the threat of violence, the manipulation of factions, or else direct conquest of the region, were able to keep nomadic groups at bay on the vast Eurasian steppes. Different Chinese dynasties chose to employ this strategy to greater and lesser extents, with many lacking the capacity or willingness to think about Xinjiang at all. Nevertheless, Xinjiang remained an important component of China's defense consider-

ations well into the nineteenth century, and even if they did not choose
to use it, the strategy laid out during the Han dynasty served as a strategic
tool that China-based dynasties to the east could wield against nomadic
confederations if desired.

More than fifteen hundred years after Han Wudi's conquest of the
region, the Qing dynasty completed their own conquest of Xinjiang in
1759 as a way to head off the growing power of a Mongol tribe known
as the Zungars. The tribe had been based in the grasslands of northern
Xinjiang and controlled a large empire that included the oases of southern
Xinjiang and appeared to threaten the Qing dynasty's holdings in Mongolia and also Tibet. Even after the conquest and the destruction of the
Zungars, an event that one well-known scholar suggests should be viewed
as a genocide, Xinjiang remained central to the imperial court's security
calculations, though in a changing manner.[4] Qing power in Xinjiang
waxed stronger in the mid- to late eighteenth century, but by the early
to mid-nineteenth it was clear that the dynasty's hold over this region,
which was expensive to maintain, difficult to supply, and far from other
Qing military garrisons, could only be tenuous. Uprisings and large-scale
rebellions by indigenous groups in the south were frequently fomented
and supported by powerful Muslim kingdoms across the border to the
west, and constantly threatened Qing authority in the region during this
period. Despite the growing cost of maintaining its presence in Xinjiang,
Qing leaders, confident in the necessity of maintaining their position in
the region in order to secure the borders of their empire, refused to relin-
quish their hard-won conquest.[5]

The importance that Xinjiang held for China's overall security continued
well into the modern period, when one might think that powerful Western
navies along China's coast might be the primary source of concern for the
Qing court in Beijing. Yet, when a massive rebellion fomented by the agents
of a Central Asian kingdom to the west threatened to permanently wrest
Xinjiang from the Qing empire in the 1860s, officials reacted in a way that
would have made a great deal of sense to their Han dynasty counterparts
nearly 2,000 years earlier. In debates waged in the Qing imperial court,
officials argued that losing Xinjiang would result in the empowerment of
fearsome enemies who would eventually threaten north China and even
Beijing. These battle-tested arguments won out, and in 1876, General Zuo
Zongtang began his famous march into Xinjiang to put down the rebellion and reabsorb the region into the Qing Empire. This campaign cost an
estimated forty million ounces of silver—a huge sum. Only a few officials
thought it could be better spent in shoring up China's navy and construct-
ing coastal defenses capable of holding off the threat from Western imperial
powers.[6] For that majority of Qing officials who continued to view Xinjiang
as central to their security concerns, it was money well spent.

XINJIANG ON THE EDGE

The end of the nineteenth century was the beginning of the end of Xinjiang's centrality in the once roiling politics of Eurasia. By 1884, Russian armies had completed their quest to smash the wealthy and powerful independent kingdoms that formerly dotted Central Asia and undercut the maneuverability of large and powerful nomadic groups in the steppes. The Russians now claimed for the tsar all the land up to Xinjiang's modern-day western and northern borders. That same year, Xinjiang, which had already been reconquered by Zuo Zongtang's armies, was officially established as a Chinese province. After more than 2,000 years of wrangling, the number of competitors for power and resources in the region was winnowed to three: the China-based Qing dynasty; Russia; and, to a lesser extent, Britain (which controlled present-day India and Pakistan to the southwest).[7]

The diverse political and economic topography of Central Asia within which Xinjiang had once played such a central role was flattened by the expansion of distant empires in the nineteenth century. The elimination of political competitors, the delineation of agreed national borders, and the channeling of trade to benefit the three empires began the process of transforming Xinjiang into a region on the periphery. Russia and China would continue to grapple over the ownership of the region and the exact line of its borders well into the twentieth century. But no matter which was successful in taking it, Xinjiang would be a frontier borderland: either part of China's northwest 2,000 miles west of Beijing, or else Russia's east, 2,000 miles east of Moscow.

The transformation of Xinjiang into an officially designated province in 1884 established it as a frontier of the Qing Empire and, after the downfall of the dynasty in 1911, as a border region attached to the westernmost edge of the new Chinese nation. Since 1949, and the rise of the Chinese Communist Party to power, there has been a widespread attempt to transform Xinjiang politically, economically, and socially by binding it more closely to China Proper. Security considerations, national pride, socioeconomic factors, and the presence of critical natural resources like oil, coal, and natural gas, have all played a role in determining this policy direction. In the last sixty years, leaders have overseen an unprecedented increase in the population of Han Chinese settlers immigrating to Xinjiang, and at the same time, have invested heavily in economic development and transportation infrastructure linking the region more closely to China Proper. Since the "reform and opening" of China in 1978, if anything these processes have been accelerated, and this former "pivot" of Eurasia, as Owen Lattimore once described Xinjiang, is now more than ever conceived as a periphery.[8]

The expansion of distant but powerful empires into Central Asia and the northern steppe initially destroyed Xinjiang's centrality, and during the past century it has morphed from an imperial frontier into a Chinese national borderland. The perception of Xinjiang as having always been a dusty periphery, which was created in the last century, is now slowly but surely being transformed into unshakable orthodoxy. Scholars and officials in China today are seeking to blur any evidence that Xinjiang was once something other than simply a "new dominion" (as its very name claims) of empires centered in China Proper or else the Chinese nation. New and ambitious scholarly projects funded by the government and aggressive attempts to counter views diverging from the historical party line have played an important role in this process and have only strengthened the impression of Xinjiang as simply a harsh backwater tacked on to China's western edge. Today, the vision of Xinjiang as a pivot is being eroded away, and without attention, may soon be forgotten completely.

SUGGESTIONS FOR FURTHER READING

Owen Lattimore traveled to Xinjiang in the 1920s and 1930s and in his travel accounts offers a fascinating description of pre-CCP Xinjiang. His works *Desert Road to Turkestan* (reprint Kodansha, 1995) and also *High Tartary* (Little, Brown, 1930) went a long way toward popularizing the exotic, isolated vision of the region. These works have been republished in recent years and are widely available.

For discussions of ancient Xinjiang, J. P. Mallory and Victor Mair's book *The Tarim Mummies* (Thames and Hudson, 2008) is a great place to start. Peter Perdue's work *China Marches West* (Harvard University Press, 2005) and James Millward's *Beyond the Pass* (Stanford University Press, 1998) both offer interesting accounts of the Qing dynasty's policies toward Xinjiang. Andrew Forbes's work *Warlords and Muslims in Chinese Central Asia* (Cambridge University Press, 1986) offers an engaging account of early twentieth-century Xinjiang, though his account is probably based too heavily on British sources.

More general histories of the region include Lattimore's *Pivot of Asia* (Little, Brown, 1950) which begins a discussion of the centrality of the region in history and also as a Cold War battleground. Millward's work *Eurasian Crossroads* (Columbia University Press, 2007) is an ambitious and engaging history of Xinjiang beginning in the prehistorical period and ending in the twenty-first century. The book *Xinjiang: China's Muslim Borderland* (M. E. Sharpe, 2004) is a recently published collection of essays on Xinjiang written by many of the best-known English-language scholars of the region. The book offers an interesting overview of Xinjiang, though it has also been extremely controversial, having been denounced by CCP political figures as well as by many important scholars of Xinjiang in China for embracing what is described as a "splittist" perspective on the region's history. To get a sense of the new orthodoxy surrounding Xinjiang's history it is worth taking a look at Li Sheng's work *Xinjiang of China: Its Past and Present* (Xinjiang People's Publishing House, 2005), an officially approved history of Xinjiang that has been translated into English.

NOTES

1. The term *China Proper* generally refers to present-day eastern and central China—areas historically dominated by ethnically "Han" Chinese. It excludes traditionally non-Han areas along the PRC's borders, including Manchuria, Mongolia, Tibet, and Xinjiang.

2. Nicola Di Cosmo, *Ancient China and Its Enemies: The Rise of Nomadic Power in East Asian History* (Cambridge: Cambridge University Press, 2002).

3. Ibid.

4. Peter Perdue, *China Marches West: The Qing Conquest of Central Eurasia* (Cambridge, MA: Harvard University Press, 2005).

5. James Millward, *Beyond the Pass: Economy, Ethnicity, and Empire in Qing Central Asia, 1759–1864* (Stanford, CA: Stanford University Press, 1998).

6. Liu Kwang-chih and Richard J. Smith, "The Military Challenge: The Northwest and the Coast," in *The Cambridge History of China* 11, part 2 (New York: Cambridge University Press, 1986).

7. Britain's role in Xinjiang would decline precipitously in the last years of the nineteenth century and the early twentieth, when policy makers came to believe that the region could not produce enough wealth to justify the large investment needed to secure it and connect it to the empire's infrastructure to the southwest.

8. Owen Lattimore, *Pivot of Asia: Sinkiang and the Inner Asian Frontiers of China and Russia* (Boston: Little, Brown, 1950).

15

Tibet

Elliot Sperling

The Tibet issue is particularly sensitive for China, not simply due to concern about Tibetan separatist sentiments but because it touches on the broader question of China's identity. The construction of that identity during the twentieth century has involved much reworking of traditional categories so that new definitions for "Chinese" and "Han" could be solidified and passed down the generations via state education. This has also entailed the construction of the category of "national minority," essentialized so that the narrative of China's identity might become the story of the country fulfilling its Marxist destiny. Modern China has incorporated diverse peoples such as the Tibetans and Mongols—peoples with a conscious historical experience of independence from China, replete with an awareness of themselves as peoples possessing their own states, states with bureaucracies operating in their own languages. Incorporation into China has necessitated their uniform reduction—along with other groups sometimes numbering only in the tens of thousands, and having no similar national history—to the common status of "minority nationalities." Marxist teleology also mandates the narrative that incorporation into China has brought great strides in social advancement, which have saved the Tibetans from a cruel feudal serfdom under which more than 90 percent of the population lived no better than slaves. These particular aspects of the Tibet issue are central to the way that Tibet is understood in modern China. And that understanding, passed down through China's educational system, is wrong in crucial ways. Nevertheless, it is on the basis of such erroneous and historically unsupportable facts that most Chinese citizens comprehend Tibet's past and present. And as a result, the unrest and discontent that permeate much of Tibetan society are viewed by many Chinese as symptomatic of Tibetan backwardness or ingratitude for all that China has done for Tibet.

It is therefore necessary in this chapter to deal with three particular perceptions that have become or, in one case, is becoming, part of the received wisdom permeating common Chinese views of Tibet. These perceptions provide the foundation for official positions that pay scant heed to real Tibetan sentiments and grievances, and support popular certitudes that see Tibetans as unwilling to recognize the benefits of modernization—that is, modernization as conceived for it by China.

TIBET AND THE YUAN DYNASTY

The assertion that Tibet has been an inalienable and inseparable part of China since the thirteenth century holds that it was the Yuan dynasty (1271–1368) established by the Mongols that effected this momentous historical event. But this is a relatively recent interpretation, appearing only after the People's Republic of China (PRC) had been established. The earlier Republic of China (ROC) expressed a different claim. On October 30, 1913, at the tripartite Anglo-Chinese-Tibetan conference (1913–1914) convened in Simla to deal with the Tibet question, the ROC delegation submitted that in the aftermath of the Tibeto-Nepalese War of 1792–1794:

> so powerless and helpless were the Tibetans that they again went to China for assistance. To their supplication China responded at once by sending over 50,000 soldiers to Tibet; and accordingly the Gurkhas were driven out of the country. Tibet was then definitely placed under the sovereignty of China.[1]

Republican China held to this basic historical claim, albeit with some variation, and maintained that, subjugation to the Mongols aside, Tibet became a full part of China only during the Qing (1644–1911). When Republican-era writers spoke of China's claim to sovereignty over Tibet, they tended to view Tibet as having been a vassal state of the Qing rather than (as the present-day Chinese position has it) an integral part of China. The terms used to describe Tibet under the Qing, *fanbang, fanshu,* and so on, are specific in that regard, and are generally rendered as "vassal state." One typical Republican-era work asserts:

> Thus, in both the 57th and 58th years of the Qianlong period (1792 and 1793), the relationship between China and Tibet was radically reformed. China's sovereignty over Tibet was firmly established and afterwards implemented in practical terms.
>
> From the time of the above-mentioned radical reform Tibet was purely reduced to a vassal state of China's. To China belonged not only suzerain rights over Tibet, but sovereign rights as well.[2]

Such comments do not mesh with current Chinese assertions on the historical status of Tibet. But evidence from earlier sources is even harder to square with China's present-day stance. Historiographers have recorded the shape of China over several dynasties. The geographic range of the state is delineated quite clearly in the chapters on geography (*dilizhi*) in official dynastic histories, and Tibet is simply not found within the Chinese state in the *Yuan History*. As a result, we find that in modern works holding that Tibet became part of the Yuan there is no agreement as to when this actually happened. And there is certainly no document from the Yuan era announcing it. Consequently, different articles from the PRC have given different dates for this incorporation, as they struggled to describe something that did not happen.[3] The Mongols dominated Tibet but never attached it to China.

The succeeding Ming dynasty (1368–1644, under which the *Yuan History* was compiled) simply had no authority in Tibet at all. When the Qing dynasty compiled the official history of the Ming it first placed Tibet within the chapters on foreign countries (*waiguo zhuan*). The completed history placed Tibet in the Western Regions (*xiyu*), alongside the realm of Tamerlane and the like. The Manchu rulers of the Qing dynasty—indeed the rest of the world that dealt with the Qing—saw Tibet as a feudal dependency within an empire, not the integral part of a unitary multinational state that Chinese are now educated to see when they learn about imperial China's past. Late Qing officials concerned with Tibetan affairs actually suggested that these be modeled after other imperialist projects, such as those of the French in Indo-China and the Americans in the Philippines.[4] There was no need to hide or disguise empires.

TIBET AND CHINA "IN ANCIENT TIMES"

This idea, that Tibet became a part of China during the Yuan dynasty, has held sway for several decades in China. But of late a new position has been put forward there, one that is more uncompromising. Since we seem to be at a moment when the two ideas both have currency, it is reasonable to deal with the new position as well. Given the disjunctions between them, however, we need to treat them separately. They both serve the same end, asserting China's historical hold on Tibet, but ultimately it is worth bearing in mind that this second position may well supersede the first.

This new position holds that Tibet has been a part of China "since ancient times," that is, since well before the Yuan. It seems to be part and parcel of a broader Chinese assertiveness on the Tibet issue, one that developed following protests in and about Tibet in 2008 that left China defensive about Tibet at the very moment, following the Beijing Olympics and the unfolding of the global financial crisis, that it found itself in a stronger position as a rising global power. Much as China has made a public show of discarding the charade that led credulous observers to think that China was amenable to a compromise with the Dalai Lama over the Tibet issue,[5] so too a hardened position over Tibet's historical status is now operative. The pronouncements vis-à-vis Tibet are significant because they show the broad agreement and even common language that characterizes positions that have been sanctioned as official policy. So it would seem with this case. Among several reports, most significant is a Xinhua news dispatch of May 5, 2008, which imparted a clear air of official authorization as it proclaimed, "[The assertion that] 'Tibet has been a part of China since ancient times' is built upon an already existing theoretical base in Chinese historical geography."

And indeed, the theoretical element in this new historical view is laid out very clearly, drawing on the work of Tan Qixiang (1911–1992), the renowned scholar of China's historical geography. The article quotes what it views as a seminal paper by him from 1981 on "Historical China and China's Dynastic Frontiers," a paper that put things very clearly:

> How do we handle the question of historical China? We take the territory of the Qing dynasty, after its complete unification and prior to the encroachment of imperialism on China, specifically China's territory from the 1750s to the 1840s, the period preceding the Opium Wars, as the historical sphere of China. What is termed historical China is this sphere. Whether it's a question of centuries or millennia, the nationalities active within this sphere are considered by us to be China's historical nationalities; the regimes established within this sphere are considered by us to be China's historical regimes. This is the simple answer. Beyond this sphere lie no Chinese nationalities or Chinese regimes.
>
> . . . Some comrades take Tufan [i.e., imperial-era Tibet] Tibet to be a part of the Tang dynasty; this goes against historical reality. The Tang and Tibet struggled many times as enemies and marital alliances and friendly relations were rare. And when there were marital alliances and friendly relations, the Tang absolutely did not control Tibet. The relationship between the Han dynasty and the Xiongnu and that between the Tang Dynasty and the Turks and Uyghurs was essentially the same. We can only recognize that Tufan, the Xiongnu, the Turks and the Uyghurs were part of historical China; but we can't say that they were part of the Han or Tang dynasties.[6]

Adding to this, the Xinhua article then goes on to state:

> [The assertion that] "Tibet has been a part of China since ancient times" is built on the base of Tan Qixiang's famous thesis. It's just as when we speak of Xinjiang, Inner Mongolia, Ningxia, the Northeast, Taiwan, Yunnan, Guizhou, Hunan and Hubei, Guangdong and Guangxi, and even Beijing and Nanjing, etc: these places have been part of China since ancient times. There's no need to

delve deeply into the question of when they fell under effective administration by the political authority of the Central Plain or of the central government.[7]

This is not isolated political rumination. Rather, it represents a new tack in the polemical case being made over Chinese historical claims to Tibet. Other articles have echoed the same premise. With a clear stamp of authority, Sun Yong, vice director of the Tibetan Academy of Social Sciences, gave an interview to *Renmin Ribao* (*People's Daily*) journalists that appeared on the paper's website on February 26, 2009, and that set out the points raised in the Xinhua piece with very precise relevance to Tibet:

> When we say today that Tibet has been a part of China since ancient times, it is an historical fact. To say "since ancient times" is not the same as saying "since the Yuan dynasty;" it is rather to say "since human activity began." In this regard saying "Tibet has been a part of China since ancient times" is also not to say "the regime in Tibet since ancient times has always been a part of the area effectively governed by political authority from the Central Plains or the political authority of the Central Government." Rather, it's to say that "the history of this piece of land, Tibet, has, since human activity began, been a part of Chinese history." . . . The famous Tibetologist Wang Furen pointed out in the 1980s that "saying Tibet entered China's territory during the Yuan dynasty is tantamount to saying Tibet had a period outside the Motherland; that prior to the thirteenth century Tibet was not within China. This does not accord with the historical fact of the evolutionary process of China's historical inseparability.
> . . . Since ancient times each of the fraternal nationalities have been creating our great Motherland all together. . . . The history of the formation and development of these nationalities is an organic part of China's history; the political regimes which they established, whether they were central dynasties or regional regimes, were all political regimes within China. Seen this way, we can reach a clear conclusion: the history of the Tibetan nationality since ancient times is a composite part of the nationality history of China.[8]

This is a change in polemical thinking and it will be interesting to follow its progress in future assertions of China's claims to Tibet. The argument's premise is strikingly simple: the boundaries reached by the Qing dynasty at its height represent historical China and within that area there is only Chinese history. While it is problematic for many scholars to consider the Qing in its entirety a Chinese state, that is irrelevant for the proponents of the "Since Ancient Times" thesis, which effectively asserts Chinese historical dominion retroactively. To the extent that this argument comes to the fore there will be no need to quibble over whether or not the Ming exercised control over Tibet following the fall of the Yuan. In fact, it may be that the weaknesses in the Yuan-based case for Chinese sovereignty over Tibet, mentioned above, have played a role in this polemical change. In any event, the new thesis treats all historical polities within the Qing borders at their furthest extent as Chinese regimes, much as historians have done with competing dynasties in China Proper during eras of division such as the Five Dynasties. Sun Yong therefore asserts that an area such as Tibet has no history other than as a part of China, starting from the time that human activity began on the Plateau. Within the bounds of this thesis there is simply no independent Tibetan history. This sounds ludicrous from the start and serves to further distance an important area of academic Tibetan Studies in China from Tibetan Studies elsewhere. But there it is.

FEUDAL TIBET

Finally, there is the question of Tibet's feudal past. Here, the nature of China's presence in Tibet is effectively represented within China—unintentionally, of course—as something akin to the "civilizing missions" of Western powers in the age of imperialism. Indeed, in response to the mass Tibetan protests of spring 2008 China declared a new holiday commemorating the suppression of the 1959 Tibetan rising: "Serfs Emancipation Day," to be celebrated every March 28. This is meant to reinforce a rigid interpretation of Tibet's history that brooks no serious questions about the fate of Tibetans in the aftermath of their "emancipation."

There is no doubt that Tibet's traditional society was hierarchical and backward. It had aristocratic estates and a bound peasantry. Most Tibetans will readily admit that the social structure was highly inegalitarian and they voice no wish to see it restored. But it was not the cartoonish, cruel "Hell-on-Earth" that Chinese propaganda has portrayed it to be. The fact is, Tibet's demographic circumstances (a small population in a relatively large land area) served to mitigate the extent of exploitation. This was quite the reverse of the situation in China in the early twentieth century, where far too little land for the large population allowed for severe exploitation by landowners. China's categorization of Tibetan society as feudal obscures the fact that this socially backward society, lacking the population pressures found elsewhere, simply did not break down as theoretically it ought to have, but continued functioning smoothly into the twentieth century. Traditional Tibetan society was not without its cruelties (the punishments visited on some political victims were indeed brutal), but seen proportionally, they pale in comparison to what transpired in China in the same period. In modern times mass flight from Tibet only happened after its annexation to the PRC.

Chinese government propaganda often illustrates its Hell-on-Earth thesis with photographs and anecdotes derived from Western imperialist accounts of Tibet. Such materials can equally be used to create a similar narrative of decadent Chinese barbarism. And indeed, they were put to that very use during the nineteenth and early twentieth centuries. Ironically, for Tibetans today there is probably no period that registers in the historical memory as cruelly and savagely as that from the 1950s through the Cultural Revolution. When the Dalai Lama's first representatives returned to tour Tibet in 1979, cadres in Lhasa, believing their own propaganda, lectured the city's residents about not venting anger at the visiting representatives of the cruel feudal past. What actually transpired was caught on film by the delegation: thousands of Tibetans descended on them in the center of Lhasa, recounting amid tears how awful their lives had become in the intervening twenty years.[9] These scenes stunned China's leadership and for some, at least, showed the depths to which Tibetan society had sunk since the era of "Feudal Serfdom."

All of these issues—the actual date of Tibet's incorporation into China, the legitimate historical boundaries of China, and the insistence on treating pre-1959 Tibet as a place mired in feudal serfdom—are anything but long-established readings of Tibetan or Chinese history. They are positions established by a state that views any concession to open and free debate on these issues as an attack on one foundation supporting the edifice of the Chinese nation as built up since 1949. And indeed, some may feel that such fears on the part of the Chinese government are legitimate. But this does not relieve scholars and students of the responsibility of weighing such assertions by the state against the actual historical record. Here we have three new Chinese orthodoxies about Tibet that deserve free and reasoned debate.

SUGGESTIONS FOR FURTHER READING

Chinese views may be seen in *The Boundary Question between Tibet and China* (Peking, 1940) and *Concerning the Question of Tibet* (Peking: Foreign Languages Press, 1959). Tibetan views are represented by Tsering Shakya, *The Dragon in the Land of Snows* (Columbia University Press, 1999). Western views are found in Elliot Sperling, *The Tibet-China Conflict: History and Polemics* (East-West Center, 2004) and "China Digs In Its Heels in Tibet," *Far Eastern Economic Review* (April 2009), and in Warren Smith Jr., *China's Tibet?* (Rowman & Littlefield, 2008).

NOTES

1. *The Boundary Question between Tibet and China: A Valuable Record of the Tripartite Conference between China, Britain and Tibet, Held in India, 1913–1914* (Peking, 1940), pp. 7–8. The same statement reports the subjugation of Tibet in 1206 by

Chinggis Khan, which never happened, and the fanciful notion of a Chinese expedition entering Lhasa in the seventh century.

2. Xie Bin, *Xizang wenti* (*The Tibet Question*) (Shanghai: Commercial Press, 1926), pp. 20–21.

3. See, for example, the sources cited in Elliot Sperling, *The Tibet-China Conflict: History and Polemics* (Washington, DC: East-West Center, 2004), pp. 24–25, which date the incorporation of Tibet into China variously to 1279, 1271, and 1264. Another work, published to make China's case in the wake of the 1959 Tibet uprising, *Concerning the Question of Tibet*, p. 190 dated the event to 1253.

4. Elliot Sperling, *The Tibet-China Conflict*, pp. 29 and 42.

5. See Elliot Sperling, "China Digs In Its Heels in Tibet," *Far Eastern Economic Review* (April 2009): 48–51.

6. "Xizang zigu yilai jiushi Zhongguo de yi bufen" [Tibet has been a part of China since ancient times], *Guangming ribao*, repr. *Xinhuawang* (May 5, 2008), http://news.xinhuanet.com/politics/2008-/05/content_8106611.htm (accessed May 14, 2009).

7. Ibid.

8. Zhang Fan, Su Yincheng, and Wang Zhiqiu, "Fang Xizang shekeyuan fuyuanzhang: Xizang zigu yilai jiushi Zhongguo de yi bufen" [Deputy Director of the Academy of Social Sciences says on a vist to Tibet: "Tibet has been a part of China since ancient times"] *Zhingguo Xizang wang* (February 26, 2009), http://big5.people.com.cn/gate/big5/xz.people.com.cn/GB/139187/139208/8871595.html (accessed May 16, 2009). My attention was originally drawn to this interview through a post about it on the website of Taiwan Xuangouzi: http://lovetibet.ti-da.net/e2642725.html (accessed May 16, 2009).

9. Tsering Shakya, *The Dragon in the Land of Snows* (New York: Columbia University Press, 1999), p. 377.

16

The Opium War and China's "Century of Humiliation"

Julia Lovell

In China today, the Opium War (1839–1842) is the traumatic inaugural event of the country's modern history. History books, television documentaries and museums chorus a received wisdom about the conflict, which goes broadly as follows. In the early nineteenth century, unscrupulous British traders began forcing enormous quantities of Indian opium on Chinese consumers. When the Chinese government declared war on opium, in order to avert the moral, physical and financial disaster threatened by the empire's growing drug habit, British warships bullied China out of tens of millions of dollars, and its economic and political independence. In this way, gunboat diplomacy, opium and the first "Unequal Treaty" of 1842 (followed by a second in 1860, concluding the "Second Opium War") brought China to its knees, leaving it incapable of resisting subsequent waves of European, American, and Japanese colonizers.

This account of the Opium War is now one of the founding episodes of Chinese nationalism. It stands for the first great call-to-arms against a bullying West, but also the start of China's "Century of Humiliation" (*bainian guochi*, a useful shorthand for everything that happened in China between 1842 and 1949) at the hands of imperialism. It marks the beginning of China's struggle to free itself from "semicolonialism and semifeudalism" (Mao's own summary of the century after 1842), and to "stand up" (Mao again) as a strong modern nation. This battle ends, naturally, with Communist triumph in 1949. As summarized by a 2007 history textbook in use in one of China's elite institutions of higher education, Peking University,

> The story of China's modern history [from the Opium War to the present day] is the history of every nationality in the country, under the leadership of the

153

Chinese Communist Party, undertaking a great and painful struggle to win national independence and liberation through the 1949 Revolution. . . . What are the aims of studying our modern history? . . . To gain deep insight into how History and the People came to choose . . . the Chinese Communist Party.[1]

Particularly since the 1990s, when the Communist Party began rallying antiforeign nationalism to shore up its own legitimacy after the Tiananmen crackdown, landmarks in the "Century of Humiliation" such as the Opium War have been called into service in successive "patriotic education" campaigns waged in textbooks, newspapers, films, and monuments. With the turmoil of the Tiananmen uprising of 1989 blamed on "Western bourgeois liberalization," the 150th anniversary of the first Opium War in 1990 offered a public relations gift to the government: the opportunity to splash editorials across the media about this "national tragedy" inflicted by the gunboats of the West. *The People's Daily* (*Renmin Ribao*, the Communist Party's official news organ) reminded its readers that,

In order to protect its evil opium trade, the British government poisoned the Chinese people . . . and openly engaged upon imperialist aggression . . . as a result of which the Chinese fell into an abyss of suffering. . . . This, as Comrade Mao Zedong pointed out, began the Chinese people's resistance against imperialism and its running dogs. The Opium War and the acts of aggression that followed it awoke in the Chinese people a desire for development and survival, initiating their struggles for independence and liberation. . . . The facts undeniably tell us that the Chinese people have only managed to stand up thanks to the leadership of the Chinese Communist Party . . . only socialism can save and develop China. . . . Raise ever higher the glorious banner of patriotism, commemorate the 150th anniversary of the Opium War.[2]

Unorthodox reappraisals of key events of the "Century of Humiliation" (especially the Opium Wars and the Allied invasion to suppress the Boxer Rebellion in 1900) can jangle high-level political nerves. In 2006, the government closed down China's leading liberal weekly, *Freezing Point* (*Bingdian*) because it ran an article by a philosophy professor called Yuan Weishi challenging textbook doctrine on the Second Opium War and the Boxers: "it viciously attacked the socialist system [and] attempted to vindicate criminal acts by the imperialist powers in invading China."[3]

In the century and a half since it was fought, the Opium War has become the tragic beginning of China's modern history, and a key prop for Communist one-party rule. Glance across a moderately detailed chronology of modern China, and it becomes obvious that internal causes of violence outnumber external: the rural rebellions of the nineteenth century that left millions dead or displaced; the civil wars of the twentieth century, both before and after 1949. Yet while contemporary China's media and publishing industries loudly commemorate acts of (assuredly shaming) imperialist aggression such as the Opium Wars, the self-inflicted disasters of the Communist period—the manmade famine of the early 1960s, the political persecutions that culminated in the extraordinary violence of the Cultural Revolution, the bloodletting of 1989—go largely ignored. This historiographical imbalance efficiently reminds the Chinese people of their country's victimization by the West and of everything that was wrong about the "old society" before the Communist Party arrived. When the West tries to criticize China, most often for its human rights record or for its lack of an independent judiciary and press, Chinese voices—both inside and outside the government—often fight back with references to events such as the Opium War. In January 2009, when the British government protested China's execution of an allegedly mentally ill British citizen, Akmal Shaikh, for heroin smuggling, the Chinese media and Internet bubbled over with references to the nineteenth century. "The words 'England' and 'opiate' equal 'Opium War,'" explained a blogger, "the start of China's modern history of being bullied and humiliated. The English have forgotten that in 1840 their forebears began blasting open China's gates with opium. But the Chinese still feel the pain acutely."[4] This essay will explore the roots of China's powerful sense of national humiliation, from the Opium War to the present day.

THE OPIUM WAR: HISTORY AND IMAGINATION

A glance at contemporary Chinese sources—both official and civilian—paints a picture of the Opium War that jars with the apocalyptic, nationalistic account prevalent in modern Chinese textbooks and museums. As the Opium War was being fought, for example, late imperial China's rulers failed to find it epochal; indeed, most of the empire—including a number of those who were supposed to be directing proceedings—had some difficulty acknowledging an Opium War with the British was happening at all. The reigning Daoguang emperor (1782–1850) had little idea he was supposed to be at war with Britain, or why, until August 1840, almost a year after the British judged that armed hostilities had commenced. After the conflict's existence was at last officially acknowledged, the emperor and his men still had trouble dignifying it with the term "war." They preferred to name it a "border provocation" or "quarrel" (*bianxin*), atomized into a series of local clashes along China's coast. The British were identified in court documents of the time as "clowns," "bandits," "pirates," "robbers," "rebels"—they were temporary insurgents against a world order still centered in the Qing state. This, in the eyes of China's rulers, was an aggravation no more worrying than the other domestic and frontier revolts the government was struggling to suppress around the same time.

Primary sources also offer intriguing insights into the complexity of interactions between ordinary Chinese people and the attacking British armies. As long as their property and lives were not directly threatened by the British, many Chinese responses to the war were governed by economic pragmatism, rather than by racial anger. To fight their war in China, the British relied on a wide array of Chinese helpers and collaborators, eager to sell supplies, to be hired as pilots up Chinese rivers, to disable government defenses, and to serve as informers, a fact corroborated by both the Chinese and the British record. (For example, Foreign Office wartime dispatches are full of useful reports filed by the British army's Chinese spy ring). The Chinese state media today work hard to convince audiences that modern China is the story of the Chinese people's heroic struggles against "imperialism and its running dogs." In reality, the story of modern China could probably also be told as a history of collusion *with* "imperialism and its running dogs." China has about as extensive a tradition of collaboration with foreigners as any country that has suffered invasion and occupation.

If you take careful note of what observers at the time reveal about this first conflict with Western imperialism, you find little clear evidence of the heroic war of People's Resistance that commentators like Mao Zedong stirringly described in his canonical essays. Instead, you find extreme social, cultural, and political fractiousness in the nineteenth-century Chinese empire; far from being a nation united against foreign invaders, late Qing China was in many respects at war with itself as well as with Britain. Time and again, Chinese sources blame defeats not on British strength, but on the collaboration of fifth columnists. Key engagements were lost because armies from different parts of China refused to cooperate with each other; in extreme cases, these armies were killing and eating each other. The hardest-fought clashes with the British sprang not from a sense of all-out national mobilization against an alien enemy, but from very specific local grievances: drunken, disorderly rambles into the countryside that generated brawls, injuries, and sometimes deaths; the raping of women; and the desecration of graves.

THE AFTERLIVES OF IMPERIALISM

Subsequent Chinese evaluations of these events, and of imperialism in general, changed relatively slowly, and in complex, ambivalent ways. As late as the 1910s, what Chinese people today now know as the Opium War (*Yapian zhanzheng*), the inaugural act of Western imperialist aggression, could remain in textbooks just one incident in China's long, difficult nineteenth century, buried beneath the more general subheadings of "Internal and External Troubles" or "the Western Migration East," and sandwiched between problems in Xinjiang and the sprawling violence of the Taiping Rebellion.

As conflicts with the West and Japan proliferated through the late Qing (the second Opium War of 1856–1860, the Sino-Japanese War of 1894–1895, the Boxer war of 1900), anti-imperialist sentiment had an important part to play in the rise of a modern Chinese nationalism, but it was combined with powerfully self-critical strains of thought. A local victim of the notorious Anglo-French looting of Beijing in 1860 blamed the catastrophe predominantly on the derelict actions of Qing ministers, rather than on European rapacity. Noted nationalist reformers of the late nineteenth century such as Yan Fu and Liang Qichao excoriated their own countrymen, as well as Western aggression, for China's predicament. Liang argued in 1898 that "the destruction of our country is not due . . . to external troubles. . . . It's due to the mental weakness of our educated men."[5] They persisted in denouncing their fellow Chinese despite the imperialist rape of north China that followed the Boxer Rebellion. The revolt, Yan Fu decided, was an "uprising of the superstitious mob and of ignorant and worthless armed bandits. . . . It was certainly a disaster for our state."[6] Even as a patriotic antiopium movement gathered steam, campaigners seemed reluctant to blame China's opium habit exclusively on imperialism. "The English use opium to speed China's demise," summarized a Shanghai poet at the end of the nineteenth century. "The Chinese do not understand and vie to smoke it; this can be called great stupidity."[7]

Mobilizing and harnessing anti-imperialist zeal after 1911 was not straightforward either. Assuredly, certain groups in Chinese society were prone to fury about instances of "National Humiliation" (such as Japan's Twenty-One Demands in 1915, or the 1919 decision at Versailles to cede Shandong to Japan). Outraged students, teachers, and writers (through articles, demonstrations, petitions, and commemoration days) drew attention to the country's mistreatment at the hands of the Great Powers. But this anger was mixed with fear that, without the vigilance of the nation's intellectual leaders, ordinary Chinese would easily forget the horrors of foreign oppression. Editorialists complained through the 1910s and 1920s that the Chinese had a serious national humiliation attention deficit disorder: "an enthusiasm for things that only lasted five minutes."[8] One newspaper cartoon from 1922 pictured a disapproving-looking individual standing by an enormous thermometer showing that the country's "National Humiliation Commemoration Fever" had dwindled to almost nothing.[9]

The rise of China's modern political parties in the 1920s, however, added a sharper sense of grievance to this ambivalent historiography. As revolutionary nationalists like Sun Yat-sen, Chiang Kai-shek, and Mao Zedong looked for causes that would rally a loose, diverse Chinese population into a disciplined, one-party nation-state, they concentrated—among other things—on anti-imperialism. By the end of this decade, the Opium War had been reinvented as the turning point in a modern history that, books and political tracts now proclaimed, was dominated by imperialist aggression. It was (ahistorically) named the "beginning of China's diplomatic defeats" after "5,000 years of isolation" from the outside world; "a humiliation to the country—the greatest ever in our history" that "brought dishonour to countless descendants."[10] Reassessment of the Opium War coincided with other anti-Western commemorations introduced after 1924: week-long anti-imperialism fiestas protesting acts of foreign violence—such as the shooting of eleven Chinese protestors by British-led constables in Shanghai on May 30, 1925. The aim of this new rhetoric was to persuade the populace to blame all China's problems on a single foreign enemy. The Opium War and later acts of aggression became a long-term imperialist conspiracy from which only the Nationalist or the Communist Parties could preserve the country.

In the 1930s and 1940s, China's preeminent political leaders, Chiang Kai-shek and Mao Zedong, both completed their own definitive judgments of the Opium War and of imperialism in general. In 1943, Chiang denounced in his book-length manifesto *China's Destiny* the "limitless evil effects" of the country's "First National Humiliation," which "cut off the lifeblood of the state" and "threatened our people's chance of survival."[11] Once Mao was finished with it (returning to it in at least fifteen separate essays), the Opium War was no longer just a turning point in modern Chinese history; it was its inaugural event: "the first lesson" of the Chinese revolution, and the start of a century of capitalist-imperialist oppression.[12] China's modern history now became "a history of struggle by the indomitable Chinese people against imperialism and its running dogs"; the Opium War—this strange, ambivalent story of collaboration and civil war—became the "people's unrelenting and heroic struggle," "a national war" against imperialism.[13] A popular history published in 1951 recycled Mao's views: "For a whole hundred years, imperialism trampled our Chinese people underfoot. . . . The founding of the People's Republic in 1949, by contrast, is the most glorious achievement of this century; our will has been forged by the painful wound of suffering."[14]

The point of remembering past bitterness was to remind the populace to savor the sweetness of the Communist present—even as the government itself caused tens of millions of deaths in manmade famines, in purges of counterrevolutionaries, and in the civil war ushered in by Mao's Cultural Revolution. By insisting on the malevolence of China's foreign antagonists, Mao's Communist Party legitimized its own use of violence against both imperialists and, more crucially, their alleged Chinese allies (Nationalists, capitalists, landlords, and anyone suspected of sympathizing with them): "In the face of such enemies," Mao dictated, "the Chinese revolution cannot be other than protracted and ruthless. . . . In the face of such enemies, the principal means or form of the Chinese revolution must be armed struggle."[15]

CONCLUSION

The complicated history of Chinese responses to modern imperialism—a history that is simplified, in Communist discourse, into the "Century of Humiliation"—does not remotely lessen the racist stridency of many nineteenth- and twentieth-century Western attitudes to China, as expressed in the writings and actions of politicians, soldiers, and popular commentators. Even as he influentially argued, in *Discovering History in China*, that historians had simplified the impact of imperialism on China, Paul Cohen wrote: "Let there be no question about it. Everyone—or, at any rate, almost everyone—today regards imperialism as bad . . . [it] had real, measurable effects."[16] As scholars like James Hevia have demonstrated, China's encounter with Western imperialism was often deforming and dehumanizing.[17] What this narrative does show, however, is how fragmented this place we call China is: how even seemingly straightforward acts of alien aggression can generate a broad variety of responses and loyalties.

And this holds also for Chinese attitudes to the Opium War today. Even as secondary school history textbooks strive to indoctrinate young minds with the "China-as-Victim" account of modern history, always starting with 1839, classroom discussions of events such as the Opium War easily lapse out of fury toward the West and into disgust at nineteenth-century China's corruption and military weakness. Start a conversation about the Opium War and someone, sooner or later, is bound to come out with the self-hating catchphrase *luohou jiu yao aida*—a social Darwinist sentiment that translates as "if you're backward, you'll take a beating." Beneath the narrative of the Opium War and the Century of Humiliation as told by contemporary Chinese nationalism lies a far more interesting story: that of a painfully self-critical and uncertain quest to make sense of the country's crisis-ridden last two centuries.

SUGGESTIONS FOR FURTHER READING

On the subject of "national humiliation" and the modern uses of history, two of the key anglophone specialists are Paul Cohen in, for example, *History in Three Keys* (Columbia University Press, 1997) and *Speaking to History: The Story of King Goujian in Twentieth-century China* (University of California Press, 2008); and William Callahan in, for example, *China: The Pessoptimist*

Nation (Oxford University Press, 2010). For a reappraisal of imperialism in China, read also Cohen, *Discovering History in China: American Historical Writing on the Recent Chinese Past* (Columbia University Press, 1986). On the politicization of history education in China, see work by Edward Vickers and Alisa Jones, and especially *History Education and National Identity in East Asia* (Routledge, 2005).

NOTES

1. *Zhongguo jin, xiandaishi gangyao* (An Outline of Modern Chinese History) (Beijing: Gaodeng jiaoyu chubanshe, 2007), p. 1.

2. *People's Daily*, June 3, 1990, p. 1.

3. "History Textbooks in China," at http://www.zonaeuropa.com/20060126_1.htm (accessed March 3, 2009).

4. "Zhongguo ren kan le gaoxing" (The Chinese People Are Delighted), at http://blog.huanqiu.com/?uid-89545-action-viewspace-itemid-406290 (accessed January 12, 2010).

5. See, for just one set of examples, *Liang Qichao quanji* (Collected Works of Liang Qichao) Vol. 1 (Beijing: Beijing chubanshe, 1999), pp. 101, 140, 99, 167.

6. Benjamin Schwartz, *In Search of Wealth and Power: Yen Fu and the West* (Cambridge, MA: Harvard University Press, 1990), p. 142.

7. Alexander Des Forges, "Opium/Leisure/Shanghai," in Timothy Brook and Bob Tadashi Wakabayashi, ed., *Opium Regimes: China, Britain and Japan* (Berkeley: University of California Press, 2000), p. 178.

8. Paul Cohen, "Remembering and Forgetting," in *China Unbound: Evolving Perspectives on the Chinese Past* (London: Routledge, 2003), pp. 161–62.

9. Ibid., p. 163.

10. See discussion and further examples in Julia Lovell, *The Opium War and Its Afterlives* (London: Picador-Macmillan, 2011), chapter 18.

11. See, for example, Chiang Kai-shek, *China's Destiny and Chinese Economic Theory* (London: Dennis Dobson, 1947) trans. Philip Jaffe, pp. 51, 55, 90, 84.

12. Mao Zedong, "Orientation of the Youth Movement," at http://www.marxists.org/reference/archive/mao/selected-works/volume-2/mswv2_14.htm (accessed February 10, 2010).

13. Mao Zedong, "The Chinese Revolution and the Chinese Communist Party," http://www.marxists.org/reference/archive/mao/selected-works/volume-2/mswv2_23.htm; "On Contradiction," http://www.marxists.org/reference/archive/mao/selected-works/volume-1/mswv1_17.htm (accessed February 10, 2010).

14. *Bainian shihua* (A Historical Narrative of the Past Century) (Shanghai: Pingmin chubanshe, 1951), p. 1.

15. Mao, "The Chinese Revolution."

16. Paul Cohen, *Discovering History in China* (New York: Columbia University Press, 1986), p. 125.

17. See, for example, James Hevia, *English Lessons: The Pedagogy of Imperialism in Nineteenth-Century China* (Durham, NC: Duke University Press, 2003).

IV

MAKING MODERN CHINA

17

Sun Yat-sen

Wasana Wongsurawat

DEMYSTIFYING THE AMBIGUOUS HERO

The Xinhai Revolution, which brought about the demise in 1911 of the imperial system that had governed China for more than 2,000 years and ushered in the dawn of the Chinese Republican era in 1912, could not have been the single-handed achievement of any one individual. Yet the mainstream historical narratives of both the Republic of China (Taiwan) and the People's Republic of China (PRC), and the general understanding of the rest of the world as well, seem to accord most of the credit for the epoch-making events of 1911 to a single person. Sun Yat-sen was not even in China when the military uprising in Wuchang on October 10, 1911, unleashed a chain of events that would later become known as the Chinese Revolution. One direct outcome of that revolution was his ascension on January 1, 1912, to the presidency of the new republic, though he ceded the position barely three months later to General Yuan Shikai, the driving force behind the Xinhai Revolution. Sun Yat-sen spent most of the remainder of his life in exile, attempting unsuccessfully to regain power. Though the success of his political career during his lifetime was modest, Sun Yat-sen's influence after his death was much more widespread. Despite the painful political gulf that continues to divide the People's Republic on the Mainland from the Republic on Taiwan, Sun Yat-sen is today honored as a national hero on both sides of the Taiwan Strait. His mausoleum on the Mainland stands at the foot of Mount Zijin (Purple Mountain), a highly prestigious site shared only by the greatest Han Chinese icon of late imperial history, Zhu Yuanzhang, the Hongwu emperor who founded the Ming dynasty (1368–1644). Across the strait, the National Dr. Sun Yat-sen Memorial Hall in Taipei City is known as "Guoli Guofu Jinianguan," which translates literally as "National Memorial for the Father of the Nation." Major universities bear his name on both sides of the Strait, and there is another in Moscow. In the persistent homage paid to his memory by Republicans and Communists alike, it would be fair to say that Sun Yat-sen succeeded where most prominent Chinese politicians of the twentieth century have failed miserably. Though Mao Zedong and Chiang Kai-shek managed to rule and become national heroes in their respective realms, both suffer damning vilification in the other's mainstream historiography. How is it possible that Sun Yat-sen, who never ruled more than a minor part of the Mainland, and that for barely three months, is so highly revered by both Communists and Guomindang (or Kuomintang, GMD or KMT) supporters? What were his true political ideals? And why do so many of Sun's followers, each proclaiming to be the true ideological heir, fight so violently against one another, leaving China profoundly divided to this day?

FROM CHAMPION OF MODERNIZATION TO ANTIDYNASTIC REVOLUTIONARY

Among the numerous accolades accorded to Sun Yat-sen, one of the most popular is that of the great revolutionary of China. Considering his track record, Sun was indeed quite prolific in his revolutionary career. He had been causing unrest, instigating revolt, and masterminding revolution ever since his adolescence. His revolutionary activities varied greatly in kind and in their degree of success—ranging from vandalizing temples and mutilating sacred idols to instigating peasant revolts, organizing industrial strikes, and toppling the ruling dynasty. Nonetheless, even a brief assessment of Sun's ideology and ideals shows them to be intriguingly mutable, prompting more questions about what sort of revolutionary the man was, and which revolution should be credited to him or to his inspiration.

Sun Yat-sen was born in the village of Cuiheng in Guangdong. Like many of his contemporaries from poor peasant families in South China, he was sent overseas to make a better living and remit money that would help to improve his family's financial situation. Sun arrived in Hawai'i at the age of thirteen and lived with his brother, who had arrived several years earlier and managed to set up a small grocery store in Honolulu. The young migrant from Cuiheng had the opportunity to further his studies in the modern/Western education system of Hawai'i, and was deeply impressed by the enormous gulf between the modernity he experienced there and the backwardness of his home village in Guangdong.

So enthusiastic was he in this newly found path of modern learning that his brother sent him back to Guangdong after five years, fearing that he would convert to Christianity.

An astute politician who often changed his standpoint in order to gain support and political advantage, Sun Yat-sen nonetheless never wavered throughout his life in his fight for the modernization of China. It was a quest that drew him into a lifelong career as a revolutionary. In 1894, after spending a few years doing basic medical studies in Hong Kong, Sun traveled to Beijing to offer his services to Li Hongzhang. Li, the governor of Zhili, was well known as the modernizing mandarin of the Self-Strengthening Movement. In offering his services, Sun wrote his own elaborate letter of introduction, expounding some of his ideas about how to strengthen China through modernization. Unfortunately, he lacked the requisite classical Chinese education, and his family background was less than illustrious: the proposal was unceremoniously rejected. Henceforth, Sun's quest for modernization would become much more radical. Turning to the common folk for support in the late 1890s and early 1900s, Sun began lobbying overseas Chinese entrepreneurs and members of secret society gangs, preaching political goals aimed at nothing less than the complete overthrow of the Qing dynasty and the establishment of a Chinese Republic. Strangely enough, the traditions of Chinese secret societies, sworn brotherhoods steeped in superstition and racism, did not seem to hinder Sun's modernizing agenda. He formally became a member of the Hawai'ian chapter of the Heaven and Earth Society (*tian di hui*), and used anti-Manchu nationalist rhetoric to recruit support from Chinese secret societies in overseas Chinese communities across Southeast Asia, Europe, and America. Anti-Manchu sentiments were deeply entrenched in Sun's nationalist propaganda, and secret societies were profoundly involved in the revolution.

A NATION-BUILDER OF EVER-COMPROMISING PRINCIPLES

Despite the prominent role of secret societies in Sun's earlier political career and in the turn of events that became known as the Xinhai Revolution itself, supporters, historians and his most distinguished biographer[1] all agree that superstition and race-based nationalism were no more than means used by Sun in hopes of achieving a far greater end. Sun was a revolutionary who sought to overturn not only the Qing dynasty of the Manchus but the entire dynastic system that had ruled China for the past two millennia. His true vision, according to followers on both sides of the Taiwan Strait, was to found a modern nation that would be governed as a republic. As the first step in realizing this vision, Sun constructed a philosophical foundation for the revolution that proved both ideologically flexible and politically useful. His "Three Principles of the People" is an eclectic collection of political and economic theories, mostly influenced by European/American schools of thought, but not without a touch of Confucianism. While the "Principles" were not particularly original, they captured the imagination not only of Sun's followers, but also of the supporters of the Revolutionary Alliance[2] across China and in many overseas Chinese communities in Southeast Asia and beyond. These principles later found their way into the fundamental state ideology of the Republic of China and comprise the cornerstone of homegrown Chinese communist ideology.

The three main components of Sun Yat-sen's "Three Principles of the People" are nationalism (民族 *minzu*), democracy (民权 *minquan*), and socialism [or livelihood] (民生 *minsheng*). While the popular English translations may appear quite straightforward, there are numerous complications and inconsistencies in Sun's explanation of this central terminology. These ambiguities left plenty of room for different interpretations by the various opposing groups among his followers.

First, the Chinese term Sun employed for "nationalism" denotes a strong racial component. *Minzu* translates as "the clan of the common people," "the race." Considering Sun's close connection to secret societies earlier in his political career, it is not surprising that his brand of nationalism reflects anti-Manchu origins. Even after the Revolutionary Alliance was established in 1905, the part of its political platform first widely propagated was "expulsion of the northern barbarians." Only after the republic was established and sovereignty claimed over all territories of the former Qing Empire did Sun find it necessary to acknowledge other ethnic groups, besides the Han, within the new Chinese nation. A fundamental concern for race and an important official nod to China's five major ethnic groups is suggested in the Republic of China's first flag in 1912. The five-color standard symbolized the Han, Mongol, Tibetan, Manchu, and Hui peoples.[3] However, Sun's brand of "nationalism" according to the "Three Principles of the People" did not end, for him, at the borders of the Chinese nation. His political career took a difficult turn in the 1910s when he found himself constantly in need of support from foreign allies. The concept of "nationalism" in the Three Principles had to be adjusted to pan-Asian ideas that were gaining influence in Japan in that period. The broader interpretation reflected the need to gain Japanese support, the drive to liberate China from the yoke of Western imperialism, and the promotion of unity among all Asians in the face of exploitation by European and American imperialists. All this makes more comprehensible the fateful decision by Wang Jingwei—one of Sun's closest associates and a man viewed by many as his political heir—to cooperate with the Japanese by leading the Nanjing puppet regime during the Second World War.

The second of the "Three Principles of the People" is the one most often translated as "democracy." However, the meaning of the Chinese characters that represent this concept is slightly more complicated. *Minquan* could be translated as "the people's power," but this does not necessarily denote liberal democracy in the sense of Cold War American ideology. Although Sun's concept of *"minquan"* may, for many, bring to mind a Western idea of constitutional government where citizens exercise their rights through representatives in a national assembly, Sun strongly believed that China needed to proceed through a prior period of "guided democracy." The Guomindang—his political party—was to be the sole governing power, leading the nation through crucial stages of development before a fully liberated, fully functioning, democratic system of government could be achieved. In fact, from 1920 onward Sun adopted a Soviet-style, party-state system as the national policy of his regime. The *dangguo* or *yi dang zhi guo* (party-state)[4] system essentially allowed the Guomindang not only to control all aspects of government, but also to effectively shepherd the activities of nongovernmental organizations and individuals alike in the Republic of China. Top state administrators were all Party personnel. The new educational system was aimed at training Party cadres as much as producing a skilled workforce for the nation. The authoritarian dictatorship of the GMD, though projected ideally as a mere temporary transition leading to a fully functioning democratic republic was, in fact, the fundamental government system of the Republic of China for the rest of Sun's biological lifetime. In fact, this regime extended far beyond the lifetime of Sun's successor, Chiang Kai-shek, and even of Chiang's successor, Chiang Ching-kuo. The *dangguo* system was not abandoned completely until the 1990s when the Republic of China, then fully established in Taiwan, entered an era of democratization. Considering the very limited extent to which constitutional democracy was actually implemented while Sun was in power, and how his immediate successors controlled the reins of government, one could not but wonder if "democracy" is really the correct translation of the second of Sun's "Three Principles of the People."

The last of Sun Yat-sen's Three Principles looks to be the most problematic. *Minsheng* is literally "the life of the people." There is a wide range of English translations for this concept—socialism, welfare state, livelihood of the people, and so on—depending greatly on the interpretation. The concept of *"minsheng"* was actually derived, in large part, from a proposal by the American political economist, Henry George, for a "Single Tax" reform in which the state would collect only one tax according to the amount of land owned by each citizen. This amounted to granting the state ownership of all land, with citizens paying rent according to the amount of land they wished to use. All other forms of taxation by the state would be abolished. Essentially, there is not a big difference between George's proposition and what is popularly perceived as a communist land reform. However, Sun stated quite explicitly that he was against the abolition of private property as he did not believe in the Marxist idea of class struggle: he doubted that capitalism was the sole reason for the proletariat's misery.[5] Furthermore, he had been garnering generous support from overseas Chinese capitalists since his early revolutionary days. To have equated *"minsheng"* with full-blown communism would not only have been an oversimplification; it would also have been quite detrimental to Sun's financial foundation and to his political career. Nonetheless, Sun's provisional government in Guangzhou received consistent support from the Comintern throughout the early 1920s in return for his willingness to accept members of the Chinese Communist Party (CCP) into the GMD. It is also noteworthy that in 1924, barely a year before his death, Sun began a policy of active cooperation with Chinese communists. The true meaning of *"minsheng"* indeed remains open for debate.

The comprehensive ambiguity of this crucial ideological term contributes greatly to Sun Yat-sen's enduring heroic status on both sides of the Taiwan Strait. To the present day, both the Guomindang and the Chinese Communist Party, while providing completely different interpretations, claim Sun's Three Principles of the People as an essential foundation of their political ideology. Both political parties also claim intimate historical and personal connections with Sun. The GMD was founded in part by Sun Yat-sen himself, and Generalissimo Chiang Kai-shek—the GMD wartime leader and successor of Sun as Party leader—was married to Sun's sister-in-law. Not surprisingly Sun Yat-sen has gained the most prestigious of all accolades. In the Republic of China on Taiwan he continues to be revered as the "Father of the Nation." On the mainland, Sun is also revered as "Forerunner of the Revolution." Close personal connections also helped to support the CCP's claim on Sun's political position, as his widow, Madame Soong Ching-ling, proved to be a staunch supporter of the Chinese Communists from the earliest years of the Chinese Civil War to the end of her life in 1981. Sun's name continues to mark major roads and academic institutions and his image remains at significant ceremonial locations on both sides of the Taiwan Strait to this day. More interestingly, in recent years the memory of Sun Yat-sen has become a sort of common ground for improving cross-strait relations. On the one hand, with the return of a GMD leader to the Taiwanese presidential office, Sun's legacy has enjoyed a new surge of public attention. On the other hand, the Communist leaders on the mainland have also decided to invoke the memory of Sun Yat-sen as a way to promote nationalism and economic reform as well as to underline their solidarity with the GMD, which by many strange twists of fate, has come to be viewed by the CCP as its chief ally against the Taiwanese independence movement.

DREAMER OF AN ERA LONG GONE OR LIVING INSPIRATION FOR A BRIGHTER TOMORROW

During his lifetime and even more since his death, Sun inspired others to pursue these dreams. Though he possessed neither the political power nor the advanced technical knowledge to achieve any practical development on his own, he aspired to modernize China. Though he had no real military training and hardly any skills in combat, he dreamed of toppling the mighty Qing Empire. Though his political philosophy pales in comparison to the great minds of his time, he was bent on being an ideologue. In the face of daunting obstacles and despite all his shortcomings, Sun did indeed contribute significantly to the immense transformations that took place in China through most of the twentieth century. He was definitely one of the greatest communicators of his time. His thoughts and ideals, though never very solid or straightforward, won many capable and devoted followers to his cause. The memory of Sun's life and aspirations and the interpretations of his ideology, probably even more than the man himself, have inspired the nation and the many varied and far-flung Chinese communities. From the Xinhai Revolution of 1911 to the "Four Modernizations" of Deng Xiaoping's regime in the 1980s, up to the present day, the legacy of Sun Yat-sen lives on, reflecting his characteristic and undaunted vitality.

SUGGESTIONS FOR FURTHER READING

Sun Yat-sen remains a popular figure for research in fields including modern history, political philosophy, and public policy, to mention only a few. Marie-Claire Bergère's *Sun Yat-sen* (Stanford University Press, 1998) is probably the most thorough study of Sun as an individual, striking a balance between the cult status afforded by nationalist Chinese historians and the fierce deconstructive rhetoric of postmodern historians of the Western Hemisphere. Bergère portrays Sun as a moderately successful politician with a kind heart and good intentions. He devoted himself to the cause of modernization with conviction though often without much originality. This is probably the most human image of Sun one could expect.

For a more complex reading of Sun's political thought, Audrey Wells's *The Political Thought of Sun Yat-sen* (Palgrave, 2001) analyzes the foundations of Sun's political theories as well as providing a broad survey of how his speeches and writings influenced the political development of newly emerging nations of the twentieth century in Asia, Africa, and beyond. It is a delightful exception to most critical works on Sun that tend to trivialize his theories while failing to first thoroughly understand them.

With the recent hundredth anniversary of the Xinhai Revolution in 2011, much has been published by way of reevaluating the revolution as well as those involved in it—with Sun Yat-sen frequently occupying center stage. *Sun Yat-sen, Nanyang and the 1911 Revolution* (ISEAS, 2011), edited by Lee Lai To and Lee Hock Guan, comprehensively surveys Sun Yat-sen's involvement as well as the revolution's impact upon Chinese both at home and in communities around the world, especially those in "Nanyang" or Southeast Asia who were the closest and most actively involved.

NOTES

1. Marie-Claire Bergère, *Sun Yat-sen* (Stanford, CA: Stanford University Press, 1998).
2. "The Revolutionary Alliance" (*tongmenghui*) was an umbrella organization of Chinese revolutionary movements founded in Japan on August 20, 1905. The two most prominent groups within this organization were the "Revive China Society" (*xingzhonghui*)—founded in 1894 and led by Sun Yat-sen—and the Zhejiang clique, "Restoration Society" (*guangfuhui*). Sun was the recognized leader of the Revolutionary Alliance from the beginning. This organization was the foundation for the Chinese Nationalist Party (*Guomindang*) after the establishment of the Republic of China in 1912.
3. Prasenjit Duara, *Rescuing History from the Nation: Questioning Narratives of Modern China* (Chicago: University of Chicago Press, 1995).
4. Chin-chin Chen, *Kangzhan qian Jiaoyü Zhengce zhi Yanjiu* (Taipei: Historical Commission, Central Committee of the Kuomintang, 1997).
5. W. Theodore De Bary, *Sources of Chinese Tradition* (New York: Columbia University Press, 1960).

18

Republican China under the Nationalists, ca. 1925–1945

Felix Boecking

The Nationalist movement was the most stable political force on the Chinese mainland between the late 1920s and the end of the Chinese Civil War in 1949. During that period, the Nationalist Party of China, the Guomindang (GMD), also formed the internationally recognized government of the Republic of China. And yet, for more than sixty years now, the history of the GMD state has mainly been viewed through the lens of its defeat in the Civil War of 1946–1949, which led to the emergence of a socialist Chinese state on the East Asian mainland. In this view, Nationalist governance was doomed to fail from the start.

Given its demonstrable achievements both before and during the second Sino-Japanese War (1937–1945), why do narratives of incompetence, insincerity, and corruption dominate the history of the Chinese Nationalist state? This chapter summarizes recent trends in anglophone historical writing on the GMD state. All these writings approach the history of the Nationalist state without seeing its defeat on the Chinese mainland in 1949 as an unavoidable outcome. I cannot offer encyclopedic coverage here; rather, I have attempted to identify the main trends of this scholarship relating to three of the most common assertions about the Nationalist regime—that it was incompetent, that it was corrupt and criminal, and that it left most of the fighting during the Sino-Japanese War of 1937–1945 to the military forces of the Chinese Communist Party (CCP).

THE GENEALOGY OF AN INTERPRETATION

Negative views of Nationalist governance fall into two broad categories: popular and academic views. The popular perception of GMD failure is

171

heavily influenced by what Hans van de Ven termed the Stilwell-White paradigm, which posited that the Nationalist regime failed because it was corrupt, authoritarian, and militarily incompetent. General Joseph W. Stilwell, the chief U.S. military advisor to the Nationalist government during the Second World War, recorded in an undated note found among his papers that the Chinese people could only expect "greed, corruption, favoritism, more taxes, a ruined currency, [and] terrible waste" from the Nationalists under Chiang Kai-shek.[1] Theodore H. White, drawing on six years' experience as *Time* magazine's correspondent in the Nationalist wartime capital, Chongqing, wrote in 1946 of both the "extravagance and debauchery of the Kuomintang's machine" and its "brutality and extortion."[2] The Stilwell-White paradigm found its most lucid expression in Barbara Tuchman's *Stilwell and the American Experience in China*. In order to demonstrate that "China was a problem for which there was no American solution," Tuchman went to great lengths to demonstrate that the Nationalist movement had been "overtaken by the compromises and corruption of climbing to power."[3]

Lloyd Eastman expressed the most influential scholarly negative view of Nationalist governance in his two books, *The Abortive Revolution* and *The Seeds of Destruction*.[4] In contrast particularly to Stilwell's views, Eastman's argument is both detailed and nuanced in giving the Nationalists credit for what he felt to be their achievements, scarce as they were in his analysis. Hence, when approaching broadly negative perspectives on the Nationalist government's record, we must take care to distinguish between scholarly views based on newly available evidence, such as those of Lloyd Eastman or Parks Coble, and politically motivated arguments, such as those of Stilwell, White, and Tuchman. As the above quotations from Tuchman's work demonstrate, these works are often as much concerned with issues outside the history of Nationalist China, such as United States foreign policy.

WAS THE NATIONALIST GOVERNMENT REALLY INCOMPETENT?

Since Eastman's *Abortive Revolution*, many English-language studies of the Chinese Nationalist Party have emphasized the perceived failure of its fiscal and budgetary policies. This crucial aspect of state building is a good test case for narratives of Nationalist incompetence. The Nationalists moved the seat of their government to Nanjing in 1927 at the end of the first phase of the Northern Expedition, a military campaign to bring more of China's territory under Nationalist control. In 1929, the Nationalist government achieved its first major foreign policy success by regaining tariff autonomy, that is, the ability to decide how much to tax imports and exports, which the imperial court had lost under the provisions of the Treaty of Nanjing at the end of the first Opium War in 1842. Because the Nationalists could now set tariffs at higher levels, the central government's annual revenue had increased nearly threefold by the beginning of the Sino-Japanese War in 1937. How was this additional revenue spent? Military expenditures plus the interest and repayments due on foreign and domestic loans together exceeded more than half the Nationalist government's spending for all but one year of this period. The importance of military expenditure is explained by China's internal conflicts of the period, and the constant threat of a Japanese invasion.

The matter of debt service offers another opportunity to examine the Nationalist government's record. When the government moved to Nanjing in 1927, new borrowing abroad was not a feasible option due to earlier successive defaults by republican governments in Beijing, and the debt inherited from previous governments. After 1929, the Nationalists used increased tariff revenue to reduce the amount of outstanding foreign and domestic loans, and as security for new domestic loans. By 1937, 10 percent of China's foreign debt was in arrears, compared to 50 percent in 1928. Both foreign and domestic bond markets were attentive to these efforts by the Nationalist government to improve China's debt service—that is, the regular payment of interest and the repayment of principal—as the rising price of government bonds demonstrates. One common indicator of bond value is their current yield.[5] The lower the price at which the bonds are sold, the higher the current yield. The current yields of China's major foreign bonds traded on the London Stock Exchange in 1937 were about half of what they had been in 1927, showing that in June 1937, on the eve of war, markets believed the government's foreign bonds to be more secure and thus worth more than they had been previously. At home, the Nationalist government consolidated its domestic debt twice in 1932 and 1936 by decreasing the interest paid on existing bonds and extending their repayment period. Despite what amounted to a partial default, these actions improved the confidence of domestic markets in the Nationalist government's fiscal probity in the medium term, since the average current yield of domestic bonds in June 1937 was one-third lower than it had been in 1928; in other words, markets valued these domestic bonds more highly too.[6] The Nationalist government's commitment to fiscal probity outlasted the beginning of war; it suspended payments on foreign loans only in January 1939, by which time the Nationalists had lost control of China's richest provinces (and hence much of their revenue base).

Prudent debt management is no guarantee of useful government spending, or the soundness of other political choices. Chiang Kai-shek's decision to spend great amounts of money on fighting the Chinese Communists was fiercely contested in China at the time. But the Nationalists' fiscal record indicates that, with regard to the prewar period, narratives that claim sweeping incompetence on the part of the government fall short of the factual record. This applies all the more when we remember that the improvement of China's government finances took place at a time when the Republic of China was fragmented politically and territorially, since the Nationalists never controlled more than six of China's twenty-eight provinces during the prewar period, and several times were challenged militarily even within those provinces. China was never unified as a country during this period.

WAS THE NATIONALIST GOVERNMENT REALLY CORRUPT AND CRIMINAL?

Even within the Guomindang, divisions continued, as is apparent from the existence of two separate Nationalist governments in 1927 during the first stage of the Northern Expedition. Joseph Esherick argued some years ago that our understanding of the Chinese Communist Party's history would be increased if historians ceased to regard the CCP as a monolithic entity.[7] The same applies to studying the history of the GMD. This means that we need to distinguish between the things that happened within and outside the Nationalist party-state's control. To some extent, "Nationalist" was a label that could be used by any local political activist. Hence extortion in the countryside, as noted by Eastman, becomes no longer necessarily a Guomindang abuse, but rather an abuse at the local level that the central institutions of the party-state failed to prevent. That failure, in itself, is revealing about the limitations of Nationalist governance. Nevertheless, applying Esherick's approach to the Guomindang allows us to be more precise about the corruption, crime, and repression to which the Nationalists undoubtedly were party. Over the course of the twentieth century, international law has moved toward recognizing the principle of command responsibility, which states that a superior's failure to prevent an offense by a subordinate, of which he is aware but which he did not order, also constitutes an offense. This approach is useful for thinking about the responsibility of the central institutions of the Nationalist party-state for abuses committed by Party members at the local level.

Chinese and foreign commentators noted a sharp increase in corrupt and criminal behavior during the early years of the second Sino-Japanese War. This observation is supported by recent research, particularly that of Frederic Wakeman. However, it has also become clear that the Nationalist government's links to organized crime, and propensity to resort to criminal means as policy tools, go back much earlier. Edward Slack and Alan Baumler have shown that the Nationalists' attitude to the domestic opium trade was at best ambivalent during the prewar years, since the government derived much-needed revenue from its opium monopoly. The ostensible purpose of this monopoly was to force the Chinese opium trade under government supervision in order eventually to eliminate opium consumption altogether. Brian Martin has documented the collusion of the Nationalists during the Northern Expedition with elements of the Shanghai underworld to suppress labor unrest. This created a loose political alliance, and the Shanghai underworld's interests in the drug trade further compromised the Nationalist government's stated policy of eradicating opium consumption. The Nationalists continued to rely on the Shanghai underworld as a political ally and occasional executioner during the prewar years.

Regardless of this, criminality, corruption and, as we have seen above, competent governance, coexisted within the Nationalist state's structure, which indicates that these things were not mutually exclusive. Hence, that the Nationalist government as a whole was corrupt and criminal may be said to be a misinterpretation, but that a large number of individuals and institutions of the Nationalist government displayed corrupt and criminal behavior is not. This, in turn, does not invalidate its governance record in other areas.

AND WHAT, EXACTLY, DID THE NATIONALIST GOVERNMENT DO DURING THE WAR?

The armed forces of the Nationalist Government and its allies withstood the Japanese invasion for eight years, by trading space for time.[8] As Hans van de Ven has pointed out, by early 1945, neither side was able to win the war, since China's inability to defeat Japan matched Japan's inability to fully occupy and consolidate its control over China. Given that it pushed the Japanese military to this point, why is the Nationalist leadership's military record even in question? The Stilwell papers leave no doubt that the Nationalist supreme military commander, Chiang Kai-shek, and his chief U.S. military advisor, Stilwell himself, were unsuited to each other temperamentally and in their leadership styles. More important, they also differed in their tactics. Stilwell was committed to the all-out offensive tactics that were adopted as the U.S. Army's doctrine during the 1930s.[9] Offensive warfare necessitated an army trained to a uniformly high standard and a defense economy to keep it supplied, neither of which China possessed in 1937; efforts to develop both were ongoing at the time. The absence of these prerequisites makes Chiang's choice of defensive warfare seem like a realistic choice. Despite Chiang's superior military experience, Stilwell's low opinion of Chiang's abilities as a military leader has stood the test of time better than the military record of the Nationalist forces.

During the war, the Chinese Nationalist polity changed, both for the better and for the worse. Of its three main aims in the realm of foreign relations—diplomatic recognition, regaining tariff autonomy, and ending extraterritoriality—the Nationalist state had achieved the first two before the war, and the last, most emblematic of China's perceived return to the world stage, by the end of the war. The Republic of China emerged from the war in 1945 with a more prominent international standing than it had had beforehand. The most visible legacy of the Nationalist party-state is the continued existence of a Republican Chinese state on Taiwan—one of the remaining unresolved issues of the Cold War in East Asia—and the continued existence of the Nationalist Party, which at the time of writing had recently returned to power in the Republic of China on Taiwan via the ballot box.

But after the Civil War of 1946–1949, the Nationalist party-state was only able to continue to exist on Taiwan, and that has much to do with the ways in which the Chinese polity changed for the worse during the war. This is illustrated again by the example of fiscal policy, an area in which central GMD governance in Nanjing was successful until the beginning of the war. That the amount of central government revenue collected increased nearly threefold between 1928 and 1937 demonstrates that the National- ists had found a sustainable way to fund their governance. However, losing control of China's wealthy coastal area because of the onset of war forced the wartime Nationalist government into adopting rapacious taxes and, ultimately, deficit financing. These new taxes contributed to the Nationalist party-state's loss of legitimacy as the war progressed, and spending more than the government could collect in revenue or borrowing led to hyperin- flation by the latter stages of the war. At the same time, opportunities for corrupt or criminal behavior increased as the institutions of the GMD state grew beyond the control of its political center. As an increasing number of Chinese people experienced such behavior, in their eyes the Nationalists increasingly lost the legitimacy to govern China.

CONCLUSION

The Second Sino-Japanese War of 1937–1945 was not the only factor in the demise of the Nationalist regime; for one, the Chinese Civil War of 1946–1949 did not have a predetermined outcome, as Arne Westad's recent research has shown. Grassroots political support for the CCP continued to increase during the Civil War. In many cases, this support was the result of CCP socioeconomic policies that promised a more equal distribution of wealth within society. The Nationalists could not and would not match these policies, and as a result their political mobilization of the general populace was weaker than that of the CCP. How Nationalist governance might have developed had it not been for the Japanese invasion in 1937 is a speculative question that historical analysis cannot answer.

However, recent works of scholarship on Republican China all stress the importance of the Sino-Japanese War of 1937–1945 in transforming the political fortunes of the Guomindang. The war is important for all three myths we have looked at in this chapter: it derailed prewar governance reforms, encouraged corrupt and criminal tendencies among members and institutions of the Nationalist party-state, and was fought at enormous human and economic cost.

It is the Second Sino-Japanese War, therefore, that had the greatest impact on the demise of Nationalist governance on the mainland; we have seen that sweeping assertions that the Nationalists were incompetent and unwilling to fight were at best exaggerated. Additional evidence of corruption and criminality within the Nationalist polity continues to surface, but here, too, a comprehensive indictment fails to convince. Since Eastman already drew attention to the transformative effects of the war, what is the difference between his argument and those made by revisionist historians more recently? The distinction lies in our increased understanding of both the achievements and failures of the Nationalist party-state. This has become possible due to improved access to archives in both the PRC and the ROC that was unthinkable even a few decades ago, together with a less heated political climate within which to debate Nationalist governance. As our understanding of the fractured nature of the Guomindang polity and the transformative effect of the second Sino-Japanese War on Chinese politics grows, so too does our appreciation of the confines within which Nationalist policy makers were operating.

SUGGESTIONS FOR FURTHER READING

The latest volume to discuss the military history of the second Sino-Japanese War is Mark Peattie, Edward Drea, and Hans van de Ven (eds.), *The Battle for China* (Stanford University Press, 2010), which offers stimulating and accessible essays, while the most recent comprehensive study of the Chinese Civil War is Arne Westad, *Decisive Encounters: The Chinese Civil War, 1946–1950* (Stanford University Press, 2003). Hans van de Ven gives a comprehensive, essential reappraisal of the Nationalist party-state and the Guomindang's war effort in *War and Nationalism in China, 1925–1945* (RoutledgeCurzon, 2003), and Julia Strauss, *Strong Institutions in Weak Polities* (Clarendon Press, 1998) provides an indispensable introduction to the frequently confusing institutional history of the Nationalist state. For a fascinating case study in the wartime decline of Nationalist governance, see

Frederic Wakeman, *Spy Master: Dai Li and the Chinese Secret Service* (University of California Press, 2003).

NOTES

1. Joseph W. Stilwell, *The Stilwell Papers*, ed. Theodore H. White (1948, reprt. New York: Da Capo, 1991), p. 317.

2. Theodore H. White, Annalee Jacoby, *Thunder out of China* (1946, reprt. New York: Da Capo, 1980), p. 312.

3. Barbara Tuchman, *Sand against the Wind: Stilwell and the American Experience in China, 1911–1945* (New York: Macmillan, 1970), pp. 531, 115.

4. Lloyd Eastman, *The Abortive Revolution: China under Nationalist Rule, 1927–1937* (Cambridge, MA: Harvard University Press, 1974) and *The Seeds of Destruction: Nationalist China in War and Revolution, 1937–1949* (Stanford, CA: Stanford University Press, 1984).

5. This is calculated by dividing annual interest payable by the percentage of the nominal value at which the bonds are traded.

6. Arthur N. Young, *China's Nation-Building Effort, 1927–1937: The Financial and Economic Record* (Stanford, CA: Hoover Institution, 1971), pp. 141, 98–99.

7. Joseph Esherick, "Ten Theses on the Chinese Revolution," in Jeffrey N. Wasserstrom, ed., *Twentieth-Century China: New Approaches* (London: Routledge, 2003), p. 53.

8. Edward Drea, Hans van de Ven, "An Overview of Major Military Campaigns during the Sino-Japanese War, 1937–1945," in Mark Peattie, Edward Drea, Hans van de Ven, eds., *The Battle for China: Essays in the Military History of the Sino-Japanese War of 1937–1945* (Stanford, CA: Stanford University Press, 2010), p. 25.

9. Hans van de Ven, "The Sino-Japanese War in History," in Peattie et al., *Battle for China*, pp. 734–35.

19

The Rise of the Chinese Communist Party

Christian Hess

The rise of the Chinese Communist Party (CCP) is a dramatic tale, full of twists and unexpected turns. The storyline is compelling enough: a small, urban-based political party, led by intellectuals, is nearly wiped out by its domestic political rivals, Chiang Kai-shek's Nationalists, only to beat the odds by transforming itself from an urban to a rural-based movement that manages to successfully lead a social revolution in the countryside while fighting a guerrilla war against invading Japanese armies. The CCP not only survived in impoverished and isolated parts of rural China, it thrived. Tens of thousands of people flocked to its rural bases to be a part of this movement. After an intense civil war with the Nationalists following Japan's defeat, the CCP won control of China and founded the People's Republic in 1949. It is, of course, still in power today, and has further reinvented itself as the architect of the stunning economic growth we witness in China today.

Both the official, CCP-sanctioned history of modern China, and to some extent Western scholarship, tend to equate modern Chinese history with the successful rise of the CCP and its revolution. But we must be careful. This is but one of the major storylines in China's rise. The primacy given to the CCP's revolution and wartime experiences gives CCP victory an air of inevitability. Interwoven into this success story are some key misinterpretations, some of which have been created and circulated by the CCP as a means to legitimate their monopoly on power, while others are perpetuated by scholarly agendas from outside the People's Republic. This chapter examines three of the main misconceptions surrounding the CCP's rise to power with the aim of revealing how and why these notions were created, and that some of the Party's key victories were far from inevitable.

THE LONG MARCH: MYTHIC JOURNEY

One cornerstone of the CCP's origin myth involves their dramatic escape from Jiangxi in southern China and arrival at a new rural base in Shaanxi in the northwest, an epic event known as "The Long March." Following their near destruction at the hands of the Nationalists in 1927, the CCP had survived in the remote hills of Jiangxi, where they built a rural Soviet (a military-protected, Party-controlled base area). By the early 1930s, the Nationalist commander Chiang Kai-shek was determined to wipe them out completely. The Nationalists launched a series of "extermination" campaigns aimed at destroying the Jiangxi base. By 1934 the CCP's territory was surrounded by Nationalist troops. One night, in October 1934, eighty thousand people departed the Jiangxi base, breaking through the blockade under the cover of darkness. Few realized that this march would not last days or even weeks, but rather months. Their destination was unclear. When they finally made it to Yan'an, the survivors, now only ten thousand, had marched six thousand miles in just over one year through some of the most inhospitable parts of China, battling the Nationalist armies and various warlords along the way. In one famous story, the CCP reached a chain bridge high across a mountain valley. Under fire from Nationalist troops on the other side, a group of commandos crawled across, hand over hand, to lob grenades at the enemy. Their daring attack ensured safe passage for the marchers.

There were more mundane but no less important struggles within the CCP itself during the Long March. It was during the course of the march that Mao Zedong and a core of leaders emerged who would rule the Party and shape its future. When Mao finally arrived at Yan'an, he marshaled the few thousand with him and asked "Are we stronger or weaker? Stronger, because you who have survived are like gold."[1] Surviving Long March veterans did indeed possess a very real symbolic and political capital within the Party, and many remained in top leadership positions well into the 1980s.

In the official retelling of the Long March story, the CCP not only survives through unimaginable hardship, but emerges as a purified, unified force. Mao Zedong and other Long March leaders appear to possess an invincibility that makes them seem destined to rule. Moreover, through their hardships, according to the story, a unity is forged among the Party, in which serious factional divisions melt away, Mao takes the helm, and they march onward toward their new base at Yan'an. Shortly after arriving in Yan'an, Mao wrote of the march, "Let us ask, has history ever known a long march to equal ours? No, never. The Long March is a manifesto. It has proclaimed to the world that the Red Army is an army of heroes, while the imperialists and their running dogs, Chiang Kai-shek and his like, are impotent."[2]

Yet the event itself is slippery historical terrain. There is little in the way of photographic or documentary evidence from the march, and we have only fleeting glimpses into the factional struggles that surrounded it. This lack of clarity gives the event a malleability that makes for a good legend. What glimpses we do catch of the decision making during the Long March reveal that contingencies and conflict were the norm. We know that Mao became the main leader during the march, but the details of his rise remain hazy. Moreover, his power was not yet total. Even in terms of deciding the final destination of the march, there was considerable debate. While Mao favored moving northward to Yan'an, there were others within the Party who had plans for a move to Xinjiang in the far northwest or Sichuan in the mountainous center. Powerful military commanders like Zhang Guo-tao, in charge of a sizable military force, competed with Mao for political influence. Zhang, for example, had led his troops into Sichuan province and upon meeting up with the rest of the Long Marchers, Zhang challenged Mao in favor of setting up a federation of bases where Zhang was in Sichuan and the rugged lands adjoining it in northwest China. Such intraparty conflict between Mao and other key leaders continued even after their arrival at Yan'an.

In reality, the Long March was more a meandering retreat than a unifying quest. It resulted in the near destruction of the CCP, and tens of thousands of its followers perished on the road. Factional conflict at the top levels of the Party intensified as their desperate situation unfolded. Had it not been for Japan's all-out invasion of China, the Nationalists might have encircled the weakened CCP once again for a final battle. Yet, in part because of such contingencies, the CCP survived and turned the defeat into a mythic victory, with the reality of a fragmented retreat transformed into a symbol of unity and perseverance, key values of the new wartime base at Yan'an.

The Long March story was propagated shortly after arriving at the new base in Yan'an. It was written about by Mao and became one of the main narratives of the Party-sponsored history of the CCP's rise to power. It resurfaced prominently during the late 1960s, when, during the Cultural Revolution, millions of "Red Guards," radicalized youths empowered by Mao to attack the CCP, donned Yan'an-style uniforms and recreated their own "Long March" journeys from provincial cities and towns to Beijing. These young new Long Marchers hoped to experience their own daring adventures on the way to greet Chairman Mao. Even in the era of reforms after Mao's death, when much of the Maoist state has been dismantled and talk of revolution replaced by market concerns, there is still a place for the Long March. Chinese satellites and astronauts are blasted into orbit on "Long March" heavy-payload rockets. Thus, this narrative has quite literally reached new heights as a symbol of progress.

DESTINATION YAN'AN: MYTHIC SYMBOL OF REVOLUTION

From 1935 until the late 1940s, Yan'an, a former trading outpost on the old Silk Road in Shaanxi province, was the center of the CCP's political, social, and cultural activity. It was during this period that Mao Zedong rose to become the head of the Party and its revolution, and at Yan'an he produced many of his most important theoretical works and policies. Despite its remote location and extreme poverty, tens of thousands of people flocked to Yan'an to join the CCP's war effort and to help build a new society. Camaraderie, hard work, thrift, egalitarianism, patriotism, and a belief in creating a better future for China became part of a core set of revolutionary values that some scholars have referred to as the "Yan'an Way."[3] Like the Long March story, there was some truth to this. At Yan'an and other rural base areas, the CCP rebuilt itself, and successfully implemented tax and rent policies with the goal of gradually increasing the wealth of the farming population. In a fractured country, scarred by incessant war, the CCP's inclusive grassroots politics, egalitarian social and economic policies, and message of unity was a powerful draw for people in China. By the early 1940s, just a few years after the Long March nearly destroyed the Party, CCP membership swelled to over 700,000.

Like the Long March, Yan'an became an instant and very potent symbol for the retooled CCP. It further refined the narrative of unity-through-struggle in the formative stages of the Party. It was the symbolic capital of the revolution, the final destination of the Long March saga. Because Yan'an was the main base where key leaders like Mao lived and operated, it tends to dominate the historical narrative of the CCP's revolution and war effort. There are several points to keep in mind when it comes to breaking through this image of centrality. First, Yan'an was only one among many rural base areas scattered throughout north China, each with its own diverse socioeconomic conditions. Second, Yan'an's symbolic power was under attack from elements within the Party shortly after the CCP's arrival there.

By the early 1940s the CCP controlled some nineteen base areas in central and north China. Within these bases, some counties were receptive to the CCP's efforts at social leveling through land reform and progressive taxation, while others were resistant, and even hostile, to these plans. For example, in the Taihang base, to the east of Yan'an, CCP leaders experienced firsthand a major uprising against their base-area government. The Party's initial, inclusive approach to building support and local governance here involved a large swath of rural society, including women and rural elites. However, after 1940, the Party switched tactics, removing many of these people from power and replacing them with CCP outsiders. Aggrieved former activists mounted an armed revolt by mobilizing an underground religious sect to take up arms against the CCP. Women comprised a large portion of the sect's membership, and captured female participants responded that they felt this organization allowed them greater freedom than the programs of the CCP. In the eyes of the local communities like this, the CCP was viewed as a political and military force made up of outsiders, strangers who believed their stay in these rural hinterlands was temporary. This was a major source of underlying tension between the Party and the people, which reached a boiling point on a number of occasions.

Some new arrivals to Yan'an were increasingly skeptical of the positive image of life in the base areas. Writers, artists, and urban intellectuals, many of whom had risked life and limb just to make the trek from Japanese-occupied coastal cities, were quick to criticize the less-than-egalitarian practices that they soon discovered characterized life there. Despite the talk of thrift and sacrifice, CCP elites, for example, enjoyed better access to food, better housing, and even enjoyed evening dance parties. Wang Shiwei, a translator who moved from Shanghai, penned a potent criticism of life in Yan'an that highlighted a darker side of authoritarianism, elitism, and the CCP's failure to truly capture the spirit of those flocking to the base. Another writer, Ding Ling, was no less critical. She had established her reputation as a leftist writer in the 1920s and was receptive to Yan'an's image as an egalitarian place. However, shortly after her arrival Ding Ling wrote a scathing critique of the CCP's policies for women, noting that in fact traditional attitudes toward women's roles continued. Both of these authors suffered during a major crackdown on dissent within the Party, launched by Mao in 1942. No sooner had the CCP built the Yan'an image than it was forced to crack down on those within the Party who sought to expose it.

Today, the Yan'an story survives and in some ways is stronger than ever. It is kept alive by television dramas that glorify the CCP's war and revolution, and in which the Yan'an days are recollected and recast as a time of past purity and unity in an age of rapid change. Occasionally, Yan'an creeps up as a story in state-owned media outlets. As part of the run-up to the gala celebrations of the PRC's sixtieth anniversary, the Xinhua News Agency ran a story in which some surviving revolutionaries and Mao's relatives visited Yan'an.[4] Yan'an the place, ignored for decades after 1949, has not been left behind in China's economic boom. It is now a major site of patriotic "red tourism," where visitors can dress up in Yan'an-style uniforms and pose for photographs at Mao's old headquarters. Well-heeled tourists are treated to revolutionary songs in modern hotels with rooms that imitate the simple cave dwellings from Yan'an's glory days.

1949: BIRTH OF "NEW CHINA"?

In founding the People's Republic of China in 1949, the CCP accomplished one of its major goals. It had defeated its chief domestic rival, the National-

ist government, and was now in charge of a new nation. Its dramatic rise
to power seemed complete. There is little in the way of mythmaking here.
This was the CCP's triumph, but it was a victory that raised new questions
for both the Party and the people of China. Was this the beginning of a
new stage of politics and society for Chinese people? Was the revolution
complete, or would it continue? Was everything from "old China" bad?

While 1949 is a watershed date in modern Chinese history, these questions remind us that dates are never perfect historical divides. The CCP did
indeed usher in a new political, social, and economic system and carried
out significant policies like land reform that fundamentally altered life
in the countryside. However, the PRC's foundations were as much past
inheritances as they were new creations. While the CCP may have reviled
the Nationalist government, it inherited from them a legacy of centralized
planning, a legal system, a transportation network, and so on. Even Japan,
whose brutal invasion scarred Chinese society from the 1930s through
1945, left certain foundations upon which the CCP built its own programs.
Japan had heavily industrialized parts of northeast China, and this area
became the industrial heart of the new People's Republic. The imperialist
factories of the enemy became the socialist factories of the people. Thus,
not everything from "old" China could be swept away, or portrayed as bad.

Moreover the CCP's own policies had a history. For the first few years
after 1949, a key challenge for Party leaders was how to carry their past
policies, forged during wartime in rural bases, forward to all of China. An
emphasis on these continuities and inheritances provides a more realistic
picture of what the CCP faced in 1949. Party leaders confronted what recent
scholarship on the early years of the People's Republic has characterized as
certain "dilemmas of victory."[5] How would it mask the legacies it inherited
from its enemies? How could it refine its message of revolution and state
building to fit urban areas that the CCP now controlled, to say nothing of
places like Tibet and Xinjiang? The most significant of these dilemmas—the
tensions between formal state-building and radical revolutionary change—
would haunt both the Party and the people in the decades to come.

CONCLUSION

What do these narratives about the rise of the CCP tell us? They exist in
most national projects, so it would be incorrect to assume that such mythmaking is unique to China. However, in the China case they do point to
something quite significant. This is a party that survived against the odds. It
is a political machine with decades of experience in fashioning tales about
its origins. Its narratives have proven to be remarkably flexible in that they
have managed to adapt through the phenomenal changes in China over

the past thirty years. When communist regimes around the globe were teetering on the brink of collapse in 1989, China too faced its own crisis. The Party acted brutally to suppress the democracy movement, headquartered at Tiananmen Square. But this was hardly a political machine about to fall apart. Rather, the CCP continued to orchestrate one of the most spectacular periods of sustained economic growth in modern history. This kind of flexibility is a recognized strength of the CCP, and has enabled it to survive for so long. But it is also a liability. There is a danger that its own narratives about sacrifice, thrift, people power, and egalitarianism might lead to increased questioning of the CCP's performance in an era when the gap between rich and poor has widened considerably. Or, such tales might reinvigorate the Party to reexamine its policies and reemphasize its role in providing broad welfare for the people. Now more than ever the world will be watching China to see how this plays out.

SUGGESTIONS FOR FURTHER READING

On the Long March and Yan'an themselves, see Sun Shuyun, *The Long March* (Harper Perennial, 2007), Helen Praeger Young, *Choosing Revolution: Chinese Women Soldiers on the Long March* (University of Illinois Press, 2001), Chen Yung-fa, *Making Revolution: The Communist Movement in Eastern and Central China, 1937–1945* (University of California Press, 1986), and Mark Selden, *The Yenan Way in Revolutionary China* (Harvard University Press, 1971).

Works that set these events in context include Rana Mitter, *A Bitter Revolution* (Oxford University Press, 2004), Maurice Meisner, *Mao's China and After: A History of the People's Republic* (Free Press, 1999), Paul G. Pickowicz and Jeremy Brown (eds.), *Dilemmas of Victory: The Early Years of the People's Republic of China* (Harvard University Press, 2007). Overt reappraisals may be found in Tony Saich and Hans van de Ven (eds.), *New Perspectives on the Chinese Communist Revolution* (M.E. Sharpe, 1995) and Jeffrey. N. Wasserstrom, *Twentieth-Century China: New Approaches* (Routledge, 2003).

NOTES

1. Quoted in Michael Dutton, *Policing Chinese Politics: A History* (Durham, NC: Duke University Press, 2005), p. 75.

2. Mao Zedong, "On Tactics against Japanese Imperialism," December 27, 1935, in *Selected Works of Mao Tse-tung*, vol. 1, http://www.marxists.org/reference/archive/mao/selected-works/volume-1/mswv1_11.htm.

3. Mark Selden, *The Yenan Way in Revolutionary China* (Cambridge, MA: Harvard University Press, 1971).

    4. Du Guodong, "Marking Mao's Legacy in Yan'an," *China View*, September 29, 2009, http://news.xinhuanet.com/english/2009-09/29/content_12124657.htm
    5. Jeremy Brown and Paul G. Pickowicz, ed., *Dilemmas of Victory: The Early Years of the People's Republic* (Cambridge, MA: Harvard University Press, 2007).

20

Simplified Characters

Imre Galambos

The perception that simplified characters are of modern origin, although largely discredited by specialists, is still common among the general population. The Chinese script is among the most important inventions of Chinese civilization and one of the key elements by which the people in China to this day define their national identity. With a documented history of over three millennia, it lies at the core of the modern vision of historical continuity, and its significance goes far beyond merely being a means of recording language and reading former writings. This is why the simplification of the script in Mainland China has also been interpreted on both sides of the Taiwan Strait as a symbolic act of defining the PRC's new identity and distancing it from the past. Taiwan, Hong Kong, and Macau continued to use traditional characters and accordingly saw themselves as heirs to the rich cultural past that in their eyes had been discontinued in the PRC.

Because simplified forms were introduced in the People's Republic as part of an effort toward mass literacy, they are often regarded as a fundamentally modern development in the history of the script. In reality, however, most of these simplified forms have been in use in the handwriting tradition since early medieval times, and the number of genuinely new forms, without historical precedents, is small. Simplification of the Chinese script breaks with tradition only in the extent of the reform, that is, the number of characters changed within a relatively short time.

Before we proceed, we should address another idea found especially among people from Taiwan (mostly students), who seem to think that traditional and simplified characters represent different languages that are mutually unintelligible. This reflects a confusion between language, script, and orthography (that is, the particular form of the characters used). Regardless of whether something is written in traditional or simplified characters, the *language* of the text remains the same (typically Mandarin), as does its *script* (Chinese). What differs is the *orthography* of some of characters, which is not unlike the differences between the British and American spellings of some words (e.g., colour vs. color, centre vs. center, catalogue vs. catalog). One can freely switch between using simplified and full forms to write the text, without the slightest change to the language or meaning. The idea that different orthography creates different languages reflects the way some people see the differences between their own writing and language and those used by people across the Taiwan Strait.

BRIEF HISTORICAL BACKGROUND OF SIMPLIFICATION

The notion that Chinese writing was in need of a large-scale reform arose along with other reform ideas during the first decades of the twentieth century, at a time of great intellectual upheaval, when contacts with the outside world inspired changes in all spheres of society. In no small part due to military defeats and humiliating political concessions suffered at the hand of leading world powers, Chinese educators and reformers recognized that their country had fallen behind other nations and, in order to succeed, had to catch up. A good example for such a transformation was modern Japan, which had launched a set of reforms starting with the early years of the Meiji era (1868–1912) and by the turn of the century managed to emerge as a major power. In contrast, China, despite its size, was unable to stand its ground against foreign powers that exerted increasing control over the country both economically and politically.

Starting from the last years of the Qing dynasty, a number of writers and scholars had been advocating the simplification of writing, or even the abolition of the Chinese script in favor of a phonetic system. However, the first official step toward simplification happened in August 1935, when 324 new forms were published as the "First Batch of Simplified Characters." After only six months, however, the characters were withdrawn, ostensibly because of opposition by a high-ranking government official. Naturally, there were also other reasons behind the failure, both cultural and political.[1] After the establishment of the PRC in 1949, education and literacy became a central objective of the new government. As the first step toward simplification, with an ultimate goal of replacing the Chinese script with a phonetic alphabet, in January 1956 the State Council accepted a list of about 1,700 simplified characters. In 1964, drawing on experience from real-life handwriting habits, a second list totaling 2,238 characters was published. An even more radical "Second-Round Character Simplification" was introduced in 1977 as part of the leftist movement.

These new characters were, however, never successfully implemented. Finally in 1986 the State Council reissued a slightly modified version of the 1964 list as the official standard.

Whether the simplification of characters achieved its purpose of eliminating illiteracy is a question open to debate. While statistics testify to the success of this endeavor, it is unclear whether this was due to the simplification of characters or to a number of other nationwide educational programs. In addition, some have questioned the true rate of literacy, or even the definition of literacy, and the effect of the writing reform in this respect.[2]

The simplification of the writing system also had its opponents, many of whom perceived wholesale orthographic changes as an attack against traditional Chinese culture and tried to protest. In the politically heated atmosphere of the 1950s, however, as the reform initiative gained state support, these intellectuals exposed themselves to increasing criticism and were eventually compelled to silence. But Taiwan and Hong Kong, where the PRC government had no direct control, continued to use traditional characters, often seeing their simplified counterparts as a negative product of Communist ideology. Thus in Taiwan, where the traditional set of characters is the only officially sanctioned standard, the characters are often informally referred to as *zhengtizi* (characters with correct or orthodox forms), in contrast with the purportedly less correct and less orthodox forms used in the PRC.

SIMPLIFICATION AS A POLITICAL SYMBOL

The concept of simplified characters as a national standard is firmly linked with the People's Republic and its Communist government. In this sense there is a clear temporal divide between written material produced prior to the 1950s and newer writings. Individuals educated in the PRC cannot read books and magazines printed before the simplification without having specifically studied traditional characters. The situation is also true the other way around, as people who grew up in Taiwan have difficulties reading text in simplified characters without prior training. The association of simplified characters with new, and traditional ones with old (that is, traditional), culture is also reflected in our English-language terminology. We habitually contrast "simplified characters," which is the literal translation of the Chinese word *jianhuazi*, with "traditional characters," which refers to what in the PRC is called *fantizi* (characters with complex forms). This term in English carries the connotation that these complex characters are the "original" or "orthodox" forms, in contrast to the new ones.

However, the notion that simplified characters are of modern origin is not an academic interpretation but rather a passive assumption among the general population. Although history books invariably mention that vulgar forms in popular use served as one of the main sources for simplified character forms, many users of the script are unaware that nearly all of these vulgar forms, and not just a few exceptional cases, go back to early medieval times. The same unawareness is also shared by Western students of Chinese, many of whom do not know that simplified forms have a long history extending over a thousand years.

Today, with China's rapidly increasing presence on the Internet, simplified characters are becoming an everyday reality for most Chinese readers, regardless of where they live. Yet because of differences in education and cultural background, simplified characters often evoke strong sentiments, especially among those who grew up using traditional forms. Naturally, PRC readers are less critical of simplified forms, as they grew up using them. At the same time, after decades of using simplified forms in the PRC, traditional characters are once again becoming used and appreciated. While simplified characters persist as the official written script, there is a growing number of academic publications—especially in traditional fields such as history and classical literature—that use traditional characters. Shop signs, company logos, and advertisements also have a marked preference for employing unsimplified forms, no doubt because of their traditional connotations and aesthetic appeal.

On the level of language and writing, over the past decades simplified characters have become a symbol of Communist China. Indeed, they are one of the most visible cultural changes instituted by the PRC government. Yet while the enforcement of writing reform during the early years of the PRC was largely a political issue, the new character forms were not invented by the Communists. The majority are traditionally attested forms with orthographies dating to medieval times. They appear in medieval manuscripts from Dunhuang or early printed editions of the Buddhist canon, all of which fall within the Chinese written tradition. For example, the simplified version of the character 愛 *ai* ("love") written as 爱 without the "heart" 心 (*xin*) radical (in the middle of the traditional character), continues to be cited by opponents of simplified forms as a case illustrating their absurdity: what kind of love is the one without heart? Yet this particular form, along with several others, in fact appears—along with other variants lacking this radical—in medieval Buddhist manuscripts, showing that the omission of the "heart" radical is a tradition going back over a thousand years, and has nothing to do with modern ideology.

THE MEDIEVAL ORIGIN OF SIMPLIFIED FORMS

Proponents of simplified characters, on the other hand, at times overstate the antiquity of the forms, tracing some of them to the Warring States period (475–221 BCE) or even earlier. The character forms 无 *wu* or 从 *cong* are commonly cited examples, as these often occur, along with their traditional forms of 無 and 從, on bronze inscriptions or bamboo slips from at least the fourth century BCE. The similarity of these pre-Qin forms to modern simplified characters, however, is merely a coincidence, and they are related only indirectly, through numerous intermediate stages. In contrast, modern simplified characters are largely based on twentieth-century *suzi* (that is, vulgar, popular, or irregular) forms, which had been in common use in informal domains of writing, such as letters, memos, diaries, and other nonprinted material. These handwritten forms in turn go back to the medieval manuscript tradition of the Tang-Song periods (seventh to twelfth centuries), the golden age of the *kai* script, which essentially remains the common style in use today. The Song period is especially important with regard to the writing habits of our modern age, not only as it is closer to us chronologically but also because this was the time when printing became widespread, and printed characters emulated the hands of renowned Tang and Song calligraphers. It is perhaps not an exaggeration to claim that Song manuscript culture provided the foundation for the handwriting habits of the entire following millennium.

The existence of nineteenth- and twentieth-century vulgar forms matching characters in medieval manuscripts testifies to the continuity of the handwriting tradition. Because many of these forms were also considered nonstandard during the Tang-Song period, they were never taught in schools and their survival is due solely to the continuity of the handwriting tradition. For example, in the eighth-century orthographic dictionary *Ganlu zishu*, the graphs 虫 *chong* and 凶 *xiong* are listed as vulgar (*su*) forms, whereas 蟲 and 兇 are identified as standard (*zheng*) ones. Moreover, while the term *vulgar* or *nonstandard* might imply orthographic inconsistency, in fact these forms are not entirely haphazard but are also bound by convention, even if this has never been officially promulgated. Millions of people have written the same character the same nonstandard way: this is a convention, even if it is different from the officially endorsed orthography. On a practical level, one cannot write with a completely random orthography, as this would preclude others from being able to read the characters. In the case of vulgar characters an unofficial standard (that is, a tradition) developed through continuous use and interaction.

As an example of vulgar forms appearing in medieval manuscripts, consider the section from a Dunhuang manuscript shown in figure 20.1. Although undated, it was most likely written in the ninth or tenth century, and records a Buddhist prayer. Even in this small section we can see that a number of characters are written with forms matching modern simplified characters (無>无 [2:6; 3:2], 彌>弥 [2:7; 3:3], 來>来 [3:6], 號 >号 [5:8]).[3] However, there are other irregular forms that do not correspond to the modern standard. Thus the character 佛 *fo* appears as 仏 [5:6], which is the standard form used today in Japan. Other nonstandard forms in figure 20.1 (for example, 發 *fa* [1:7], 願 *yuan* [1:8], 等 *deng* [3:9]) are completely different from modern simplified characters. Finally, we can also see several characters (for example, 終 *zhong* [4:3], 變 *bian* [6:8]) that match the standard traditional characters which were used in China prior to the simplification, and are still used in Taiwan.

This Buddhist prayer testifies to the remarkable diversity of nonstandard character forms in medieval manuscripts, many of which were handed down informally through the process of copying texts, and survived to our modern age. An example of vulgar forms appearing in handwritten texts during the early twentieth century can be seen in figure 20.2, which features a Chinese translation of a travel account, with this particular copy having been completed around 1914. This section of the text illustrates several interesting phenomena: the characters 門 *men* and 謂 *wei* are written as 门

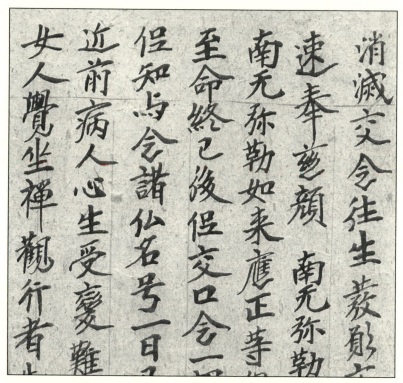

Figure 20.1. Section of a Dunhuang Manuscript. Copyright The British Library Or.8210/S.522. Image used with permission from the International Dunhuang Project's online database: http://idp.bl.uk, accessed on March 5, 2010.

[4:5] and 谓 [6:1], respectively, matching their modern simplified forms. The character 覌 *guan* [1:6] is written with 又 (*you*) as its left side, as in the modern simplified form, yet the component 見 (*jian*) on the right remains unsimplified—this form in fact matches the form for this character introduced in the short-lived simplification reform of 1935. Other characters (羅 *luo* [3:5], 漢 *han* [3:6], 籍 *ji* [6:2] and 禦 *yu* [6:6]) appear in their full traditional forms. Finally, the characters 得 *de* [1:3] and 處 *chu* [3:3] are using vulgar forms that had been around since the Tang dynasty but do not match their modern standard forms (得; 處 or 处). For example, the character 得 *de*, which is written the same way in both the PRC and Taiwan, consists here of the combination of the components 彳 + 导.

The forms appearing in this manuscript copy were all part of the handwriting habits of the early twentieth century. Yet most of them originated from the medieval manuscript tradition and have been in continuous use over the past millennium or so. Many of the same vulgar forms are also used in Taiwan, although they remain strictly in the informal domain of handwritten memos and letters, and never appear in print. In the PRC, at the time of simplifying the characters, the reformers borrowed from these nonstandard forms that were already known to and used by most literate people. Since the simplification also meant an enforcement of a new

Figure 20.2. Section from a Travel Account Copied around 1914 (Liu Jiaping, ed., *Zhongguo guojia tushuguan cang guji zhenben youji congkan* (Rare Travel Accounts in the Collection of the National Library of China) (Beijing: Xianzhuang shuju, 2003), vol. 1, p. 555). Image used with kind permission of the National Library of China.

standard, not all vulgar forms were included, especially when there were multiple forms for the same character. Sometimes vulgar forms were not adopted, even if this would have made perfect sense. For example, the popular form 仏 *fo* was commonly used in Tang-Song manuscripts instead of the character 佛 (although only in noncanonical texts such as commentaries or popular literature), yet the modern Chinese standard uses the traditional full form. In contrast with this, the form 仏 *fo* was adopted in Japan after 1945 and remains the standard way of writing the character there. This testifies to the somewhat arbitrary nature of the reform with respect to selecting simplified forms from the large pool of nonstandard forms in use. Only a portion of these were adopted and codified; the others remained in the informal domain and continue to be used unofficially in handwritten material.

SUMMARY

Contrary to a common assumption of nonspecialists that simplified forms have been mainly invented in Communist China, the vast majority of forms sanctioned by the simplification committees during the twentieth century derive from vulgar forms used in contemporary handwriting culture going back to early medieval times. These forms were familiar to most literate people at the time of the reforms and a sudden shift to this new standard was reasonably expected not to pose a major challenge. In turn, the handwritten forms of the twentieth century stem from the manuscript tradition of the Tang and Song periods, and in many cases have come down to us unchanged: the majority of modern simplified characters occur in medieval manuscripts from Dunhuang. At the same time, these documents also include many irregular forms that differ from the modern standard, bearing witness to the incredible orthographic diversity of manuscript culture. The simplified characters of the PRC merely adopted a large number of informal forms as the official standard. Yet with a thousand-year history, simplified characters cannot be regarded as a modern invention.

SUGGESTIONS FOR FURTHER READING

Roar Bökset, *Long Story of Short Forms: The Evolution of Simplified Chinese Characters* (Stockholm University Press, 2006), is a valuable, book-length treatment of the subject, in which historical overview is contrasted with field data. Bökset draws attention to the extraordinary diversity of informal handwritten forms used in China both before and after the reforms, many of which have been geographically restricted. He also shows that the enforcement of a simplified standard did not eradicate the use of forms not included in the new standard. This is by far the best book on the simplification of characters.

Chen Ping, *Modern Chinese: History and Sociolinguistics* (Cambridge University Press, 1999), points out the political motives behind reforms of language and writing, including the simplification of the script. Chapter 9, "Simplification of the Traditional Writing System," provides a general introduction to the subject, including its historical background and the pros and cons of the system. It is a useful summary of the vast literature regarding the reform.

Victor H. Mair, "Modern Chinese Writing," in Peter T. Daniels and William Bright (eds.), *The World's Writing Systems* (Oxford University Press, 1996), includes, after an introduction to the modern Chinese writing system, a "Comparative Table of Sinitic Characters," which is a convenient comparison of over a hundred character forms used in China, Taiwan, and Japan, in a visually accessible way. The reader can visualize the differences and similarities between these three most commonly used character sets, and see that at times the same character is written differently in all three regions.

Zhao Shouhui and Richard B. Baldauf, *Planning Chinese Characters: Reaction, Evolution or Revolution?* (Springer, 2007), deals specifically, in Chapter 1, "Making *Hanzi* Accessible: Three Simplification Movements in Modern Times," with the simplification of the Chinese script during the twentieth century. Although the book's statements regarding the historical evolution of Chinese writing are sometimes debatable, it nevertheless gives a detailed description of modern events, followed by analysis of the political and cultural forces behind them. It also displays a thorough familiarity with primary sources and secondary literature, and thus is useful reading for anyone interested in the subject.

NOTES

1. Zhao Shouhui and Richard B. Baldauf, *Planning Chinese Characters: Reaction, Evolution or Revolution?* (London: Springer, 2007), pp. 31–38.

2. John DeFrancis, *The Chinese Language: Fact and Fantasy* (Honolulu: University of Hawaii Press, 1984), pp. 214–215.

3. The first number in the brackets is the row number, counting from the right, and the second is the character number. Where the character occurs more than once, I use a semicolon to separate the instances.

21

The One-Child Policy

Barbara Mittler

If I had a second child, they would have taken away my bonus and the bonuses of everyone else in my work group. I would punish everyone. Moreover, I wouldn't get any raises in my salary or any extra coupons to support a second child. So, *when you have two children, your income would be even lower than if you had just one child.*

—Urbanite in her late twenties in 1980[1]

I was born in this environment, and, to me, it's always been like this. *People respect the policy and no one needs to challenge it because we don't want many kids anyway.* One child is good for couples. An only child is not hard to raise and doesn't give parents too much trouble. I do not want more than one. I know some people who don't want any children.

—Male urbanite, age twenty-four in 2005

In January 1979, the People's Republic of China (PRC), in an attempt to limit its rapid population growth to a manageable level, introduced what has become known as the "One-Child Policy." According to official statistics, the program has reduced the Chinese population by some 400 million, yet in spite of its obvious success and important effects on the growth of world population, and by association the global environment, this birth-planning policy has been controversial from the beginning. Critics inside and outside China have challenged it for violating human rights. It is condemned for its rigid, "dictatorial" implementation and due to concerns about its economic and social consequences. The policy has been held responsible for an increase in forced abortions and female infanticide, and it is considered the crucial factor behind China's growing gender imbalance

(with many more boys being born than girls). Critics fear the policy's del-
eterious effects on the physical safety of girls, on the psychological health
and behavior of children, and on the social system more generally. As the
policy comes of age, in its thirtieth year, its demographic effects are ever
more visible: China has an increasingly aging population and the One-
Child Policy is assumed to exacerbate this problem.

   There is criticism within China by policy makers and academics alike,
many of whom see no need to continue the policy, as the birth rate is fall-
ing drastically with increasing economic development, and the national
average is below the replacement level of 2.0 children. However, among
the Chinese public one finds an almost complete unawareness of the
controversy that the One-Child Policy has provoked. Indeed, many urban
residents, two of whom are quoted above, appear quite content with the
policy, and there is little popular protest in rural areas either. Why is this
so? Why do many Chinese agree with the restrictions that the policy im-
poses on individuals and their family planning? Why do they not abhor
the sexual discrimination that it entails? Why do they not consider the
demographic difficulties that the policy aggravates? Do they not see the
growth of all too many "Little Emperors"—spoiled children who may turn
out to be undisciplined, selfish, greedy, and disrespectful? This essay will
offer a rereading of some of the complex entanglements of social, cultural,
historical, geopolitical, demographic, and environmental and ecological
elements connected to China's One-Child Policy. It may thus serve to explain why statements like those above are typical, and why polls continue
to find support for the policy, not just in urban areas, but all over China:
the idea that the Chinese must hate the One-Child Policy appears to be
without foundation.

THE BEGINNINGS: MALTHUSIANISM AND MAOISM

Historically speaking, the 1979 policy, which has been called "one of the
greatest experiments in demographic control in world history,"[2] is yet another attempt in a daunting, Malthusian struggle that successive Chinese
governments have faced ever more intensively since the eighteenth century.
They have had to stabilize two key factors: access to resources—food among
them—and population growth. At the time that China came in contact with
early modern Europe, her population had grown to 150 million. Within
just one more century it was 300 million. By 1850, estimates would peg
China's population at around 450 million; by 1955, it was said to be 585
million. Until about 1960, it grew by an estimated annual average of 13
million, and from 1961 even more rapidly, by about 17 million people per
year. And yet, if up to 1970 fertility had been high and relatively stable at

about six births per woman, by the end of the 1970s the fertility rate had dropped to significantly fewer than six births. What had happened?

There have been (often contested) periods of pride in China's population size both in premodern and modern times: a large population can be both an asset and a danger. Throughout the 1950s, the Chinese leadership was divided over advice by leading sociologists such as Ma Yinchu, who warned of a Malthusian catastrophe if the asymmetrical relationship between food supply and population growth were disregarded. Throughout, the question of how to feed China's growing population remained troublesome to China's rulers, foremost among them the pro-natalist Mao Zedong. The *wan-xi-shao* or Later-Longer-Fewer campaign, first promulgated in 1970 by Premier Zhou Enlai, was an apparent compromise between differing views on population control: it advocated *later* (marriage), *longer* intervals (between births) and *fewer* (births per couple). By improving access to birth control techniques, it became increasingly possible for couples to realize these prescriptions. Thus, China's fertility rate dropped precipitously by the end of the 1970s.

The only apparently new policy of 1979 was simply a more forceful continuation of that earlier campaign. When foreign publications speak of it as the "One-Child Policy," they are picking up on one of its prominent slogans: "Giving birth to just one (child) is good" (*zhi sheng yige hao*). In Chinese, however, the policy is actually called, quite neutrally, the "Birth-Planning Policy" (*jihua shengyu zhengce*). Drafting of a national law had begun in 1978, but no such law was codified until 2001, so in effect central government left implementation of this policy to provincial and local governments, resulting in great variation in interpretation across time and space. From its very beginnings, however, it was never nationally enforced as a One-Child Policy but was characterized in its implementation by local diversity and exceptionalism.

NEVER JUST ONE CHILD? LOCAL DIVERSITY AND EXCEPTIONALISM

A map of China's birth rates today therefore shows (figure 21.1) two larger segments of about equal size, mostly rural and minority areas in Western and Central China, with an average rate of 1.5–2.0 and 2.0–3.5, respectively. The much smaller remaining segment could be divided again into a larger section featuring a birth average of 1.3–1.5, and another, the smallest, broadly spread over the eastern parts of the map—the segment featuring the greatest urbanization—with a birth rate of 1.0–1.3.[3] This map clearly illustrates that the so-called "One-Child Policy" has never really been enforced as such.

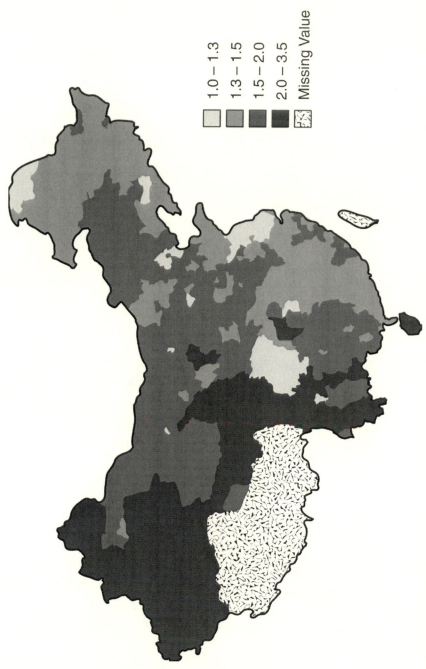

1.0 – 1.3
1.3 – 1.5
1.5 – 2.0
2.0 – 3.5
Missing Value

Figure 21.1. China's Birth Rates. From Wang Feng, "Can China Afford to Continue Its One-Child Policy?" Asia Pacific Issues 77 (2005): 3.

Indeed, it has been so far from being universally implemented that it is in fact untrue to say that Chinese families generally have been restricted to one child since 1979. Although all over China couples have been and continue to be encouraged to apply for the one-child certificate in order to participate in the scheme of benefits that accompany it (and about 63 percent of them do so),[4] many families have taken advantage, instead, of the numerous and locally divergent exception schemes. These allow, for example, for couples whose first child is a girl to have another child; for couples from minorities to have more than one, even more than two; and for couples made up of children with one-child certificates to have two; and so on. With these many exceptions in place, the "One-Child Policy" from its beginnings has been closer to being a "Two-Child Policy," although this fact may not have been well known to everyone, even within China.[5] And even today, the targeted goal of the One-Child Policy is a total fertility of 1.7 births per woman.

While the very use of the phrase "One-Child Policy" is ironic in itself, especially as employed by foreign media who thus use the Chinese Communist Party's own propaganda language, this usage is crucial to the policy's reception outside China. This in turn fosters the credibility of abominable stories of women killing their child from a first marriage in order to be able to have another after remarriage; of couples taking to hormone treatment to instigate multiple births that are exempt from punishment; of primitively executed abortions after a fetus has been identified as female; or of the pressures imposed on single children who are their parents' (and grandparents') white hope and who are therefore expected (and obliged) to do extremely well. The last of these stories usually highlights the enormous pressures on these children, allegedly causing a drastically increased suicide rate among those whose burden is exacerbated by their responsibility not only for their parents but for two sets of grandparents. And then there are reports on the public monitoring of menstruation tables, of surplus males searching for "appropriate" wives, or of kidnappings of boys.[6]

None of these stories is untrue, but they are more likely the exception than the rule. Each of them points to one or another of the major problems with the policy. Accordingly, workers in family planning are officially admonished "not to be too rigid," but instead to "become buddies" with the couples concerned and to "avoid demanding uniformity in everything."[7] Clearly, it is both necessary and feasible for China to practice de facto tolerance of an average birth rate of two. Such leniency answers to the fact that children remain crucial to the labor force in rural areas, for example; it is also based on concern about the care of old people in a society that has recently dismantled established systems of social security and offers only limited provision for the care of the aged. It may even be simply pragmatic: oftentimes local cadres have been quite dependent on collecting fines for "surplus" children to pay for much-needed local infrastructure projects. It is also no coincidence that crucial to a cadre's performance evaluation are elements other than rigidity in carrying out the One-Child Policy. Rather than trying to prevent excess births, cadres have used these as fund-raising tools, collecting penalties for infractions and investing them locally.

RECONSIDERING SEXISM, WOMEN'S EMANCIPATION AND THE ONE-CHILD POLICY

Finally, but most crucially only if one follows the news, tolerance regarding the One-Child Policy may be needed in the attempt to curb the effects of sexism (that is, the strong preference for male children) which continues to be lethal to female babies. Patterns of selective abortion, infant abandonment, and even infanticide indicate that girls continue to be less welcome as family members in China. However, it also turns out that prenatal sex selection may have reduced postnatal sex discrimination: official propaganda promoting girls and women has facilitated changes in social views and practices. Moreover, the new political economy has begun to cause change. Daughter-parent ties were traditionally weak after marriage because girls "married out" into a new family and had little relation with their own parents. But recently, "even" girls are turning out to be "useful" to their parents as they now provide more and better support to their elderly parents than before. Today's young married women have increased autonomy and can, if they wish, use this to strengthen ties with their natal families. The position of women in Chinese society is changing accordingly: girls who have survived infancy and not been abandoned to an orphanage were obviously wanted: they received just as much care as their male counterparts. The daughter-exception rule itself has begun to affect the way girls are perceived in Chinese society. Though the policy is born of son preference, it may eventually serve to equalize the value of girls and boys, rather than to reinforce girls' disadvantage.

Tolerance and leniency in applying the policy have worked well, and in view of the sharply declining birth rate in urbanized China it appears even more rational to practice them. Among the urban couples eligible under the current policy to have two children, the majority say that they have voluntarily chosen to have only one child, and they cite economic considerations as their primary reasons.[8] Even among minorities—officially permitted to have two children, and whose acceptance of the one-child certificate may thus be considered voluntary—one child is often the choice of the day.[9] The benefits of accepting a one-child certificate are quite attractive: they may include a health allowance for the child; allotment of more land; retaining more grain; longer maternity leave; larger food ration allocation; better housing; priority for child and health care; old-age pension; and preference in education, employment, and ownership of private land. The end of state-guaranteed employment and other benefits in the cities, from child care to pensions, means that the cost of child rearing has risen drastically. Thus many young couples voluntarily eschew having more children in response to economic and social pressures, and in accordance with their own personal career and life goals.

In China's larger cities—sites of cosmopolitanism and consumerism—career and physical appearance have become increasingly important for both women and men. In addition, work opportunities outside the family combined with growing levels of education mean that childbearing has become a lower priority for many. The birth-planning policy complements these developments. While it remains controversial to what extent opting for one child could also be considered a way of allowing women to achieve their goal of social equality, it is clear that a fundamental shift in perception has occurred. As the government's birth-planning policy is still in force, it is easy to jump to the conclusion that current low fertility is both caused and maintained by it, thereby ignoring fertility-depressing forces associated with economic and social transformations. As China's economy is increasingly integrated into the global economy, however, so is China's demographic regime: for nearly two decades China's fertility has been below replacement level: it appears that government control is no longer necessary to maintain low fertility. If China's birth-planning policy were to be phased out now, it would be unlikely to lead to an unwanted baby boom.

Naturally, not every Chinese agrees with the restrictions imposed by the policy. Some complain that due to the fine system, to stick to one or few children is economically more viable than to have more. Conversely, few would consider that to be a major concern: indeed, it is argued repeatedly that it is easier to take good care of just one child (or few of them), especially for independent and working parents (including mothers). Many also consider that it is better for China as a nation to restrict the number of children born.

GLOBAL CONSIDERATIONS

The demographic difficulties that the policy aggravates are problems shared with many industrialized countries, and internationally established solutions have been implemented more recently, with old-age facilities coming into prominence, not only in urban areas. Even sexual discrimination, currently a serious problem, with an evidently unbalanced birth rate of girls and boys, may eventually disappear: already we see a revaluation of girls and women not just in urban but also rural areas: as most grown-up daughters in China today are economically independent, they are considered better caretakers of their elderly parents than sons. Daughters thus become ever more desirable.

From a global perspective, too, the success of China's birth-planning policy is important: world population and demands on resources are significantly curbed. China has achieved dramatic results, creating a birth rate similar to that of developed nations. While the One-Child Policy is often criticized for abridging human rights, the Chinese government insists that a state must weigh an individual's rights against the welfare of society as a whole. This includes taking preventive measures to avoid possible famine, environmental degradation and pollution; should the welfare of one individual or his/her family be considered more important than that of the collective?

It appears—also from the opinions quoted above—that it is untrue that the One-Child Policy is abhorred in China: it is a majority view that the nation needs to control population growth. Even Chinese human rights activists, with rare exceptions, do not oppose the One-Child Policy. Such activists, themselves mostly relatively educated urbanites, share their government's aim to raise living standards by, among other means, reducing population. Under these circumstances, China's birth-planning policy seems not just legitimate but desirable, and not just from China's perspective. However, whether it is in fact necessary to enforce it in the rigid manner which has been applied until now, remains debatable.

SUGGESTIONS FOR FURTHER READING

Christopher Reed provides a thorough overview of the history of Chinese attempts at birth planning and population control in, "Malthusian Survivalism: The One-Child Policy and Its Importance in Limiting China's Population," *NIRA Review* (1998). Thomas Scharping's *Birth Control in China 1949–2000* (Routledge, 2003) surveys birth control policies and demographic change since 1949, while Tyrene White, *China's Longest Campaign* (Cornell University Press, 2006), studies the political dimension of these policies since 1949: How did the Communist Party impose birth control and why does it persist with it? For the period of Deng Xiaoping and before, Susan Greenhalgh, *Just One Child* (University of California Press, 2008) thoroughly describes the formation of China's One-Child Policy.

Cecilia Millwertz, *Accepting Population Control* (Curzon, 1997), is a classic study of the policy and its effects especially on women. Nie Yilin and Robert Wyman base their findings on a myriad of qualitative interviews with Shanghai couples expressing their views on the One-Child Policy: "The One-Child Policy in Shanghai: Acceptance and Internalization," *Population and Development Review* 31, no. 2 (2005), while Vanessa Fong studies a generation of single children and their social, economic, and psychological makeup in, *Only Hope: Coming of Age under China's One-Child Policy* (Stanford University Press, 2004).

Finally, Wang Feng argues against the need to continue with the One-Child Policy, in "Can China Afford to Continue Its One-Child Policy?" *Asia Pacific Issues* 77 (2005).

NOTES

1. The interview snippets quoted here are taken from Nie Yilin and Robert J. Wyman, "The One-Child Policy in Shanghai: Acceptance and Internalization," *Population and Development Review* 31, no. 2 (2005): 323, 325. My emphasis added.

2. Christopher A. Reed, "Malthusian Survivalism: The One-Child Policy and Its Importance in Limiting China's Population," *NIRA Review* (1998): 13.

3. This map is published in Wang Feng, "Can China Afford to Continue Its One-Child Policy?" *Asia Pacific Issues* 77 (2005): 3.

4. Zhenzhen Zheng, Yong Cai, Feng Wang, and Baochang Gu, "Below-Replacement Fertility and Childbearing Intention in Jiangsu Province, China," *Asian Population Studies* 5, no. 3 (2009): 330.

5. Significantly, the decisions allowing for exceptions nationwide (made in 1984 and 1988 respectively) were never directly reported to the Chinese people. See Susan Greenhalgh, "The Evolution of the One-Child Policy in Shaanxi, 1979–88," *China Quarterly* 122 (1990): 200.

6. These examples are based on a survey of the *Guardian* and its reporting on the One-Child Policy between 2005 and 2010.

7. Cf. John Bongaarts, "An Alternative to the One-Child Policy in China," *Population and Development Review* 11, no. 4 (1985): 588.

8. Zheng et al., "Below-Replacement Fertility and Childbearing Intention," 329.

9. Chai Bin Park and Jing-Qing Han, "A Minority Group and China's One-Child Policy: The Case of the Koreans," *Studies in Family Planning* 21, no. 3 (1990): 161–70.

22

The Cultural Revolution, 1966–1976

Marjorie Dryburgh

Was the Cultural Revolution a shocking aberration in China's modern history, or a logical outcome of Mao's revolution, or both? How closely was it controlled from above, and what did ordinary Chinese think about it? Did it hold back China's development, and was it the reaction against Cultural Revolution policies that pushed China into rapid modernization after 1976? This essay will suggest that, while the decade was marked by very visible and violent turmoil, we need to understand also that this was a complicated period, and that the experiences of those years affected different people in different ways.

Our understanding of the Cultural Revolution has been shaped by a wide range of sources. It appears as a formative experience in dozens of autobiographies and in recent Chinese literature and film; academic careers have been devoted to analyzing the politics, the economy, and the arts of those years. In these sources we face conflicting views that are not just different, but in some cases entirely incompatible with each other.

Mao Zedong and his supporters claimed, in Chinese government films, press releases, and propaganda posters, that the Cultural Revolution was a step toward socialist utopia; and public dissent from this or any other official view in China was almost impossible. Outside China, however, observers were reporting "purges," "struggle," and "chaos": an editorial in the London *Times* from January 1967 referred to "meaningless fanaticism," and "careless slaughter." The argument was established that the "Cultural Revolution" was a form of collective madness, or that it was simply a smokescreen for brutal power struggles led initially by Mao Zedong himself and his ally, Lin Biao, and later by the "Gang of Four," the radical group headed by Mao's wife, Jiang Qing. This was reinforced by episodes such as the two-year detention in Beijing of Reuters correspondent Antony Grey, and the publication of eyewitness accounts such as the polemic *Chinese Shadows* by Belgian scholar Pierre Ryckmans, writing as Simon Leys. After Mao's death in 1976 and the arrest of the Gang of Four, the "Cultural Revolution" became shorthand for everything that the Party wished to disown from its past, and it is not uncommon to find "development" in China today measured in terms of distance from Cultural Revolution thinking and practice.

The message of personal memoirs of the Cultural Revolution has been that the negative evaluations are the true ones; violence and suffering have also been central to many fictional narratives. Commonly told stories of the genre of "scar literature," and of films produced in China and overseas, underline the victimization of some who had been loyal servants to the revolution, as in Bertolucci's *Last Emperor* (1987) and Tian Zhuangzhuang's *Blue Kite* (1993), and the pressures that fear of persecution place on personal relations are central to the plot of Chen Kaige's *Farewell My Concubine* (1993) and Deng Yimin's *Troubled Laughter* (1979). We live in times when great value is attached to acknowledging the full truth of historical abuses and the suffering of victims, and the commemoration of those who suffered is a very common theme as the Cultural Revolution is discussed.

The majority view in academic writing has also been strongly negative. However, recent research emphasizes that the Cultural Revolution affected different people at different times in different ways. It would be impossible to cover these complexities in a short essay: instead, let us first sketch the movement's origins, and then focus on two commonly discussed questions: The question of violence against people allows us to consider the human costs of the Cultural Revolution and also the question of responsibility; the handling of education and culture allows us to see that the Cultural Revolution project was in some ways more ambiguous than it seems. Nor should we forget that the aftermath of those years is also a sensitive matter. As personal stories and photographs of the Cultural Revolution circulate in China, they evoke memories that differ widely, according to individual experiences: While some who grew up in the Cultural Revolution have prospered since 1978, economic reform has brought unemployment and inequality to others.

CHARTING THE CULTURAL REVOLUTION

The first steps toward "Cultural Revolution" were taken as an associate of Mao published a critique of a historical play, *Hai Rui Dismissed from Office* (for time line of events see figure 22.1). The play, by historian Wu Han, reworked the tale of an imperial official punished for telling inconvenient truths to his superiors. Commissioned in 1961 to discourage false reporting by local officials, the play was read in 1966 as an attack on Mao and his allies. A campaign was launched, first against Wu Han, then against officials accused of protecting him, then against an "anti-Party clique," and finally against "revisionism" in the highest levels of the Party. Calls for "Cultural Revolution" to restore ideological purity were followed by mass rallies in cities, the persecution of Mao's opponents, and upheaval led by radical "Red Guards" loyal to Mao in schools and universities (see time line). As senior figures such as Liu Shaoqi tried to control the universities, Mao aligned himself with the rebels and moved to isolate his critics.

Party infighting was mirrored in offices, factories, and neighborhoods by attacks on the "Four Olds" (thinking, culture, customs, and habits) and the search for "bad elements," who were evicted from their homes or "struggled" against at public rallies; tensions between Red Guard factions erupted into open fighting that persisted until many were sent to the countryside in 1968. By 1969, as the army moved to restore order in the cities, bitter power struggles had spread to rural areas. The balance of power in the Party shifted again after 1971 when Lin Biao—creator of the Mao cult of personality—was killed in a plane crash, allegedly fleeing China after a plot to assassinate Mao. There were also policy shifts, as moves were made to build relations with the United States and Japan, and some publishing restrictions were eased. Despite the launch of new campaigns—"Criticize Lin Biao, criticize Confucius" in 1974—and the heavy penalties attached to "counterrevolution," some popular dissent was also visible.

VIOLENCE IN THE CULTURAL REVOLUTION

The human costs of the Cultural Revolution were recognized in the Party's official judgment in 1981: "The Cultural Revolution . . . was responsible for the most severe setbacks and the heaviest losses suffered by the Party, the state, and the people since the founding of the People's Republic." Cultural Revolution violence was widespread and severe. Prominent victims included revolutionary veterans Liu Shaoqi (who was purged in 1966, and

Figure 22.1. Timeline of Cultural Revolution Events

1966	Cultural Revolution launched: formation of "Red Guard" groups on university campuses
1968	Millions of educated youth sent to the countryside
1969	Army moves to restrain Red Guard activity in cities
1971	Death of Lin Biao
1972	President Nixon visits China; normalization of relations with Japan
1974	"Criticize Lin Biao, criticize Confucius" campaign
1976	Death of Mao Zedong and arrest of "Gang of Four"

died in prison in 1969), Peng Dehuai (purged 1966, died 1974) and Deng Xiaoping (purged 1966 and 1975). Others targeted included artists such as novelist Lao She (committed suicide, 1966), and countless teachers, officials, workers, and students. Many victims were "bad elements"—former landlords, rich peasants, counterrevolutionaries—and their families; others were attacked because of their attitudes and opinions. Sometimes, what mattered most then was how those attitudes and opinions could be portrayed by people in power: accusations could not be challenged by pointing to material evidence that someone was not a "class enemy" or "capitalist roader." The high value attached to revolutionary fervor, as portrayed in figure 22.2, stifled concerns over the violence that many suffered.

Some evidence of the violence was produced covertly: press photographer Li Zhensheng took striking, illicit photographs of public rallies and meetings, concealing them for years before they were published in 1988; other evidence comes from the official press and from local histories published in China after 1978, indicating some official willingness to acknowledge abuses. However, this offers no simple explanations of that violence.

The central Party authorities appeared to condone the chaos, as official propaganda exhorted people to "smash the reactionary line" or to "bombard the capitalist headquarters." Mao Zedong has been singled out in this respect, but despite his undoubted influence, he was not alone in his tolerance of violence. Red Guard fighting in the cities, against authority figures and rival Red Guard factions, is well documented, and the spread of activism to the countryside was marked in places by mass killings of "bad elements."

What is less clear is the relation between central rhetoric and local action. New research on mass killings shows that these were much more common in some provinces than in others, and that most took place in rural areas where central state control was weakest, as local power holders moved to establish themselves, seizing on central pronouncements about the threat posed by class enemies to justify mass killings, while ignoring specific warnings to avoid "excessive" violence. The vagueness of central pronouncements undoubtedly (possibly deliberately) made it much easier to justify local violence; yet we need to consider why some local actors took fuller advantage of that than others, how we understand local responsibility for violence, and what the local social and political conditions were that made violence so much more common in some places than in others.

CULTURES OF THE CULTURAL REVOLUTION

The Cultural Revolution had an immediate and profound impact on education, scholarship, and cultural life. In schools and universities the authority of teachers and administrators over students was challenged, university

Figure 22.2. "Criticize the Old World and Build a New World with Mao Zedong Thought as a Weapon," http://chineseposters.net/gallery/e15-699.php.

entrance examinations were suspended, and scholars were subject to grow-ing political pressure and, in many cases, open persecution. Mass culture in theaters, cinema, and broadcasting was increasingly dominated by a hand-ful of approved works, prompting the grim joke, "eight hundred million people watching eight shows."

The impact of these changes is reflected in memoirs—most accounts translated into English were written by teachers, students, and other "in-tellectuals"—and in film and fiction. In the film *Blue Kite*, for example, the first clear signs that the boy Tietou sees of impending upheaval comes as classes are suspended and pupils drag the head teacher into the schoolyard and forcibly cut off her hair; in *To Live* the suspension of specialized medical training leaves hospital staff unable to deal with life-threatening emergencies.

We are told that the Cultural Revolution created a "lost generation" who were deprived of schooling, as ideology dominated teaching, the technical and scientific skills needed for economic development were not developed, and personal ambitions were unfulfilled. The film *Gaokao 1977* (*Examina-tion 1977*, released 2009) shows the hunger of a generation of high school graduates for university education once normal admissions resumed. It is easy to see this as a massive act of educational vandalism and to take ref-erences to revolutionary education and autodidacticism (see figure 22.3) far less seriously. This is the message of many of the Cultural Revolution memoirs published outside China, and studies of the post–Cultural Revo-lution life chances of those whose experience is typically reflected in those memoirs—highly educated, often the children of "intellectual" families, of-ten relatively privileged before the Cultural Revolution—confirm that they saw great costs and few benefits from those years. However, it is important to see the disruption of urban schools and advanced education in context: While changes in the cities have widely been reported in negative terms, rural educational reform may have had very different effects.

China faced difficult choices in the distribution of resources between elementary education for the many and advanced education for the few, a problem common to developing and developed countries. Education policy in the 1950s and early 1960s, drawing on the Soviet model, con-centrated funding on the higher levels of education to promote rapid economic development. It emphasized abstract learning over application and tolerated serious inequalities of access to elementary education, par-ticularly in rural areas. This was always controversial; and the demand that more "workers, peasants, and soldiers" be admitted to education reflected these inequalities as well as radical, Maoist ideology. Despite the disruption in urban schools, new rural schools were set up and more students were enrolled. Since 1978, however, resources have been shifted back to elite, urban, and advanced teaching; rural schools are often less well funded and

Figure 22.3. "The Brigade Reading Room," http://chineseposters.net/gallery/e12-124.php.

some remote communities experience serious problems in recruiting and retaining teachers: the problems of access to education have not gone away.

Suzanne Pepper argues that education between 1968 and 1976 was designed in outline by central guidance, locally managed and jointly funded; in some ways, it was highly experimental. Official statistics show a sharp rise in secondary enrollments, from major cities such as Beijing and Shanghai to rural areas of provinces such as Guangdong and Fujian, where the reach of education had previously been more limited. Schools now offered more practical, applied education, and middle-school study usually involved a manual labor or work-study assignment. The rigid examination system governing progress between school years and access to elite schools was abandoned: selection had been seen as a key guarantee of educational quality, and Pepper notes suggestions by some educators that expansion was achieved only by sacrificing educational standards.

Local studies of education reform challenge this interpretation. Pre–Cultural Revolution education, with its emphasis on college admissions and abstract skills, was ill adapted to the needs of rural China, and Cultural Revolution educational reforms were important in fostering rural economic development. While traditionally minded teachers distrusted the new emphasis on practice and application, and many educated young people resented being sent to the countryside, these reforms created a new pool of usable technical skills in rural areas that the pre–Cultural Revolution system simply had not developed. Han Dongping's work shows that the Cultural Revolution years in his fieldwork county were marked by rising literacy rates, by greater mechanization of agriculture that liberated farmers from backbreaking toil and improved rural diets as productivity rose, and by the establishment of growing numbers of industrial enterprises producing increasingly sophisticated goods for local use.

This more applied education motivated rural students. Where schools offered to equip students to meet the challenges that they expected to find at work, rates of enrollment and completion both rose. After 1978, the central authorities chose once again to focus funding on elite, "key point" schools designed to prepare students for the college entrance examination system; new rural schools were closed and the take-up of education declined in many rural counties. Cultural Revolution education policy was very effective in places in its core project of extending access to basic and technical education. That progress is in stark contrast, though, with massive costs to the urban education system and some of its students and teachers. New studies raise important questions for future investigation into Cultural Revolution education and its socioeconomic impact; the policy question on the distribution of educational funding remains a pressing one today.

Studies on other areas of cultural life similarly indicate that the stories of rigid uniformity may not reflect the whole picture, particularly by the early

1970s. On one hand, it is well established that Cultural Revolution attacks on scholars and scholarship continued and intensified a trend established far earlier: obituaries of the eminent sociologist Fei Xiaotong (1910–2005) record the destruction of his papers and his exile to the countryside in 1969, but point also to the suppression of sociology as a discipline and the persecution of Fei as an individual that dated from the 1950s. On the other hand, new research on the history of paleoanthropology, the science of human origins, shows a genuine commitment by some scholars to popularizing their findings and to creating a "mass science." Popular engagement revealed tensions between experts and the public and exposed scientists to criticism as the public interpreted scientific ideas in the light of Marxist-Leninist thinking, yet the discussions suggest that some readers were as willing to think critically about socialist orthodoxies as others were to rebuke the scientists. Finally, recent studies of film, theater, fine arts, and literature have cast doubts on some earlier judgments about the cultural life of the Cultural Revolution: Although Simon Leys dismissed Cultural Revolution drama as "a handful of models that eight hundred million people now know by heart, but that have not yet generated a single imitation," more recent work has shown that, despite the stifling orthodoxy of state-sponsored culture, the encouragement of amateur production fostered regional adaptations of official works, as well as an emerging underground cultural scene.

The Cultural Revolution is still difficult to research. However, recent work has done much to develop our understanding of those contentious years and to raise new questions. It has confirmed, for example, that persecution of individuals was widespread but that we need to think about how we understand those abuses, questions of responsibility, and the long-standing tensions and divisions that provoked violence in different places and times. Studies of educational reform emphasize the genuine inequalities that it addressed and some of the constructive aspects of reform for previously neglected rural areas. Research on science and the arts indicates that mass engagement was taken seriously by some and that this paradoxically may have allowed some variation on the ideological orthodoxies that some accounts of the Cultural Revolution have presented as set in stone.

SUGGESTIONS FOR FURTHER READING

Online

China in 1972—a collection of photographs taken by Professor William A. Joseph, Wellesley College, during a research visit to China, http://www.wellesley.edu/Polisci/wj/China1972/intro.html

Chinese Posters 1925—Present: Propaganda, Politics, History—from the collection of Professor Stefan Landsberger, held at the International Institute of Social History, Amsterdam, http://www.chineseposters.net/

The Cultural Revolution—University of Maine booklist, updated 2008, http://hua.umf.maine.edu/China/culturr.html

Morning Sun—companion to the film of the same name, this site collects texts, images, and audiovisual materials from the Cultural Revolution, http://www.morningsun.org/

Picturing Power: Posters of the Cultural Revolution—from the collection of the University of Westminster, UK, http://kaladarshan.arts.ohio-state.edu /Exhibitions/picturingPowerExhibit.html

Red-Color News Soldier: An Exhibition—photographs of public meetings taken illicitly by photojournalist Li Zhensheng, http://red-colornewssoldier.com/

The Cultural Revolution on Film

Farewell My Concubine (dir. Chen Kaige, 1993)
The Blue Kite (dir. Tian Zhuangzhuang, 1993)
To Live (dir. Zhang Yimou, 1994)

Memoirs and Eyewitness Accounts

There are numerous Cultural Revolution memoirs. The best known is probably Jung Chang's *Wild Swans* (1992); but there are many more useful works than can be mentioned here. Most works available in English were written by Chinese who have since left to live outside China, though memoirs of the period are also published in China. The earliest examples, reflecting the experience of the Red Guard generation and their parents, include Liang Heng, *Son of the Revolution* (1984) and Nien Cheng, *Life and Death in Shanghai* (1988); and later, Anchee Min, *Red Azalea* (1995); Rae Yang, *Spider Eaters: A Memoir* (1998). Two more recent books reflect the younger child's perspective: Chun Yu, *Little Green* (2005), a book of poems, and Chen Jiang Hong, *Mao and Me* (2008), a picture book. Simon Leys's *Chinese Shadows* (1974) is partisan and extremely contentious, but it is probably the most readable of the contemporary foreign critiques of the Cultural Revolution.

Academic Work

There are many fine scholarly works on the Cultural Revolution. This essay has been informed by research published by the following: Roderick McFarquhar, Michael Schoenhals, Wang Shaoguang, Yang Su, and Philip Huang on Cultural Revolution politics and violence; Suzanne Pepper, Joel Andreas, Han Dongping, Paul Clark, and Sigrid Schmalzer on education and culture; and David J. Davies and Mobo Gao on Cultural Revolution memory.

23

China's Political System

Hai Ren

The image of China as a communist state comes from two major sources. First, the Chinese Communist Party (CCP) has been the only ruling party in China since the late 1940s when it established the People's Republic. Unlike the Soviet Union and other Eastern European communist governments that collapsed at the end of the cold war, the CCP still appears to maintain its absolute authority and power in the Chinese government. In recent years, communist parties from countries such as Russia, Vietnam, Cuba, and North Korea have been eager to learn from the CCP about how to maintain or regain power over their governments. Second, in North America and Western Europe, we commonly equate democracy with capitalism and authoritarianism with communism. When the media report such issues as human rights, citizens' protests, and government controls in China, for example, they usually portray China as an antidemocratic, authoritarian, and communist state. This kind of media representation also contributes to the idea that China is a communist state.

To challenge this notion, we need to develop a critical understanding of important events and activities that mark historical breaks in modern and contemporary Chinese history. It is undeniable that China has undertaken an unprecedented transformation since 1978, whether in terms of economic development, improved standard of living, or individual freedom of expression. China also plays an increasingly important part in the global economy, international affairs, and global security. However, we need a more nuanced understanding of the CCP's historical transformation, especially of how changes to the CCP are tied to the reconstitution of the Chinese nation-state. In the following, my discussion will demonstrate how the Communist party-state shifted from its original mission of only

representing the working classes to the current constitution that encompasses the representation of capitalists and private property owners. Once
we understand this radical change, we can answer the question of whether
China is still communist or a different kind of state.

THE PROLETARIAT STATE

From its establishment in 1921 to its reforms beginning in the late 1970s,
the leaders of the CCP faithfully followed the Russian leader Vladimir
Lenin's theory of the proletariat state—the way in which the proletariat
could establish their own state through revolutionary struggles. Practically, this means that the Party engaged in revolutionary struggles to overthrow the old state and establish a new one that politically represented
only the proletariat. Under the guidance of the Third International of
the Communist Party (also known as "the Comintern," an organization
established by Lenin in 1919), this historical mission was written into
the Party's founding agenda and was further developed by Party leaders.
In the CCP's history, Mao Zedong played the key role in theoretically articulating the CCP's role within the framework of the proletariat state. He
extended Lenin's theory to define the Chinese proletariat in terms of the
figure of the peasant after investigating the living conditions of peasants
in Hunan in 1925–1926. In his 1929 letter to Li Lisan, a prominent CCP
leader who believed that the CCP should focus on urban workers' struggles, for example, Mao argued: "For in the revolution in semi-colonial
China, the peasant struggle must always fail if it does not have the leadership of the workers, but the revolution is never harmed if the peasant
struggle outstrips the forces of the workers."[1] Thus, for Mao, the peasant
represented an important figure of the Chinese proletariat.

During the war against the Japanese invasion (1937–1945), Mao published a long essay entitled "New Democratic Theory" (1940) in which he
considered the Chinese revolution as part of a worldwide revolution. Compared with the bourgeois revolutions in Europe and the Bolshevik Revolution in Russia, Mao argued, the Chinese revolution was unique because it
took place in "a semi-colonial, semi-feudal state," which had formed since
the first Opium War in 1840. The CCP gradually emerged as the leader
in this revolution after a series of failures by other groups, including the
Nationalist Party under the leadership of Sun Yat-sen. For Mao, it was the
CCP's historical responsibility to take the lead in radically revolutionizing
the semi-colonial, semi-feudal state. A key to the success of this revolution
was to build a new state that completely replaced the old one.

On the eve of the establishment of the People's Republic, Mao wrote
another important essay, "On the People's Democratic Dictatorship" (June

30, 1949), to commemorate the CCP's twenty-eighth anniversary. This article outlined two fundamental principles of the new socialist state: (1) it was organized under "the leadership of the working class"; and (2) it would ally itself with the world proletariat of the socialist countries. These two principles permeated the government policies of socialist China. In the 1950s, Mao's government eliminated all forms of private ownership and their associated productive relations. Many capitalists, especially those who owned factories, left the mainland for Hong Kong and Taiwan. Those who stayed—like the landowners in the countryside—were deprived of their private property and capital. Meanwhile, the populations, including government officials and ethnic minorities, were classified into various class groups. To delineate clear boundaries between the people and the enemy and between the working class and their associated classes (for example, intellectuals), class struggle became a dominant practice in everyday lives. During the Cultural Revolution (1966–1976), Mao's government attempted to follow the principle of the working class as "the master of the state" to radically transform the way in which the state operated. At that time, Mao believed that the state was shifting away from its sole purpose of existence, which was to represent "the people" (*renmin*) or the working classes. Mao's death in 1976 opened up an opportunity for other CCP leaders to reformulate the Party's principles of representation.

GOVERNANCE TO ACHIEVE ORDER

The CCP leaders engaged in a heated debate in reassessing the historical role of the Cultural Revolution and the role of Mao in the Chinese Revolution. Deng Xiaoping's government declared the Cultural Revolution a complete failure that caused chaos in the Chinese state. This decision was codified through passage of the Communiqué of the Third Plenum of the Eleventh Central Committee of the Communist Party of China in 1978. Once the Cultural Revolution was rejected, a whole sequence of practices associated with Mao as a political leader, Maoism, and Mao's socialist experiment were reevaluated. By 1989 when the government repressed the social movement led by college students' demonstrations around the country, the Maoist state's politics of the working classes, as practiced in the Cultural Revolution, was finally displaced by a new politics of governing the population only for the purpose of maintaining a coherent order in the nation-state.

The development of this new governmental strategy, as I will show below, means that the Communist Party–controlled Chinese state became able to serve the capitalists who were rejected by the Maoist state. In 1978, Deng Xiaoping's government launched "reforms and opening," a process intended to revitalize the Chinese economy. After a series of heated debates about whether a market economy was socialist or capitalist, the government soon realized that economic development ultimately must reinforce and strengthen the leadership of the CCP in ruling the Chinese state. Over the years, economic reforms have enabled state-owned enterprises to become more efficient and effective. They have also allowed the development of private enterprises. In the political realm, the government's representation of the capitalists and legitimation of private property ownership has required radical changes to the state's constitution. This has taken place through the process of managing national reunification issues, which revolve around the status of Hong Kong, Macau, and Taiwan.

The reincorporation of capitalist Hong Kong into socialist China, an event that took place during the same period of economic reforms (1978–1997), has done what no other contemporary event could have done: it provided both the historical precondition for and the primary process of China's political reconstitution, which involved legal representation for the capitalists. Under British rule, Hong Kong was recognized not simply as a capitalist economy, but as one of the freest market economies in the world. The Sino-British Joint Declaration of 1984 that set out the conditions for Hong Kong's return to China (in 1997) called for Hong Kong to retain its capitalist system and a measure of political autonomy for a period of fifty years, a provision commonly referred to as "one country, two systems" (*yiguo liangzhi*) and viewed by the Chinese as a potentially long-term arrangement. This framework was first proposed by Deng Xiaoping during the Sino-British negotiation process in the late 1970s. It was later extended to create various types of special economic and political zones, enabling practical coexistence between socialist and capitalist spaces. Beginning in 1980, the government established a series of four special economic zones in Guangdong and Fujian provinces, where nonsocialist systems—not only private markets but also private controls of the economy and the population—were developed. In 1984, the year of the signing of the Sino-British Joint Declaration, the government expanded the special economic zone concept to another fourteen coastal cities and to Hainan Island. Deng Xiaoping's visit to the special economic zones in 1992 reaffirmed economic development as the "indisputable truth" of China's future, and the development of capitalist economic zones became the national norm. Throughout the 1990s, many priority development regions and export processing zones were established across the country. In 1997, Hong Kong became the first special administrative region of the People's Republic of China, and two years later, Macau became the second.

Parallel to the normalization of capitalist economic zones is the proliferation of numerous privately controlled zones through urban real estate development projects. Each of these was to be structured around a concept, such as a high-tech park, an ethnic town, a theme park, a shopping mall, a gated community, a business center, and the like. As each city becomes a collection of these built environments, the drama of market experimentation wrestles with the disjunctures arising between socialist and capitalist modes of social relations. In urban residential real estate, for example, the shift toward private ownership has explicitly resulted from changes of governmental policies. As early as 1988, the National People's Congress (NPC) amended the constitution to allow the transfer of land use rights. Urban housing began to be seen as a commodity. In 1990, the NPC passed an ordinance allowing cities to sell long-term leaseholds on state land and retain the profits. Next year, the State Council announced that home ownership should become the norm among urban residents. The process was led by big cities such as Shanghai and Guangzhou. The most decisive policy shift came in July 1998, when State Council Circular No. 23 announced that, as of year's end, employers would be out of the housing business. By 2002, the government announced that 80 percent of previously collectively owned housing stock was in private hands. Practically, the socialist system of welfare housing had vanished, and the bulk of urban housing stock had become capitalized, privately owned assets.

The legal framework of one country, two systems, upon being translated into political and economic practices in China, shaped the reconstitution of the Chinese state. By casting reunification with Hong Kong as an uncompromisable issue of national sovereignty, the Chinese government made this a default justification for all political, economic, social, and cultural changes. To represent new groups of the people like the capitalists from Hong Kong and private property owners, the CCP has had to modify its party constitution and amend the national constitution. Thus, in 1998, less than a year after Hong Kong's return (on July 1, 1997), Jiang Zemin, the secretary-general of the CCP and the president of China, asked Party members to propose new theories to account for the new political representation. In 2000, he proclaimed "Three Represents" (*sange daibiao*) as the new theory of political representation. According to this, the CCP represents "the developmental requirement of the advanced productive forces in China," "the progressive direction of the advanced culture in China," and "the fundamental interest of the vast majority of the people."[2] In 2003, the Third Plenum of the Sixteenth Central Committee of the Communist Party of China formally incorporated this theory into the revised Party constitution. Meanwhile, the Chinese government formally changed its English translation from the Chinese Communist Party to the Communist Party of China (CPC). Therefore, when the Three Represents and property rights became formally institutionalized, the transformation of the Communist Party–led state from a state of the working classes to one that encompasses new classes (including the capitalist class) was completed.

The development of capitalist spaces such as special economic zones and their associated social relations has allowed some Chinese to accumulate

wealth very rapidly. Past and present Communist Party officials and their relatives have more access to opportunity for accruing wealth. For them, capitalist
practices unfold a horizon of "freedom" to pursue a lifestyle oriented toward
cosmopolitan or international norms. In Beijing's real estate, for example, one
can visit Chateau Zhang Laffitte, a 1.5-square-mile estate modeled after Chateau Maisons-Laffitte, a landmark designed by the French architect Francois
Mansart (the creator of Versailles) in 1650. This $50-million private palace
was built by Zhang Yuchen, a fifty-eight-year-old Communist Party member
and former senior official at Beijing's municipal construction bureau. Zhang's
wealth was accumulated through building and selling California-style single-
family houses in the Changping District, a suburb of Beijing.

In contrast, those who lack access to social and political capital are affected negatively. They become marginalized as subjects in need, whether
as landless peasants or laid-off workers. Rapid urban growth and construction projects across the country often demand the demolition of old,
low-rise, and relatively cheap buildings and their replacement with new,
high-rise, and significantly more expensive buildings. Conflicts between
developers and property owners appear frequently in the media and on the
Internet. Moreover, as developers acquire land from surrounding rural areas
for their projects through deals with rural officials, the farmers who have
collectively worked the land under socialism have been dispossessed. As
many as seventy million farmers have lost their land to development over
the past decade. They now form a category of the new poor who have lost
their livelihoods as an effect of the economic reforms. Some of them have
joined the flow of migrant laborers to the global factories located around
major cities and in the development zones.

CHINA'S TRANSFORMATION

By 2004, government officials and scholars in China began to discuss consequences of China's transformation. The Chinese economist Yu Wenlie
summarizes four major problems:

1. The increasing gap between the rich and the poor challenges the socialist distribution system.
2. The privatization of state-owned enterprises and "state-owned assets"
   contradicts the socialist "collective ownership system."
3. The government's "malfunctions" or "misbehaviors" in the market
   damage the socialist market economic system.
4. "The urban-rural twofold economic structure" and the increasing economic gaps between regions caused the unbalanced development of
   the national economy.

These shifts have turned Chinese society from one of the world's most equal societies to one of its most unequal. China has become a risk society in which responsibility for employment, welfare, education, health, poverty alleviation, and environment have become redistributed from government to nongovernmental organizations and from the collective to the individual.

It is in this new social, economic, and political context that president Hu Jintao in 2005 proposed the framework of the "harmonious society" (*hexie shehui*) as the emphasis of the government. It covers six aspects: democracy and the rule of law, fairness and justice, sincerity and friendliness, full-scale vitality, stability and orderliness, and harmony between humans and nature. Scholars and policy makers use this formulation to debate the proper way to address the problems of increasing socioeconomic inequality. "Free market" economists argue that the current existence of inequality, despite being a problem of social harmony, should be maintained for the sake of developing a more "efficient" society, even if this means that some must be sacrificed. Scholars on the left, by contrast, argue for the elimination or amelioration of the effects of inequality so as to pursue the idea of the harmonious society. Despite holding different positions on the problem of social inequality, both sides generally share a common concern about the urgency for developing a middle-class society as a way of safeguarding the stability and security of the Chinese state.

Based on the above historical understanding of major changes of the transformation of the Chinese state, it would be reasonable to argue that China in the twenty-first century is not a communist state that only represents and serves the working classes. Nor is it a capitalist state as legitimized by such principles as democracy and liberty. Instead, China is now a *neoliberal* state, which refers to both the Chinese nation-state under a hybrid capitalist-socialist system, and China as a country where economic rationalism penetrates all aspects of society, even domains such as the political and the cultural that are usually incommensurable or incompatible with the economic realm. The transformation of China from a communist or socialist country to a neoliberal state was made historically possible by the Chinese government's resumption of sovereignty over Hong Kong in 1997 and politically practical by the fundamental changes of the way in which the Communist Party represents the people of China.

SUGGESTIONS FOR FURTHER READING

Jonathan D. Spence's *The Search for Modern China* (Norton, 1999) offers a useful general account of modern Chinese history. Wang Hui's

"Depoliticized Politics, from East to West," *New Left Review* 41 (September–October 2006) gives a sophisticated statement of political changes from the late 1970s to the early 1980s. Hai Ren's *Neoliberalism and Culture in China and Hong Kong: The Countdown of Time* (Routledge, 2010) provides an in-depth analysis of the connections between the reconstitution of China and the historical event of Hong Kong's return to China in 1997.

NOTES

1. Jonathan Spence, *The Search for Modern China* (New York: Norton, 1999), p. 388.

2. *Renmin ribao* (*People's Daily*), May 16, 2000, p. 1.

24

Tiananmen 1989

Fabio Lanza

On the night between June 3 and 4, 1989, the tanks of the People's Liberation Army crushed (with literal brutality) a popular movement that, for
seven weeks, had focused the world's attention on Beijing's Tiananmen
Square. Starting on April 15, when the first groups of Beijing residents
gathered in the Square to commemorate the death of the former Chinese
Communist Party (CCP) secretary, Hu Yaobang, the demonstrations caught
everybody—including the Chinese government—by surprise. And this allowed for a brief relaxation of the grip of censorship: the protests, which
by April 21 drew hundreds of thousands of people into the streets of the
capital, were shown on Chinese national television and reported in Chinese
newspapers. Western media quickly followed suit and in May, when foreign
journalists moved into Beijing en masse to report on the first Sino-Soviet
summit since the 1950s, they ended up telling the story of a popular protest instead. For weeks, evening newscasts in half of the world opened with
reports from Tiananmen.

It is difficult to overestimate the role of the media not only in the evolution of the events of 1989—the protestors quickly realized that they
were being filmed and demonstrations assumed even more the form of
political theater staged for the Chinese and the global audience—but also
in our understanding of the movement. The protestors and the world media had to construct a narrative while the events were still unfolding and
the situation was very confused. Out of their serendipitous collaboration
came a story that still circulates today: Tiananmen 1989 was a student
movement for democracy.

This narrative emerged through oversimplifications, purposeful self-
representation, simple mistakes, and a winnowing out of discordant voices.

It also proceeded from a particular view of the evolution of Chinese politics and society in the previous decade. Many Western commentators had before conveyed the idea that Deng Xiaoping, leader of the CCP, was indeed moving China forward, and that the economic reforms he had initiated in 1978 represented just the first step of a process of transformation toward a "liberal," "democratic" China. The students' calls for "democracy" and the "rule of law," then, were seen to embody a proreform statement, in opposition to an "antireform," conservative faction within the Communist leadership. After the June 4 massacre, media commentators and experts of all sorts expressed very bleak views on the future of China. If the 1989 protests reflected a fight between proreform and antireform factions within the Chinese government, June 4, they argued, meant the victory of the antireform conservatives. As a consequence, the process of change would forever be halted, Deng's legacy would be forever bloodied, and the events of 1989 would be both unforgettable and unforgivable.

Twenty years later, it is obvious that those forecasts were wrong. And in large part, they were wrong because they moved from an assessment of the protests that was meant to fit a news soundbite rather than being the result of an accurate analysis.

STUDENTS AND CITIZENS

The view of Tiananmen 1989 as a "student movement for democracy" was produced and is still perpetuated largely by Western media: academic publications and even firsthand journalistic accounts have since offered more nuanced depictions. Moreover, unlike most of the other issues discussed in this volume, 1989 is principally a Western obsession. It can be remembered and reproduced only outside the People's Republic of China, because any discussion of Tiananmen 1989 within the country is still political taboo.

There was a specific moment in the early days of the protest that synthesizes both the construction of a particular view of the movement and its contradictions. It took place on the day of Hu Yaobang's funeral, April 22. It was a strange scene: inside the Great Hall of the People, the somber and rushed farewell to an already deposed leader was taking place. Outside, the actual people, hundreds of thousands of them, had gathered to offer their homage. From the crowd, three students moved out, carrying a petition; they climbed the stairs of the Great Hall, and in a very iconic gesture, they knelt down. There was no contact at this stage between the two sides; nobody came out to receive the petition. However, the scene was highly symbolic. By kneeling down, as imperial subjects, the students were indirectly indicating that the communist state was just another incarnation of the Chinese Empire of old. But also, by presenting a petition to the new emperors, they were claiming for themselves not just the position of generic subjects, but of loyal and upright imperial officers: they were inscribing themselves in a tradition of intellectuals' participation in government that went back hundreds of years. The kneeling scene was then directly communicating two things: the government was not listening to the people and the students were claiming for themselves the role of representatives of the people.

Accordingly, the demonstrations were immediately labeled a "student protest," but, when we talk of hundreds of thousands of participants, it is quite obvious that these were not all "students." Rather, to the chagrin of the government, people from all walks of life joined them in the Square, including a sizable contingent of workers. Likewise, in the following weeks and months, while students organized and were in the forefront of the movement, all of their initiatives—from the marches of April 27 and May 4, to the hunger strike and the occupation of the Square from May 13—would have been unthinkable without the active involvement of the general citizenry in a much larger social upheaval. We can thus dispel the first part of our simplified narrative: Tiananmen 1989 was *not just* a student movement. Rather, it is precisely in this reductive label that we can see one of the crucial contradictions of the 1989 Spring, the disparity between those who represented the movement (students) and the diverse interests they embodied and reflected: those of workers, small merchants, and citizens at large. People gathered in April and May to voice a shared dislike of corruption and a shared fear for the future; they found the banner of "democracy" carried by the students wide enough to include their specific grievances. But the vagueness of these code words masked what were sometimes radically different understandings of the nature of China's predicament, and conflicting ideas of what the post-Mao reforms meant. Therefore, to catch a glimpse of what the Spring of 1989 was about, we have to start from the so-called reform era.

THE IMPACT OF THE REFORM ERA

The protests of 1989 came after a decade of massive changes. In 1978, two years after the death of Mao Zedong, Deng Xiaoping was the undisputed leader of the party-state, and he launched a program of reforms with the stated goal of "modernizing" the country. The reforms configured a complete reversal of the socialist system of production and a gradual shift toward a market economy. This transformation was to happen in stages, and always under the control of the state and the CCP.

Up to 1984, the reforms were largely limited to the countryside. The rural communes of the Mao era were dismantled, collective ownership erased, fields were parceled out and allotted to families, and local markets were reestablished, while the state remained the largest buyer of rural products. Production increased, prices of rural products went up, and the state encouraged the development of local enterprises in the countryside, which prospered. Farmers were better fed, better housed, better off.

In these first few years of the Deng era, very little was done to alter the situation in the cities. The main reason was that it was a complex and integrated system. Everything in the socialist city depended on the workplace (or *danwei*), be it a hospital, a school, or one of the huge urban industrial enterprises. The workplace provided lifetime employment, usually referred to as the "iron rice bowl." With that came health care, schooling for children, and food stamps for the basic commodities, like flour and rice. The price of other commodities was fixed by the state. To introduce even a few elements of a market economy was going to produce massive shocks to the lives of city residents.

In 1985, new policies were launched based on the premise of the separation of politics from management: that is, the state and the party abdicated direct control of enterprises to their managers, while at the same time creating a partially free labor market for new employees and allowing for a two-price structure. Starting in 1985, a very strange and confusing system developed in the cities: you still had commodities at fixed prices and others at market prices; you had an army of "lifetime" workers clinging desperately to their "iron rice bowl" while new younger workers were hired without any of those guarantees; more importantly, you had the perfect breeding ground for corruption. Deng had said "To get rich is glorious." "Somebody," he had added "will get rich first." Not surprisingly, the people who got rich first were the politically connected technocrats, as well as the sons and daughters of the Party leaders.

In the meantime, city people were not faring well. Since 1985 urban residents had experienced raging inflation: sure, there were more commodities available, but many, if not most, were priced out of the reach of the average Chinese. Frustration was compounded by a growing sense of fear and insecurity: the commoditization of labor initiated in 1985 was a harbinger or more radical changes to come. The media discussed openly the smashing of the "iron rice bowl." This affected not only workers, but everybody employed by a state enterprise, including low-level officials: their purchasing power already slashed by inflation, they faced a near future without any safety net at all.

But there were also those who were dissatisfied with the current state of the reforms for completely different reasons. The government leadership was aware of the social price of the transformation it had started and moved with extreme caution. Therefore, in the late 1980s, the pace of the reforms proceeded slowly and haltingly. Too slowly to satisfy managers, interest groups, entrepreneurs, and those intellectuals working within the state: they were unhappy not because of the social costs of the reforms, but because of the continuous adjustments and slow pace of change. They wanted full privatization, full pricing reform, and a completely unobstructed labor market. Like many of the urban residents, they were in support of the reform project, but rather than decrying its social effects, they were pushing the government to ignore them.

Among the dissatisfied and the disgruntled, intellectuals occupied a special place. In the early years of the Deng era, intellectuals were the most vocal and enthusiastic supporters of the reforms. What Deng had promised under the name of "modernization" was a technological, scientific, and economic revolution; it was unthinkable to pursue that path without fostering the development of a technocratic elite, that is, without putting intellectuals in charge. It seemed that the "historic" place of intellectuals in China was to be reclaimed. Intellectuals had therefore welcomed the reforms: they expected to be valued, appreciated, and compensated, in both earnings and status.

Throughout the second half of the 1980s, enthusiasm gave way to disillusionment and eventually to dismay and anger. Those intellectuals who had participated directly in formulating the reform policy or in articulating its propaganda message benefited immensely from the reforms, both economically and in terms of power and leadership. The others, and especially those in the nontechnological disciplines, felt they had been left behind, and that their comparative position in society was worsening. Many students—and students are considered "intellectuals" in China—saw for themselves a future not much different than other social groups, like workers, state employees, and so on: a state job, with a shrinking and increasingly fragile iron rice bowl, in a society where a small group was accumulating ill-gotten wealth and prestige. Students and intellectuals then shared with urban residents the same sense of insecurity and fear, as well as resentment toward corruption. But to these they added a peculiar ambivalence, a continuous oscillation between the disillusionment they felt with their present situation and the hope, unfulfilled but not extinguished, of being, once again, the guiding light of the nation.

WHAT DID THE PROTESTERS WANT?

The students who emerged as the leading voice of the 1989 movement manifested this ambivalence. From the very first days of the protests, student leaders spoke both as "students" and as representatives of a much larger set of constituents, the people. The April petition, for example, included different kinds of demands, ranging from freedom of the press to more money for education, to the release of the income data for all high officials. In the following weeks, students combined parochial requests (better salaries for professors, better living conditions) with calls for "democracy" and the "rule of law."

It is difficult to come up with a single idea of what students and protesters meant when they advocated for democracy. In some instances, "democracy" meant the existence of a public sphere, an arena in which intellectuals were to play a central role. In others, it implied a government that served the interests of the people. This did not mean the desire that common citizens should run the government: it was rather the idea of a government for the people, but not by the people. Students, in particular, expressed doubts that the Chinese people were ready for "real" democracy. As a consequence, this was not a uniformly antigovernment or antiparty movement: many believed that the Communist Party, with the support of intellectuals, could be an agent of reform, and could actually serve the people's interests. Despite the attacks against individuals within the government, many students did not favor a radical change of system, something that got lost in the media representation of the protests.

In general, we can see the call of students for democracy as a confused reflection of a tension that existed within Chinese society: as mentioned earlier, by the late 1980s, two different sets of impulses were driving the reforms. On the one hand, interest groups were pulling the state toward an increasing privatization, a complete dismantling of public welfare, and a rule of law meant only as protection of powerful interests and of legal contracts. On the other hand, the majority of urban residents were calling on the Communist Party to respect its mission to "serve the people." And this did not mean a return to the Maoist past or the rolling back of the reforms. Rather here it meant the redistribution of resources in a more equitable way, social justice, and a democratization of economic life (in other words, the ability for common people to have a say in what happened in their workplace, in their city). "Rule of law" here meant the protection of the interests of the people, not an elite. And it was this second set of claims with which the people of Beijing identified the slogans of "democracy" and "rule of law" espoused by the students. However, the students (and it was not completely their fault) were largely incapable of representing these claims and especially to formulate any practical proposal that would move in that direction. In a sense, they were incapable of understanding that this was much more than a student movement, that it had grown beyond them and had sparked the participation of other social forces.

CONCLUSION

In conclusion, the Beijing Spring of 1989 was not simply a student movement for democracy. While students were the protagonists, they were not the only actors. This was revealed in the cruelest form during the repression of June Fourth, when the majority of victims were not students, but citizens of Beijing who stood in the way of the advancing troops on the way to Tiananmen. Later that night, the students vacated the Square seemingly without casualties.

As for "democracy," the term is always extremely vague. In this particular case, it came to include ideas diverse and at times contradictory: freedom of speech and assembly as well as an improved economic and social status for the students; the right to independent organizations for the workers; redistribution of wealth and social justice for urban residents; all combined with the shared criticism of corruption and very ambivalent positions vis-à-vis one-party rule. In this sense, to call Tiananmen 1989 a movement for "democracy" does not add much to our understanding.

SUGGESTIONS FOR FURTHER READING

A more complex analysis has been offered by Wang Hui in his *China's New Order: Society, Politics, and Economy in Transition* (Harvard University Press, 2003). Wang views the movement as the multifaceted expression of a crisis in the reforms and a conflict over their directions. The failure of the 1989 social movement also quelled this debate and opened the way for a new set of economic reforms that institutionalized the social problems at the center of the protests.

Two books offer an inside-the-party view of the 1989 Spring: *The Tiananmen Papers*, compiled by Zhang Liang and edited by Andrew Nathan and Perry Link (Public Affairs, 2001), retells, through original Party documents, the decision making within the Communist leadership. Zhao Ziyang's newly unveiled "secret memoir" *Prisoner of the State* (Simon and Schuster, 2009), offers the perspective of the Party secretary who was ousted because he was considered "soft" on the 1989 protesters.

Probably the most thorough sociological analysis of student activism in 1989 is Zhao Dingxin's *The Power of Tiananmen: State-Society Relations and the 1989 Beijing Student Movement* (University of Chicago Press, 2001). Jeffrey Wasserstrom and Elizabeth Perry's edited volume *Popular Protest and Political Culture in Modern China* (Westview, 1994) places 1989 in a larger historical and cultural context.

For an exhaustive collection of original documents check *Cries for Democracy: Writings and Speeches from the 1989 Chinese Democracy Movement* (Princeton University Press, 1990), edited by Han Minzhu. There is also an interesting documentary film, *The Gate of Heavenly Peace*, directed by Carma Hinton and Richard Gordon, with original footage and interviews.

Finally, the list of firsthand accounts by journalists and eyewitnesses is too long and exceeds the space of this text. I will just mention the most recent one, Philip J. Cunningham's *Tiananmen Moon: Inside the Chinese Student Uprising of 1989* (Rowman and Littlefield, 2009).

Index

About the Contributors

Elif Akçetin, Lecturer
Department of History, Durham University, UK
BA, Smith College, Massachusetts; MA, Boğaziçi University, Istanbul; PhD, University of Washington

Bridie Andrews, Associate Professor of History
Department of History, Bentley College, Massachusetts, USA
BSc, University of Edinburgh; PhD, Cambridge University

Tim Barrett, Research Professor of East Asian History
Departments of the Study of Religions and of History, School of Oriental and African Studies, London, UK
BA, Cambridge University; PhD, Yale University, Connecticut

Felix Boecking, Lecturer in Modern Chinese Economic and Political History
School of History, Classics and Archaeology, University of Edinburgh, UK
BA, Oxford University; PhD, Cambridge University

Michael C. Brose, Associate Professor
Department of History, University of Wyoming, USA
BS, Seattle Pacific University; MSc, University of British Columbia; MA, University of Washington; PhD, University of Pennsylvania

Marjorie Dryburgh, Lecturer
School of East Asian Studies, University of Sheffield, UK
BA, Durham University; PhD, Durham University

241

Imre Galambos, Lecturer in Pre-Modern Chinese Studies
University of Cambridge, UK
MA, ELTE University, Budapest; MA, University of California at Berkeley;
PhD, University of California at Berkeley

Stanley E. Henning, Independent scholar
Hawai'i, USA
BA, Virginia Military Institute; MA, University of Hawai'i

Christian Hess, Assistant Professor
Faculty of Liberal Arts, Sophia University, Japan
BA, University of California at Davis; MA, University of California at San
Diego; PhD, University of California at San Diego

Clara Wing-chung Ho, Professor
Department of History, Hong Kong Baptist University, Hong Kong
BA, University of Hong Kong; MPhil, University of Hong Kong; PhD,
University of Hong Kong

Judd Kinzley, Assistant Professor
Department of History, University of Wisconsin–Madison, USA
BA, Macalester College, Minnesota; MA, Washington University in St. Louis;
PhD, University of California at San Diego

Fabio Lanza, Associate Professor
Departments of East Asian Studies and History, University of Arizona, USA
BA, University of Venice, Ca' Foscari; MA, Columbia University, New York;
PhD, Columbia University, New York

Peter Lorge, Assistant Professor of History and Asian Studies
Department of History, Vanderbilt University, Tennessee, USA
BA, University of Texas at Austin; MA, University of Reading; PhD, University
of Pennsylvania

Julia Lovell, Senior Lecturer
Department of History, Classics and Archaeology, Birkbeck College,
University of London, UK
BA, Cambridge University; MPhil, Cambridge University; PhD, Cambridge
University

Rana Mitter, Professor of the History and Politics of Modern China
Institute for Chinese Studies, Oxford University, UK
BA, Cambridge University; PhD, Cambridge University

Barbara Mittler, Professor
Institut für Sinologie, Ruprecht-Karls-Universität Heidelberg, Germany
BA, Oxford University; PhD, Heidelberg University

Ruth Mostern, Associate Professor
School of Social Sciences, Humanities and Arts, University of California–
Merced, USA
BS, Georgetown University, Washington DC; MA, University of California at
Berkeley; PhD, University of California at Berkeley

Peter C. Perdue, Professor
Department of History, Yale University, Connecticut, USA
BA, Harvard College, Massachusetts; MA, Harvard University, Massachusetts;
PhD, Harvard University, Massachusetts

Hai Ren, Associate Professor
Departments of East Asian Studies and Anthropology, University of Arizona,
USA
BA, Sichuan University; MA, University of Washington; PhD, University of
Washington

Andres Rodriguez, Lecturer in Modern Asian History
School of Humanities, University of Southampton, UK
BA, Universidad Catolica de Chile; MPhil, Oxford University; DPhil, Oxford
University

Tansen Sen, Associate Professor
Department of History, Baruch College, City University of New York, USA
BA, Beijing Languages Institute; MA, Peking University; PhD, University of
Pennsylvania

Elliott Sperling, Associate Professor
Department of Central Eurasian Studies, Indiana University, USA
BA, Queens College, City University of New York; MA, Indiana University;
PhD, Indiana University

Naomi Standen, Professor of Medieval History
School of History and Cultures, University of Birmingham, UK
BA, London University, Queen Mary College; PhD, Durham University

Wasana Wongsurawat, Lecturer
Department of History, Chulalongkorn University, Bangkok, Thailand
BA, University of Chicago; MSt, Oxford University; DPhil, Oxford University

Ling Zhang, Assistant Professor
Department of History, Boston College, Massachusetts, USA
BA, Peking University; MPhil, Cambridge University; PhD, Cambridge University